Praise for *Low-Code AI*

Everyone from those in tech-adjacent roles to aspiring data scientists and
ML engineers can benefit from the project-based approach and no-code and low-code
solutions presented in this wonderfully written book.

—*Eric Pilotte,*
Global head of Technical and Business Training Delivery, Google Cloud

Low-Code AI is what I have been looking for to help jumpstart learning AI.
This book provides an easy-to-follow guide that helps those of us who want to harness
the power of AI for data-driven decision making, but that do not yet have years of ML
coding experience. I am grateful for this highly accessible book and feel seen!

—*Shana Rigelhaupt,*
Product manager, The Carey Group, and aspiring citizen data scientist

Low-Code AI is a very special book that manages to strike the right balance
between practical low-code recipes to get started with ML and in-depth explanations
that are accessible to beginners. A great read to start a journey in AI
from scratch and build quality intuition in this always-changing field.

—*Benoit Dherin,*
ML engineer, Google Cloud

Whether you are familiar with coding or are a beginner,
this excellent and detailed guide unlocks the potential of ML,
illustrated through real-world use cases and hands-on problems.

—*Michael Munn,*
Research software engineer, Google Cloud

Low-Code AI
A Practical Project-Driven
Introduction to Machine Learning

Gwendolyn Stripling, PhD
& Michael Abel, PhD

Beijing · Boston · Farnham · Sebastopol · Tokyo

Low-Code AI

by Gwendolyn Stripling and Michael Abel

Published by O'Reilly Media, Inc., 1005 Gravenstein Highway North, Sebastopol, CA 95472.

O'Reilly books may be purchased for educational, business, or sales promotional use. Online editions are also available for most titles (*http://oreilly.com*). For more information, contact our corporate/institutional sales department: 800-998-9938 or *corporate@oreilly.com*.

Acquisition Editor: Nicole Butterfield
Development Editor: Corbin Collins
Production Editor: Clare Laylock
Copyeditor: nSight Inc.
Proofreader: Piper Editorial Consulting, LLC

Indexer: BIM Creatives, LLC
Interior Designer: David Futato
Cover Designer: Karen Montgomery
Illustrator: Kate Dullea

September 2023:   First Edition

Revision History for the First Edition
2023-09-13:   First Release

See *http://oreilly.com/catalog/errata.csp?isbn=9781098146825* for release details.

978-1-098-14682-5

[LSI]

Table of Contents

Preface. ix

1. How Data Drives Decision Making in Machine Learning. 1
   What Is the Goal or Use Case?   1
   An Enterprise ML Workflow   4
      Defining the Business Objective or Problem Statement   5
      Data Collection   6
      Data Preprocessing   7
      Data Analysis   9
      Data Transformation and Feature Selection   10
      Researching the Model Selection or Using AutoML (a No-Code Solution)   11
      Model Training, Evaluation, and Tuning   12
      Model Testing   13
      Model Deployment (Serving)   14
      Maintaining Models   14
   Summary   15

2. Data Is the First Step. 17
   Overview of Use Cases and Datasets Used in the Book   17
      1. Retail: Product Pricing   18
      2. Healthcare: Heart Disease Campaign   18
      3. Energy: Utility Campaign   19
      4. Insurance: Advertising Media Channel Sales Prediction   19
      5. Financial: Fraud Detection   20
      6. Energy: Power Production Prediction   21
      7. Telecommunications: Customer Churn Prediction   21
      8. Automotive: Improve Custom Model Performance   22
   Data and File Types   23

Quantitative and Qualitative Data   23
Structured, Unstructured, and Semistructured Data   24
Data File Types   25
How Data Is Processed   26
An Overview of GitHub and Google's Colab   27
Use GitHub to Create a Data Repository for Your Projects   27
Using Google's Colaboratory for Low-Code AI Projects   30
Summary   48

3. Machine Learning Libraries and Frameworks. 49
No-Code AutoML   49
How AutoML Works   58
Machine Learning as a Service   62
Low-Code ML Frameworks   66
SQL ML Frameworks   67
Open Source ML Libraries   68
Summary   70

4. Use AutoML to Predict Advertising Media Channel Sales. 71
The Business Use Case: Media Channel Sales Prediction   71
Project Workflow   72
Project Dataset   73
Exploring the Dataset Using Pandas, Matplotlib, and Seaborn   73
Load Data into a Pandas DataFrame in a Google Colab Notebook   74
Explore the Advertising Dataset   75
Use AutoML to Train a Linear Regression Model   85
No-Code Using Vertex AI   86
Create a Managed Dataset in Vertex AI   86
Select the Model Objective   87
Build the Training Model   93
Evaluate Model Performance   98
Model Feature Importance (Attribution)   101
Get Predictions from Your Model   103
Summary   111

5. Using AutoML to Detect Fraudulent Transactions. 113
The Business Use Case: Fraud Detection for Financial Transactions   113
Project Workflow   114
Project Dataset   115
Exploring the Dataset Using Pandas, Matplotlib, and Seaborn   116
Loading Data into a Pandas DataFrame in a Google Colab Notebook   116
Exploring the Dataset   118

Exporting the Dataset 131
Classification Models and Metrics 132
Using AutoML to Train a Classification Model 134
 Creating a Managed Dataset and Selecting the Model Objective 135
 Exploring Dataset Statistics 136
 Training the Model 137
 Evaluating Model Performance 140
 Model Feature Importances 141
 Getting Predictions from Your Model 142
Summary 145

6. **Using BigQuery ML to Train a Linear Regression Model.** **147**
The Business Use Case: Power Plant Production 147
Cleaning the Dataset Using SQL in BigQuery 148
 Loading a Dataset into BigQuery 149
 Exploring Data in BigQuery Using SQL 154
Linear Regression Models 160
 Feature Selection and Correlation 163
 Google Colaboratory 166
 Plotting Feature Relationships to the Label 170
 The CREATE MODEL Statement in BigQuery ML 175
Introducing Explainable AI 178
 Explainable AI in BigQuery ML 179
 Exercises 182
Neural Networks in BigQuery ML 183
 Brief Overview of Neural Networks 183
 Activation Functions and Nonlinearity 185
 Training a Deep Neural Network in BigQuery ML 187
 Exercises 190
Deep Dive: Using Cloud Shell to View Your Cloud Storage File 190
Summary 192

7. **Training Custom ML Models in Python.** **193**
The Business Use Case: Customer Churn Prediction 193
Choosing Among No-Code, Low-Code, or Custom Code ML Solutions 194
Exploring the Dataset Using Pandas, Matplotlib, and Seaborn 196
 Loading Data into a Pandas DataFrame in a Google Colab Notebook 196
 Understanding and Cleaning the Customer Churn Dataset 199
 Transforming Features Using Pandas and Scikit-Learn 213
Building a Logistic Regression Model Using Scikit-Learn 218
 Logistic Regression 219
 Training and Evaluating a Model in Scikit-Learn 221

Classification Evaluation Metrics 223
Serving Predictions with a Trained Model in Scikit-Learn 225
Pipelines in Scikit-Learn: An Introduction 228
Building a Neural Network Using Keras 231
Introduction to Keras 231
Training a Neural Network Classifier Using Keras 232
Building Custom ML Models on Vertex AI 237
Summary 248

8. Improving Custom Model Performance **249**
The Business Use Case: Used Car Auction Prices 249
Model Improvement in Scikit-Learn 250
Loading the Notebook with the Preexisting Model 251
Loading the Datasets and the Training-Validation-Test Data Split 251
Exploring the Scikit-Learn Linear Regression Model 253
Feature Engineering and Improving the Preprocessing Pipeline 256
Hyperparameter Tuning 261
Model Improvement in Keras 266
Introduction to Preprocessing Layers in Keras 266
Creating the Dataset and Preprocessing Layers for Your Model 267
Building a Neural Network Model 270
Hyperparameter Tuning in Keras 272
Hyperparameter Tuning in BigQuery ML 276
Loading and Transforming Car Auction Data 276
Training a Linear Regression Model and Using the TRANSFORM Clause 279
Configure a Hyperparameter Tuning Job in BigQuery ML 281
Options for Hyperparameter Tuning Large Models 285
Vertex AI Training and Tuning 286
Automatic Model Tuning with Amazon SageMaker 286
Azure Machine Learning 286
Summary 286

9. Next Steps in Your AI Journey **289**
Going Deeper into Data Science 289
Working with Unstructured Data 290
Generative AI 294
Explainable AI 295
ML Operations 298
Continuous Training and Evaluation 299
Summary 300

Index **301**

Preface

Artificial intelligence (AI) can be defined as the broad field of study where computers show intelligence. The phrase "show intelligence" is vague; it could be interpreted as a computer making a decision that we would expect from a living being. The concept of AI has existed since ancient times, at least in mythology. A famous example of this is the Greek myth featuring Talos, a bronze automaton made to protect Europa from invaders who wished to kidnap her. As the centuries passed, basic forms of AI passed from the realm of myth to real life.

In modern times, AI has found its home in augmenting human abilities and automating decision making and other processes that are time-consuming for people. Expert systems, first developed in the 1970s, are one such example of modern AI. An expert system leverages a knowledge base, a collection of facts and rules, and an inference system to synthesize new knowledge. The main disadvantage of an expert system is that it needs domain expert time and effort to create the facts and rules for the knowledge base.

In recent decades, another form of AI has become more ubiquitous. Machine learning (ML) is the discipline of having computers learn algorithms from the data provided rather than the programmer having to provide the algorithms. Another way to phrase this in contrast to expert systems is that ML is about using data to discover the rules versus having experts write the rules for you.

ML touches almost every industry nowadays. In retail, ML is used for demand forecasting, predicting the expected sales of products or services months in advance. The travel industry uses ML to recommend points of interest and destinations to customers based on their past travel history and other information. In healthcare, ML can be used to not only determine if an X-ray image contains a healthy or diseased lung, but it can also pinpoint the region of the X-ray image that led to the determination for medical experts to explore in more detail. The list of active uses of ML could fill up an entire book on its own. In this book we focus on a few specific

ML use cases to get you started, including advertising media channel sales, energy production, and customer churn just to name a few.

With so many applications of ML in industry, it is exciting to explore the different possibilities. One assumption that many make is that ML is solely a field of study for the experts. That is, unless you have a large amount of background knowledge across many different fields (computer science, mathematics, statistics, and so on), you have no hope of using ML in practice. That is simply not the case.

In recent years, the concept of a *citizen data scientist* has become much more common. A citizen data scientist is someone who does not necessarily have a formal education and/or role in data science or related fields but can perform some data science work alongside other domain-specific expertise they bring to the table. Many easy-to-use tools have been developed for ML that are available to this group of people, and the goal of this book is to enable and encourage more people to become citizen data scientists.

Who Should Read This Book?

The goal of this book is to teach readers how to frame ML problems for structured (tabular) data, prepare their data for ML workflows, and build and use ML models using different no-code, low-code, and some basic custom code solutions. You will go through step-by-step processes to understand these objectives within the framing of a specific business problem. The primary audience for this book are business analysts, data analysts, students, and aspiring citizen data scientists who seek to learn how to apply ML to their work very quickly using automated machine learning (AutoML), BigQuery ML (using SQL), and custom training in Python. Some basic familiarity with data analysis is assumed, but you don't need to be an expert to benefit from going through this book.

Anyone considering a career move into data science and/or ML engineering may also find this book to be a great first step toward their goal. ML practitioners will likely find this book to be too basic for their needs, but they may find discussions on some of the tools being used to be helpful if they are unfamiliar.

No prior knowledge of ML or a specific programming language is required, but readers will find the book a little easier to read with some basic knowledge of programming concepts, Python, and SQL. We include references to additional foundational material within context throughout the book. In addition to ML concepts and use case–based examples, you will also explore different tools such as Jupyter Notebooks and basic use of the Linux terminal.

What Is and Isn't in This Book

This book was created as a first step for those who wish to become ML practitioners, not as a book to turn you into an ML expert. We do not cover the theory of ML in detail, nor do we cover all of the topics from statistics and mathematics needed to be a successful data scientist. We cover the theory that is needed for the projects discussed in this book as a way to ease you into working on ML projects, but going farther than that would be beyond the scope here. We do, however, give many references to resources where you can dive deeper if you are interested in doing so.

Chapters 2 and 3 discuss many different types of data that can be used in ML problems and different tools that can be used in practice. However, no single book can cover every single circumstance with every available tool. We focus on use cases with structured data and only pursue a light discussion around ML for unstructured data in Chapters 2 and 9. Some of the most exciting applications (AI-powered chatbots and image generation, for example) use unstructured data, but in practice most applications of ML in business and industry focus on problems involving structured data.

In terms of tools, we focus on a narrow range of tools so that you can focus on the business use cases. Packages in Python such as NumPy, Seaborn, Pandas, scikit-learn, and TensorFlow are popular across all industries, and we cover those alongside many of the use cases in this book. Jupyter Notebooks are also an industry standard used to interactively run Python code in a notebook environment.

We use Google Colab, a free Jupyter Notebook service, for running our notebooks. Additionally, we will use other Google Cloud tools, such as Vertex AI AutoML for no-code ML model training and BigQuery for SQL data analysis and training ML models using SQL. Other major cloud providers, such as Microsoft Azure and Amazon Web Services (AWS), offer similar services for running Jupyter Notebooks, AutoML, analyzing data with SQL, and training ML models using SQL. We highly encourage and recommend that you explore the other tools that we mention but do not use here. Links for more information and documentation are included throughout the entire book.

Conventions Used in This Book

The following typographical conventions are used in this book:

Italic
: Indicates new terms, URLs, email addresses, filenames, and file extensions.

`Constant width`
: Used for program listings, as well as within paragraphs to refer to program elements such as variable or function names, databases, data types, environment variables, statements, and keywords.

`Constant width bold`
Shows commands or other text that should be typed literally by the user.

`Constant width italic`
Shows text that should be replaced with user-supplied values or by values determined by context.

This element signifies a tip or suggestion.

This element signifies a general note.

This icon indicates a warning or caution.

Using Code Examples

Supplemental material (code examples, exercises, etc.) is available for download at *https://oreil.ly/supp-lcai*.

This book is here to help you get your job done. In general, if example code is offered with this book, you may use it in your programs and documentation. You do not need to contact us for permission unless you're reproducing a significant portion of the code. For example, writing a program that uses several chunks of code from this book does not require permission. Selling or distributing a CD-ROM of examples from O'Reilly books does require permission. Answering a question by citing this book and quoting example code does not require permission. Incorporating a significant amount of example code from this book into your product's documentation does require permission.

We appreciate, but do not require, attribution. An attribution usually includes the title, author, publisher, and ISBN. For example: "*Low-Code AI* by Gwendolyn Stripling and Michael Abel (O'Reilly). Copyright 2023 Gwendolyn Stripling and Michael Abel, 978-1-098-14682-5."

If you feel your use of code examples falls outside fair use or the permission given above, feel free to contact us at *permissions@oreilly.com*.

O'Reilly Online Learning

 For more than 40 years, *O'Reilly Media* has provided technology and business training, knowledge, and insight to help companies succeed.

Our unique network of experts and innovators share their knowledge and expertise through books, articles, and our online learning platform. O'Reilly's online learning platform gives you on-demand access to live training courses, in-depth learning paths, interactive coding environments, and a vast collection of text and video from O'Reilly and 200+ other publishers. For more information, visit *https://oreilly.com*.

How to Contact Us

Please address comments and questions concerning this book to the publisher:

O'Reilly Media, Inc.
1005 Gravenstein Highway North
Sebastopol, CA 95472
800-889-8969 (in the United States or Canada)
707-829-7019 (international or local)
707-829-0104 (fax)
support@oreilly.com
https://www.oreilly.com/about/contact.html

We have a web page for this book, where we list errata, examples, and any additional information. You can access this page at *https://oreil.ly/LowCodeAI*.

For news and information about our books and courses, visit *https://oreilly.com*.

Find us on LinkedIn: *https://linkedin.com/company/oreilly-media*.

Follow us on Twitter: *https://twitter.com/oreillymedia*.

Watch us on YouTube: *https://youtube.com/oreillymedia*.

Acknowledgments

This book exists only because of the generous support and time of many people. We would like to thank our fellow Googlers—Enrica Filippi, Mona Mona, Benoit Dherin, and Michael Munn—for their detailed review of this book. The quality of exposition and technical details greatly benefited from their expertise. We also want to thank our coworkers—Rich Rose, Patrick Bentley, Yoanna Long, Esra Duygun, and Concepcion Diaz—for their support and feedback. Last but not least, we want to thank our managers—Kelly Thompson, Eric Pilotte, and Sree Upadhyayula—for their unwavering support for this endeavor.

A big thank you to the O'Reilly team for all their collaboration in bringing this dream to life and their patience with two writers excitedly navigating this process for the first time. We wish to thank Nicole Butterfield for believing in our project and vision from the beginning and Clare Laylock for her work in getting this book ready for print. We would like to thank Corbin Collins for his hard work and editorial expertise throughout the entire process.

Michael would like to thank his wife Jackie for her incredible support and patience throughout this entire process of writing this book, his daughter Mia for her knack of always finding the right time to interrupt work to play with the keyboard and bring a smile to his face, and his parents, Ben and Rita, for fostering his love of mathematics and computers for as long as he can remember.

Gwendolyn would like to thank her life partner, Nada Velimirović, for her unwavering support during this amazing journey, and her daughter, Saskia, and pets, Ginger and Wonton, for their incredible ability to know when to provide a hug, ask for a lap, and whine for a short walk. She would also like to thank her family: her father and mother (thank you for the DNA); her sister Belinda (thank you for seeing me); her sister, Gloria Taylor Williams, and her husband, Charles Williams; her brothers, Maurice Cobb and Carlos S. Armstrong; and her uncle, Tony Hall. She so appreciates her niece, Katrina Marie Burage, and nephew, Carlos S. Armstrong Jr., for all of their amazing support during this journey! She'd also like to thank her dear friend Christina Ramirez, who has always believed and supported her out-of-the-box thinking!

## CHAPTER 1

How Data Drives Decision Making in Machine Learning

This chapter explores the role of data in the enterprise and its influence on business decision making. You also learn the components of a machine learning (ML) workflow. You may have seen many books, articles, videos, and blogs begin any discussion of the ML workflow with the gathering of data. However, before data is gathered, you need to understand what kind of data to gather. This *data understanding* can only be achieved by knowing what kind of problem you need to solve or decision you need to make.

Business case/problem definition and data understanding can then be used to formulate a no-code or low-code ML strategy. A no-code or low-code strategic approach to ML projects has several advantages/benefits. As mentioned in the introduction, a no-code AutoML approach enables anyone with domain knowledge in their area of expertise and no coding experience to develop ML models quickly, without needing to write a single line of code. This is a fast and efficient way to develop ML applications. A low-code approach enables those with some coding or deep coding experience, to develop ML applications quickly because basic code is autogenerated—and any additional custom code can be added. But, again, any ML project must begin with defining a goal, use case, or problem.

What Is the Goal or Use Case?

Businesses, educational institutions, government agencies, and practitioners face many decisions that reflect real-world examples of ML. For example:

- How can we increase patient engagement with our diabetes web app?
- How can we increase our student feedback numbers on course surveys?

- How can we increase our speed in detecting cyberattacks against our company networks?

- Can we decrease the number of spam emails entering our email servers?

- How do we decrease downtime on our manufacturing production line?

- How can we increase our customer retention rate?

- How do we reduce our customer churn (customer attrition) rate?

In each of those examples, numerous data sources must be examined to determine what ML solution is most appropriate to solve the problem or aid in decision making. Let's take the use case of reducing customer churn or loss rate—using a very simplistic example. *Churn prediction* is identifying customers that are most likely to leave your service or product. This problem falls into a supervised learning bucket as a classification problem with two classes: the "Churn-Yes" class and the "Churn-No" class.

From a data source perspective, you may need to examine customer profile information (name, address, age, job title, employment statement), purchase information (purchases and billing history), interaction information (customer experiences interacting with your products [both digitally and physically]), your customer service teams, or your digital support services. Popular data sources of customer information are customer relationship management systems, system ecommerce analytics services, and customer feedback. In essence, everything the customer "touches" as a data point should be tracked and captured as a data source.

The nature of the decision you must make is tied directly to the data you will need to gather to make that decision—which needs to be formulated into a problem statement. Let's say you are in charge of marketing for a company that makes umbrellas, and the *business goal* is to increase sales. If you reduce the selling price of your existing umbrellas, can you predict how many umbrellas you will sell? Figure 1-1 shows the data elements to consider for this option.

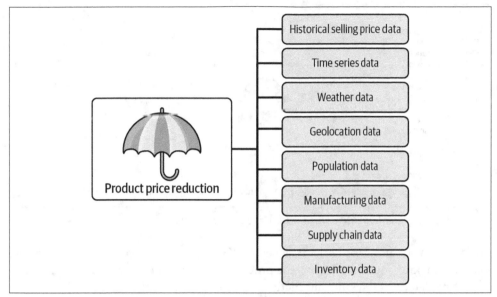

Figure 1-1. Data elements that impact a price reduction strategy to increase sales.

As you can see in this data-driven business illustration, your business goal (to increase sales) takes on a new dimension. You realize now that to understand a product price reduction, you need to include additional data dimensions aside from the selling price. You will need to know the rainy seasons in specific regions, population density, and whether your inventory is sufficient to meet the demand of a price reduction that will increase sales. You will also need to look at historical data versus data that can be captured in real time. Historical data is typically referred to as *batch*, whereas real-time data capture is typically called *streaming*. With these added dimensions, the business goal suddenly becomes a very complex problem as these additional columns may be required. For any organization, there could ostensibly exist dozens of discrete data sources—with each source requiring certain skills to understand the relationships between them. Figure 1-2 is an illustration of this challenge.

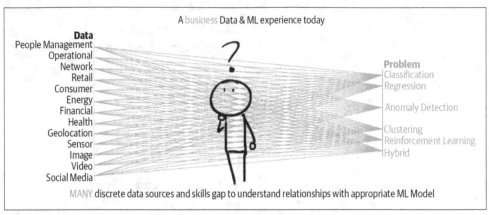

Figure 1-2. A typical business data and ML experience today.

So what is your use case here? It depends. You would need to undergo a business decision-making process, which is the process of making choices by asking questions, collecting data, and assessing alternative resolutions. Once you figure out the use case or business goal, you can use the same data to train machines to learn about your customer patterns, spot trends, and predict outcomes using AutoML or low-code AI. Figure 1-3 shows our umbrella example as a business use case that then leads to data source determination, ML framework, and then a prediction.

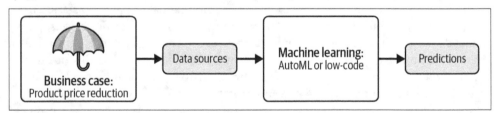

Figure 1-3. Business case that leads to predictions using ML framework.

An Enterprise ML Workflow

While decision-making processes help you identify your problem or use case, it is the ML workflow that helps you implement the solution to your problem. This section presents a typical ML workflow. In our ongoing umbrella example, you could use your data to train an ML model using an AutoML service that provides a no-code solution for running unsupervised ML clustering. From there, you could examine *clusters* of data points to see what patterns were derived. Or, you could decide to simply focus on historical data so that you could predict a specific target based on a certain number of data input features. What would your enterprise ML workflow look like? Not surprisingly, it is data-driven and requires decision making in the process.

The ML workflow can be shown as a series of steps, and the steps can be combined into phases. Figure 1-4 shows the 10 steps, and then we briefly discuss each. Later chapters provide more detailed examples of each step.

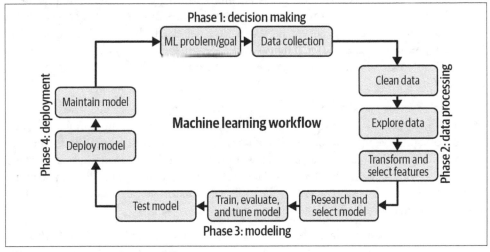

Figure 1-4. Ten-step ML workflow.

Defining the Business Objective or Problem Statement

The ML workflow starts with defining a specific question or problem with a defined boundary. In this phase you are attempting to define scope and feasibility. The right question will lead you to what data is required and potential ways data must be prepared. It is important to note that any question that may arise in analyzing data can be grouped in one of the five ML categories as shown in Table 1-1. Let's continue with our umbrella example.

Table 1-1. Categories of analyzing data

Algorithm/model	Problem or question
Regression problem	How many umbrellas do you expect to sell this month/season?
Classification problem	Did they buy straight umbrellas (A) or foldable umbrellas (B)?
Clustering problem	How many straight umbrellas were sold by month or by region?
Anomaly detection problem	Did the company sell more umbrellas in the Mojave Desert than in Portland, OR?
Reinforcement learning	Company policy is to only ship to customers with a balance owed of $500 or less. Can a manufacturing robot be trained to extract, package, load, and ship straight umbrellas to our customers based upon this policy?

Data Collection

In the early part of the 21st century, companies, universities, and researchers typically relied on local servers/hard drives or data centers to host their database applications and store their data. Relying on on-premises data centers or even renting server space in a data center was costly: server infrastructure needed to be maintained, software needed to be updated, security patches had to be installed, physical hardware was swapped out, and so on. In some cases, large amounts of data were stored across a cluster of machines.

Today, to save on costs, enterprises and educational institutions have moved to the cloud to host their database applications and store their data. Cloud storage, a service offered by cloud vendors to store files, allows you to upload different file formats or can be configured to automatically receive files from different data sources. Because most ML models are trained using data from files, storing your data in a cloud storage *bucket* makes for easy data collection. Cloud storage buckets can be used for storing both structured and unstructured data.

Another option to store data files for data collection is *GitHub* (*https://github.com*), a service designed for collaborating on coding projects. You can store data in the cloud for future use (for free), track changes, and make data publicly available for replication. This option has strict file size limits of 100 MB, but there is an option to use Git Large File Storage (LFS), an open source GitHub extension for versioning large files. Git LFS replaces large files such as datasets, audio samples, graphics, and videos with text pointers inside Git, while storing the file contents on a remote server like GitHub.com or GitHub Enterprise (*https://github.com/enterprise*).

The challenge of data collection is compounded within large organizations, where many different types of operations management software such as enterprise resource planning, customer relationship management, and production systems exist and may run on different databases. Data may also need to be pulled from external sources in real time, such as Internet of Things (IoT) sensor devices from delivery trucks. Thus, organizations are challenged with collecting not only structured data, but also unstructured and semistructured data formats in batches or real time (streaming). Figure 1-5 shows various data elements that feed data collection for structured, unstructured, and semistructured data.

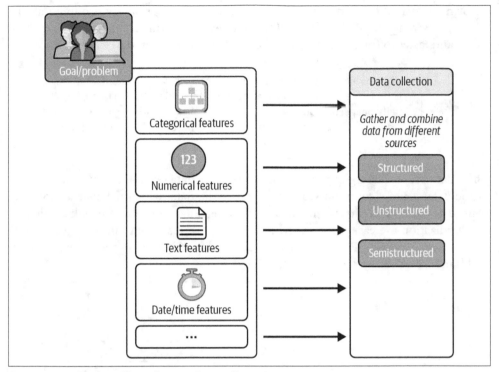

Figure 1-5. Goal/problem flow to data collection.

 It is possible to have streaming structured data. Structured versus unstructured is a property of data format. Streaming versus batch is a property of latency. Chapter 2 presents more information on data format and properties.

Data Preprocessing

To perform data cleanup you'll need to deal with missing data values, duplicates, outlier data, formatting issues, or data that is inconsistent due to human error. This is because real-world data is raw and messy and filled with assumptions. One assumption could be that your data has a normal distribution, meaning that data is symmetrically distributed with no skew, and that most values cluster around a central region, with the frequency of the values decreasing further away from the center (mean or average).

Suppose your data showed, for the first time, an increase in the number of umbrellas sold in August in Palm Springs, the California desert town. Would your data be normally distributed, or would this be considered an outlier? Would it skew the results of predictions for monthly umbrella sales in August? When data does not have a normal distribution, it needs to be *normalized*, made *normal* by grouping all the records in a range of [0,1] or [−1,1], for example. You normalize a dataset to make it easier and faster to train an ML model. Normalization is covered in Chapter 7.

 This min-max normalization example can have detrimental effects if there are outliers. For example, when scaling to [0,1], it essentially maps the outlier to 1 and squashes all other values to 0. Addressing outliers and anomalies is beyond the scope of our book.

Thus, data preprocessing can mean normalizing the data (such that numeric columns in the dataset use a common scale) and *scaling* the data, which means transforming your data so that it fits within a specific range. Fortunately, normalization and standardization are easily performed in Python with just a few simple lines of code (*https://oreil.ly/50v98*). Figure 1-6 shows actual data before and after normalization and standardization.

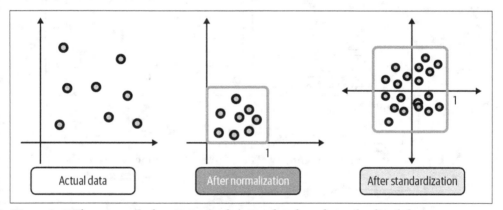

Figure 1-6. Three images showing actual, normalized, and standardized data.

 Collecting data from a single source may be a relatively straightforward process. However, if you are aggregating several data sources into one file, make sure that data formats match and that any assumptions regarding time-series data (or timestamp and date ranges needed for your ML model) are validated. A common assumption is that the data is stationary—that the statistical properties (mean, variance, etc.) do not change over time.

Data Analysis

Exploratory data analysis (EDA) is a process used to explore and analyze the structure of data. In this step, you are looking to discover trends, patterns, feature relevance, and correlations, such as how one variable (feature) might correlate with another. You must select relevant feature data for your ML model based on the type of problem you are trying to solve. The outcome of this step is a feature list of input variables that can potentially be used for ML. Our hands-on exercise using EDA can be found in Chapter 6.

Figures 1-7 and 1-8 are a result of an EDA process plotted using Seaborn, a Python data visualization library (see Chapter 6 for more detail on the dataset). Figure 1-7 shows an *inverse* relationship between *x* and *y*. Figure 1-8 shows a *heat map* (or correlation matrix) and illustrates that more energy is produced when temperatures are lower.

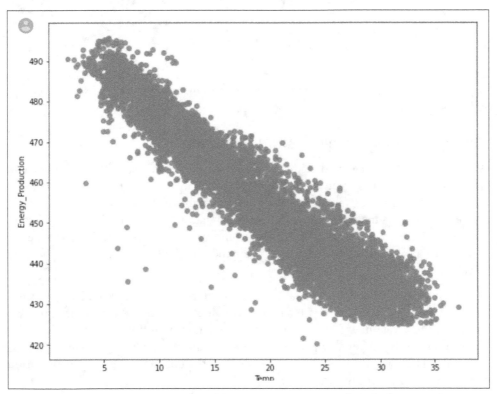

Figure 1-7. Seaborn `regplot` showing that more energy is produced when temperatures are lower.

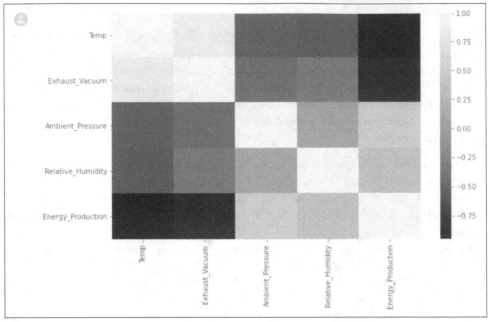

Figure 1-8. Seaborn correlation matrix (heat map) showing a strong inverse relationship between Temp *and* Energy_Production, *-0.75.*

Data Transformation and Feature Selection

After data has been cleaned and analyzed, you obtain a list of the features you think you need to help you solve your ML problem. But might other features be relevant? This is where *feature engineering* comes into play, where you *engineer* or *create new* features that were not in the original dataset. For example, if your dataset has separate fields/columns for month, day, and year, you can combine all three for a "month-day-year" time feature. Feature engineering is the final step before feature selection.

In reality, feature selection occurs at two stages: after EDA and after data transformation. For example, after EDA, you should have a potential list of features that may be candidates to create new features—for example, combining time and day of week to get an hour of day. After you perform feature engineering, you then have a final list of features from which to select. Figure 1-9 shows the position of data transformation and feature selection in the workflow.

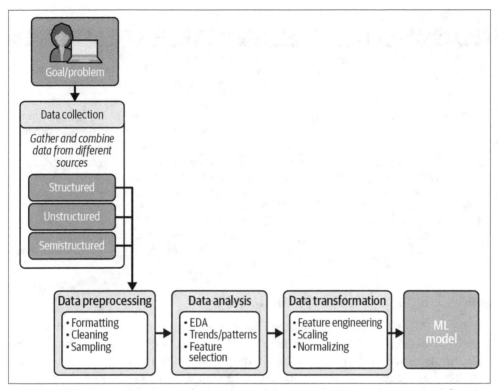

Figure 1-9. Position of data transformation and feature selection in the ML workflow.

Researching the Model Selection or Using AutoML (a No-Code Solution)

In this step, you either research the model that will be best for the type of data that fits your problem—or you could use AutoML, a no-code solution that, based on the dataset you uploaded, selects the appropriate model, trains, tests, and generates evaluation metrics. Essentially, if you use AutoML, the heavy lifting of model selection, model training, model tuning, and generating evaluation metrics is done for you. Chapter 3 introduces AutoML, and Chapter 4 starts getting hands-on with AutoML. Note that with a low-code solution, you would need to know what model to select.

Although AutoML might cover about 80% of your ML problems, you may want to build a more customized solution. In that case, having a general understanding of the types of problems ML algorithms can solve is helpful. Choosing the algorithm is solely dependent upon the problem (as discussed earlier). In Table 1-2, a "Description" column is added to further describe the ML model problem type.

Table 1-2. Describing the model type

Problem or question	Problem	Description
How much or how many umbrellas?	Regression problem	Regression algorithms are used to deal with problems with continuous and numeric output. These are usually used for problems that deal with questions like *how much* or *how many*.
Did they buy straight umbrellas (A) or foldable umbrellas (B)?	Classification problem	A problem in which the output can be only one of a fixed number of output classes, like Yes/No or True/False, is called a classification problem. Depending on the number of output classes, the problem can be a binary or multiclass classification problem.
Company policy is to only ship to customers with a balance owed of $500 or less. Can our manufacturing robot be trained to extract, package, load, and ship straight umbrellas to our customers based upon this policy?	Reinforcement learning	Reinforcement algorithms are used when a decision is to be made based on experiences of learning. The machine agent learns the behavior using trial and error in interaction with the continuously changing environment. This provides a way to program agents using the concept of rewards and penalties without specifying how the task is to be accomplished. Game-playing programs and programs for temperature control are some popular examples using reinforcement learning.

Model Training, Evaluation, and Tuning

Before an ML model can be deployed to a production environment, it has to be trained, evaluated, and tested. Training an ML model is a process in which stored data instances are fed (input) into an ML model (algorithm). Since every stored data instance has a specific characteristic (recall our umbrella examples of the different types, prices, regions sold, and so forth), patterns of these data instances can be detected using hundreds of variables, and the algorithm is thus able to learn from the training data how to make a generalized prediction based on the data.

Every ML model needs to not only be trained but also evaluated. Thus, you hold out a sample of data, called a *validation dataset*. The validation set measures how well the model generalizes to unseen or new data. The training error is used to determine how well the model fits the data because that is what the model is trained on.

Model evaluation metrics should be chosen or defined so that they align with the problem or business goals. Model tuning should improve the model performance as measured by the evaluation metrics. For example, how accurate were the sales of umbrella predictions during the month of December? Can these predictions be generalized for future forecasting efforts? Note that satisfactory performance is something that should be dictated by the business needs and should be agreed upon before starting any ML engagement.

 The validation set is also used to determine if the model is overfitting. Chapter 8 discusses overfitting.

Model Testing

There is no way to know if your umbrella prediction app can be generalized for future forecasting efforts without testing the model. Once the training dataset is used to fit the model to the data, and the validation dataset is used to improve model accuracy, you test the model on data it has never seen before. Testing data is used to assess model performance.

For example, let's say you want to build an application that can recognize an umbrella's color or pattern based on images of the umbrellas. You train a model by providing it with images of all umbrellas that are each tagged with a certain color or pattern. You use that model in a mobile application to recognize any umbrella's color or pattern. The test would be how well the model performs in differentiating between umbrella colors and patterns.

Figure 1-10 shows the relationship between the training, validation, and testing datasets.

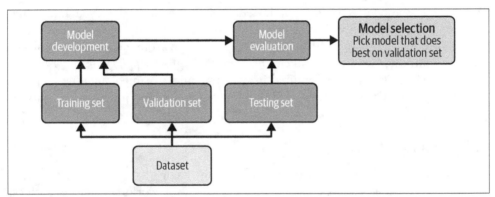

Figure 1-10. Relationship between training, validation, and testing datasets in model deployment and model evaluation.

Figure 1-11 illustrates this relationship among the training, validation, and test datasets in five process steps. For simplicity, the arrow going back to the dataset in Step 5 is not shown, since once a model is deployed as an application and it begins collecting data, new data enters the *pipeline* that may *skew* the original model's results. (At this point you enter the fascinating realm of machine learning operations, or MLOps, which is beyond the scope of the book.)

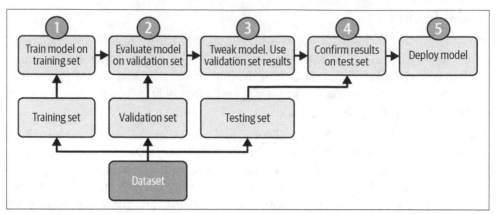

Figure 1-11. Five process steps of the ML workflow.

Model Deployment (Serving)

Once the ML model is trained, evaluated, and tested, it is deployed into a live production environment where it can be used. Note that by the time the model reaches production, it more than likely has a web app frontend (using a browser) that communicates with the production system through an *application programming interface* (API). Data can be captured in real time and streamed (ingested) into an MLOps pipeline. Or data can be captured in batch and stored for ingestion into the pipeline. Or both.

Maintaining Models

Models can become *stale* when predictions do not align with the original business goal or use case metrics. Staleness might occur when the world changes or business requirements change. These changes then impact the model. Post-deployment, you need to monitor your model to ensure it continues to perform as expected. Model and data drift is a phenomenon you should both expect and be prepared to mitigate through regular retraining using MLOps. Let's look at an example of data *drift*, which means changes in the data that you trained with and the data that is now being received from the web app.

In our umbrella example, a region that once experienced heavy rainfall is now experiencing drought conditions. Similarly, a region that once experienced drought conditions is now experiencing heavy rainfall. Any prediction tied to weather and climate and the need for umbrellas and umbrella type will be impacted. In this scenario, you would need to retrain and test a new model with new data.

Summary

Businesses, educational institutions, government agencies, and practitioners face many decisions that reflect real-world examples of ML, from increasing customer engagement to reducing customer churn. Data—its collection, analysis, and use—drives the decision making used in ML to determine the best ML strategic approach that provides real world solutions to real-world problems.

While decision-making processes help you identify your problem or use case, it is the ML workflow that helps you implement the solution to your problem. An enterprise ML workflow is data-driven and requires decision making in the process. The ML workflow can be shown as a series of 10 steps, and the steps can be combined into four phases:

1. Decision making

2. Data processing

3. Modeling

4. Deployment

Each phase of the ML workflow can be implemented using AutoML or low-code AI. AutoML does all of the heavy lifting for you. AutoML will train the model, tune it, test it, and present you with evaluation metrics. Your role is simply to evaluate the metrics and determine if they meet your business objective or solve your problem. AutoML is recommended for quick experiments and prototypes. It is also used in production environments. A low-code approach enables those with some coding or deep coding experience to use autogenerated code that can be further customized during any phase of the ML workflow.

In this chapter, you learned about data collection and analysis as part of the ML workflow. Chapter 2 provides an overview of the datasets used in the book, where to find data sources, data file types, and the difference between batch, streaming, structured, semistructured, and unstructured data. You also get hands-on experience using basic Python code to help you perform EDA and solve dirty data problems.

Data Is the First Step

This chapter provides an overview of the use cases and datasets used in the book while also providing information on where to find data sources for further study and practice. You'll also learn about data types, and the difference between batch and streaming data. You'll get hands-on practice with data preprocessing using Google's free browser-based open source Jupyter Notebook. The chapter concludes with a section on using GitHub to create a data repository for the selected projects used in the book.

Overview of Use Cases and Datasets Used in the Book

Hopefully, you picked up our book to learn ML not from a math-first or algorithm-first approach but from a project-based approach. The use cases we've chosen are designed to teach you ML using actual, real-world data across different sectors. There are use cases for healthcare, retail, energy, telecommunications, and finance. The use case on customer churn can be applied to any sector. Each of the use case projects can stand on its own if you have some data preprocessing experience, so feel free to skip ahead to what you need to learn to upskill yourself. Table 2-1 shows each section, its use case, sector, and whether it is no-code or low-code.

Table 2-1. List of use cases by industry sector and coding type

Section	Use case	Sector	Type
1	Product pricing	Retail	N/A
2	Heart disease	Healthcare	Low-code data preprocessing
3	Marketing campaign	Energy	No-code (AutoML)
4	Advertising media channel sales	Insurance	No-code (AutoML)
5	Fraud detection	Financial	No-code (AutoML)
6	Power plant production prediction	Energy	Low-code (BigQuery ML)

Section	Use case	Sector	Type
7	Customer churn prediction	Telecommunications	Low-code (scikit-learn and Keras)
8	Improve custom model performance	Automotive	Custom-code (scikit-learn, Keras, BigQuery ML)

1. Retail: Product Pricing

This section begins with a use case designed to illustrate the role of data in decision making. In this use case, you are in charge of marketing for a company that makes umbrellas, and the *business goal* is to increase sales. If you reduce the selling price of your existing umbrellas, can you predict how many umbrellas you will sell? Figure 2-1 shows the data elements that may impact a price reduction strategy to increase sales.

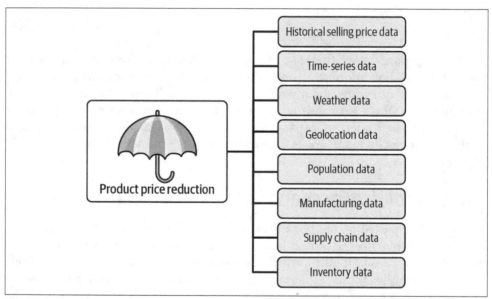

Figure 2-1. Data elements that impact a price reduction strategy to increase sales.

2. Healthcare: Heart Disease Campaign

In this one, you are a healthcare consultant and are given data on heart disease mortality for populations over the age of 35 in the United States. The goal is to analyze the heart disease mortality data and suggest a possible use case in a heart disease prevention campaign. For example, one possible use case would be to track trends in heart disease mortality over time or to develop and validate models for predicting heart disease mortality. This dataset is dirty. Some fields have missing values. One field is missing. In working through these issues, you learn to import data into a Python Jupyter Notebook, analyze it, and fix dirty elements. Figure 2-2 shows the data elements that contribute to your analysis.

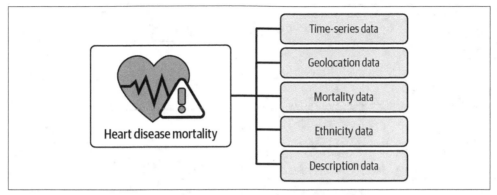

Figure 2-2. Data elements for a heart disease mortality use case.

3. Energy: Utility Campaign

Here, you are a business analyst working for a utility company. You are tasked with developing a marketing and outreach program that targets communities with high electrical energy consumption. The data has already been preprocessed. You do not have an ML background or any programming knowledge. You elect to use AutoML as your ML framework. Figure 2-3 shows the data elements that contribute to your model.

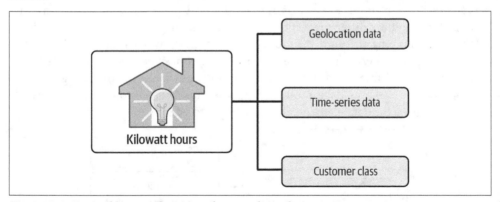

Figure 2-3. Data elements that contribute to the utility energy campaign.

4. Insurance: Advertising Media Channel Sales Prediction

In this section, you work on a team charged with developing a media strategy for an insurance company. The team wants to develop an ML model to predict sales based on advertising spend in various media channels. You are tasked with performing exploratory data analysis and with building and training the model. You do not have an ML background or any programming knowledge. You elect to use AutoML as your ML framework. Figure 2-4 shows the data elements that contribute to your model.

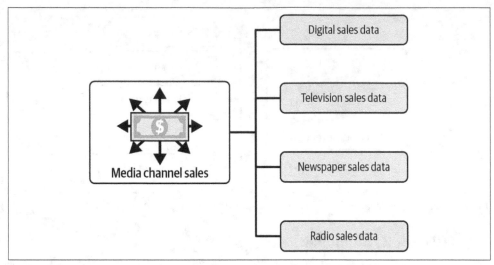

Figure 2-4. Data elements that contribute to media channel sales prediction.

5. Financial: Fraud Detection

Your goal in this project is to build a model to predict whether a financial transaction is fraudulent or legitimate. Your new company is a mobile payment service that serves hundreds of thousands of users. Fraudulent transactions are fairly rare and are usually caught by other protections. However, the unfortunate truth is that some of these are slipping through the cracks and negatively impacting your users. The dataset in this section consists of transaction data that has been simulated to replicate user behavior and fraudulent transactions. You do not have an ML background or any programming knowledge. You elect to use AutoML as your ML framework. Figure 2-5 shows the data elements that contribute to your model.

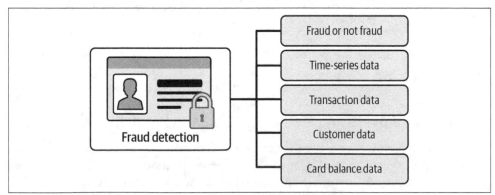

Figure 2-5. Data elements that contribute to a fraud detection model.

6. Energy: Power Production Prediction

Your goal in this project will be to predict the net hourly electrical energy output for a combined cycle power plant (CCPP) given the weather conditions near the plant at the time. The dataset in this section contains data points collected from a CCPP over a six-year period (2006–2011) when the power plant was set to work with a full load. The data is aggregated per hour, though the exact hour for the recorded weather conditions and energy production is not supplied in the dataset. From a practical viewpoint, this means that you will not be able to treat the data as sequence or time-series data, where you use information from previous records to predict future records. You have some Structured Query Language (SQL) knowledge from working with databases. You elect to use Google's BigQuery Machine Learning as your ML framework. Figure 2-6 shows the data elements that contribute to your model.

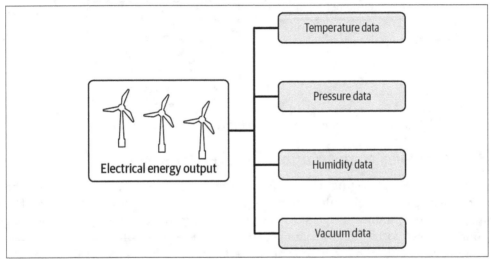

Figure 2-6. Data elements that contribute to the electrical energy output model.

7. Telecommunications: Customer Churn Prediction

Your goal in this project will be to predict customer churn for a telecommunications company. *Customer churn* is defined as the *attrition rate* for customers, or in other words, the rate of customers that choose to stop using services. Telecommunications companies often sell their products at a monthly rate or via annual contracts, so *churn* here will represent when a customer cancels their subscription or contract in the following month. The dataset contains both numeric variables and categorical variables, where the variable takes on a value from a discrete set of possibilities. You have some Python knowledge and find AutoML very powerful, yet are looking to learn low-code solutions that allow you to have a bit more control over your model.

You elect to use scikit-learn and Keras as ML frameworks. Figure 2-7 shows the data elements that contribute to your model.

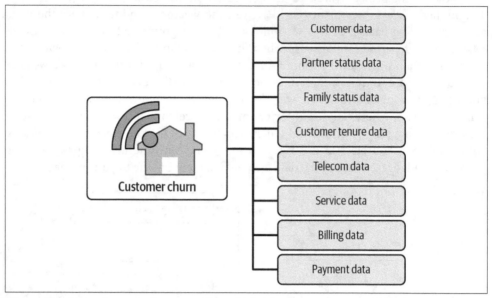

Figure 2-7. Data elements that contribute to the customer churn model.

8. Automotive: Improve Custom Model Performance

Your goal in this project (as a newer member of an ML team) will be to improve the performance of an ML model trained to predict the auction price of used cars. The initial model is a linear regression model in scikit-learn and does not quite meet your business goals. You will ultimately explore using tools in scikit-learn, Keras, and BigQuery ML to improve your model performance. The training, validation, and testing datasets used for training the linear regression model have been supplied to you as CSV files. These datasets have been cleaned (missing and incorrect values have been remedied appropriately), and the code that was used to build the scikit-learn linear regression model has also been provided. Figure 2-8 shows the data elements that contribute to your model.

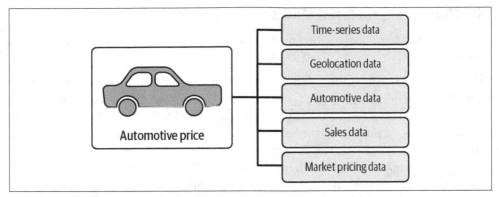

Figure 2-8. Data elements that contribute to the automotive pricing model.

Data and File Types

Data is really the first step, so let's go over some basic terminology and concepts around data. If you are already familiar with the differences between quantitative and qualitative data; between structured, semistructured, and unstructured data; and batch and streaming data, then skip to "An Overview of GitHub and Google's Colab" on page 27, where you can start creating the Jupyter Notebook in GitHub.

Quantitative and Qualitative Data

In data analysis, you work with two types of data: quantitative and qualitative. If it can be counted or measured, and given a numerical value, it's quantitative data. Quantitative data can tell you how many, how much, or how often—for example, how many people visited the website to view the product catalog? How much revenue did the company make this fiscal year? How often do the machines that manufacture your umbrella handles break?

Unlike quantitative data, qualitative data cannot be measured or counted and can include almost any non-numerical data. It's descriptive, expressed in terms of language rather than numbers. Why is this distinction important in ML? If you have qualitative data, then you need to preprocess it so that it *becomes* quantitative—that is because you cannot feed qualitative data into an ML model. You will learn how to handle some qualitative data in subsequent chapters.

Structured, Unstructured, and Semistructured Data

Data can be grouped into three buckets: structured, unstructured, and semistructured.

Structured data is information that has been formatted and transformed into a well-defined data model. A data model is a way of organizing and structuring data so that it can be easily understood and manipulated. Data models are used in a variety of applications, including databases, software applications, and data warehouses. Structured data is well organized. Table 2-2 shows the schema and data type used in Chapter 4's Advertising Media Channel Sales Prediction use case. Note that there is a column name and column type. There are four columns of numeric (quantitative) data that feed into the AutoML model.

Table 2-2. Schema and field value information for the advertising dataset from Chapter 4

Column name	Column type	Notes about field values
Digital	Numeric	Budget of advertisements in digital
Newspaper	Numeric	Budget of advertisements in newspaper
Radio	Numeric	Budget of advertisements in radio
TV	Numeric	Budget of advertisements in TV

Here are some examples of structured data:

- Customer records
- Product inventory
- Financial data
- Transaction logs
- Website analytics data
- Log files

Unstructured data is data that is not structured or tabular or formatted in a specific way. Here are some examples of unstructured data:

- Social media posts
- Chats (text)
- Videos
- Photos
- Web pages
- Audio files

Semistructured data is a type of structured data that lies between structured and unstructured data. It doesn't have a tabular data model but can include tags and semantic markers for records and fields in a dataset. Semistructured data is, essentially, a combination of structured and unstructured. Videos may contain meta tags that relate to the date or location, but the information within has no structure.

Here are some examples of semistructured data:

- CSV, XML, JSON files
- HTML
- Email (Emails are considered semistructured data because they have some structure, but not as much as structured data. Emails typically contain a header, a body, and attachments. The header contains information about the sender, recipient, and date of the message. The body of the message contains the text of the message.)

Figure 2-9 compares unstructured, semistructured, and structured data.

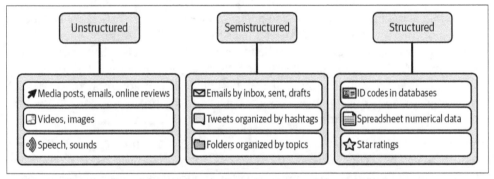

Figure 2-9. Unstructured, semistructured, and structured data examples.

Data File Types

You just learned about the different types of data, and several file types were mentioned. There are many different types of data file formats, each with its own purpose. Table 2-3 shows some of the most common data file types.

Table 2-3. Common data file types

Common data file types	Common file extensions
Text files are files that contain plain text. They are typically used to store documents, such as letters, reports, and code.	Some common text file extensions include .txt, .csv, .tsv, .log, and .json.
Spreadsheet files are files that contain data in a tabular format. They are typically used to store financial data, sales data, and other tabular data.	Some common spreadsheet file extensions include .xls, .xlsx, and .csv.
Image files are files that contain images. They are typically used to store photos, graphics, and other visual content.	Some common image file extensions include .jpg, .png, and .gif.
Audio files are files that contain audio recordings. They are typically used to store music, podcasts, and other audio content.	Some common audio file extensions include .mp3, .wav, and .ogg.
Video files are files that contain video recordings. They are typically used to store movies, TV shows, and other video content.	Some common video file extensions include .mp4, .avi, and .mov.
Webpage files are files that contain webpages. They are typically used to store HTML code, CSS code, and JavaScript code.	Some common webpage file extensions include .html, .htm, and .php.

How Data Is Processed

There are two main modes of how data is processed: batch processing and real-time processing. Batch processing is a mode of data processing where data is collected over a period of time and then processed at a later time. This is a common mode of data processing for large datasets, as it can be more efficient to process the data in batches than to process it in real time. Real-time processing is a mode of data processing where data is processed as soon as it is collected. This is a common mode of data processing for applications where the data needs to be processed quickly, such as fraud detection or stock trading.

The frequency of how data is processed can also vary. Continuous processing is a mode of data processing where data is processed continuously, as it is collected. This is a common mode of data processing for applications where the data needs to be processed in real time. Periodic processing is a mode of data processing where data is processed at regular intervals. This is a common mode of data processing for applications where the data does not need to be processed in real time, such as financial reporting.

The mode and frequency of how data is processed depends on the specific needs of the application. For example, an application that needs to process large datasets may use batch processing, while an application that needs to process data in real time may use real-time processing. Table 2-4 summarizes the different modes and frequencies of data processing.

Table 2-4. Summary of the different modes and frequencies of data processing

Mode	Frequency	Description
Batch processing	Intermittent	Data is collected over a period of time and then processed at a later time.
Real-time processing	Continuous	Data is processed as soon as it is collected.
Periodic processing	Intermittent	Data is processed at regular intervals.

Batch data and streaming data are two different types of data that are processed differently.

- *Batch* data is data that is collected over a period of time and then processed at a later time.
- *Streaming* data is data that is processed as it is received.

Batch data requires data to be collected in batches before it can be processed, stored, analyzed, and fed into an ML model.

Streaming data flows in continuously and can be processed, stored, analyzed, and acted on as soon as it is generated. Streaming data can come from a wide variety of distributed sources in many different formats. Simply stated, streaming data is data that is generated continuously and in real time. This type of data can be used to train ML models that can make predictions in real time. For example, a streaming data model could be used to detect fraud or predict customer churn.

An Overview of GitHub and Google's Colab

This section talks about how to set up a Jupyter Notebook and GitHub project repository. The GitHub repository can hold your datasets and the low-code project notebooks you create—such as the Jupyter Notebooks mentioned in this book.

Use GitHub to Create a Data Repository for Your Projects

GitHub is a code repository where you store your Jupyter notebooks and experimental raw data for free. Let's get started!

1. Sign up for a new GitHub account

GitHub offers personal accounts for individuals and organizations. When you create a personal account, it serves as your identity on *GitHub.com*. When you create a personal account, you must select a billing plan for the account.

2. Set up your project's GitHub repo

To set up your first GitHub repo, see the full steps in the "Use GitHub to Create a Data Repository for Your Projects" page in Chapter 2 of the book's GitHub repo (*https://oreil.ly/supp-lcai*). You can also refer to GitHub documentation (*https://oreil.ly/1iJ-w*) on how to create a repo.

Type a short, memorable name for your repository; for example, low-code book projects. A description is optional, but in this exercise, enter **Low-code AI book projects**. Choose a repository visibility—in this case, the default is Public, which means anyone on the internet can see this repository. Figure 2-10 shows what your setup should look like.

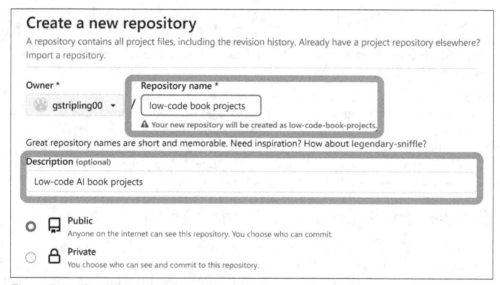

Figure 2-10. Create a new repository page.

Have GitHub create a *README.md* file. This is where you can write a long description for your project. Keep the other defaults: `.gitignore` lets you choose which files not to track, and a license tells others what they can and can't do with your code. Lastly, GitHub reminds you that you are creating a public repository in your personal account. When done, click "Create repository." Figure 2-11 shows what the page should look like.

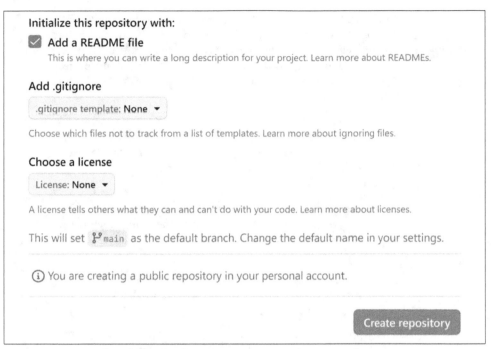

Figure 2-11. Initialize the repo settings.

After clicking "Create repository," the repo page appears, as shown in Figure 2-12.

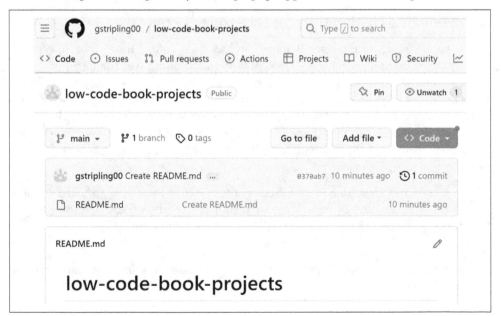

Figure 2-12. Your GitHub repo page.

In the next section, you will create a Jupyter Notebook in Google's Colaboratory. You will save the notebook file from Colab into GitHub, which will create a file under the *Main* branch. Creating a file in GitHub is a great way to improve collaboration on a project. It provides a number of features that can help teams work more effectively together:

Version control
GitHub tracks changes to files. This means that everyone who has access to the file can see the changes that have been made, and they can revert to a previous version if necessary.

Pull requests
Pull requests allow collaborators to propose changes to a file. This gives everyone a chance to review the changes before they are merged into the main branch.

Issues
Issues can be used to track bugs or feature requests. This allows everyone to collaborate on solving problems and adding new features.

Comments
Comments can be added to files to provide feedback or ask questions. This allows for a more collaborative way of working on code.

Using Google's Colaboratory for Low-Code AI Projects

Years ago, if you wanted to learn Python, you had to download the Python interpreter and install it on your computer. This could be a daunting task for beginners, as it required knowledge of how to install software and configure your computer. Today, there are many ways to learn Python without having to install anything on your computer. You can use online IDEs (integrated development environments) that allow you to write and run Python code in a web browser. You can also use cloud-based Python environments that provide you with access to a Python interpreter and all the libraries you need to get started.

These online and cloud-based resources make it easier than ever to learn Python, regardless of your level of experience or technical expertise. Here are some of the benefits of using online and cloud-based resources to learn Python:

No installation required
You can start learning Python right away, without having to download or install any software.

Access from anywhere

You can use online and cloud-based resources to learn Python from anywhere, as long as you have an internet connection.

Affordable

Online and cloud-based resources are often free or very affordable.

Easy to use

Online and cloud-based resources are designed to be easy to use, even for beginners.

You build your low-code Python Jupyter Notebook using Google's Colaboratory, or Colab. Colab is a hosted Jupyter Notebook service that requires no setup to use, while providing access to computing resources, including graphical processing units (GPUs). Colab runs in your web browser and allows you to write and execute Python code. Colab notebooks are stored in Google Drive and can be shared similarly to how you share Google Docs or Sheets.

Google Colaboratory is free to use, and there is no need to sign up for any accounts or pay for any subscriptions. You can share your notebooks with others and work on projects together.

1. Create a Colaboratory Python Jupyter Notebook

Go to Colab (*https://colab.research.google.com*) to create a new Python Jupyter notebook. Figure 2-13 shows the home screen.

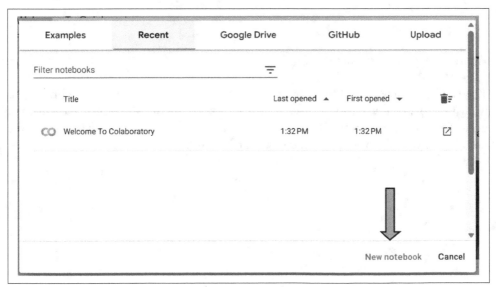

Figure 2-13. Google Colab home page.

Title the notebook in the title bar as shown in Figure 2-14 (A) and expand to show the table of contents (B). Then click the + Code button (C) to add a cell to hold your code. The + Text button allows you to add text, such as documentation.

Figure 2-14. Title notebook and add a new cell code.

2. Import libraries and dataset using Pandas

Once you have added the code cell, you need to import any libraries you will need. In this simple example, you'll just import Pandas. Type **import pandas as pd** into the cell and run it by clicking the arrow, as shown in Figure 2-15.

Figure 2-15. Code to import Pandas.

The Pandas library is used for data analysis. Typically, when you import a library, you want to provide a way to use it without having to write out the words *Pandas* each time. Thus, the *pd* is a short-hand name (or alias) for Pandas. This alias is generally used by convention to shorten the module and submodule names.

The dataset is from the *data.gov* website. It is entitled "Heart Disease Mortality Data Among US Adults" (*https://oreil.ly/yq1hY*) (Figure 2-16).

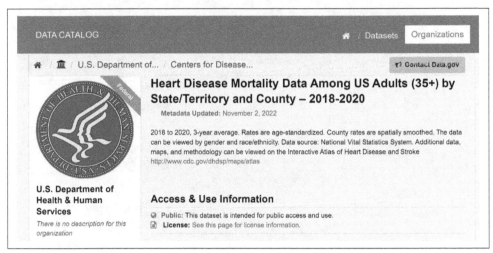

Figure 2-16. Heart disease mortality data among US adults by region.

Scroll down the page until you get to the section shown in Figure 2-17. Now, there are two ways you can import the file into your Jupyter Notebook. You can download the file to your desktop and then import it, or you can use the URL. Let's use the URL method. Click on the Comma Separated Values File shown in Figure 2-17, which takes you to the URL download shown in Figure 2-18.

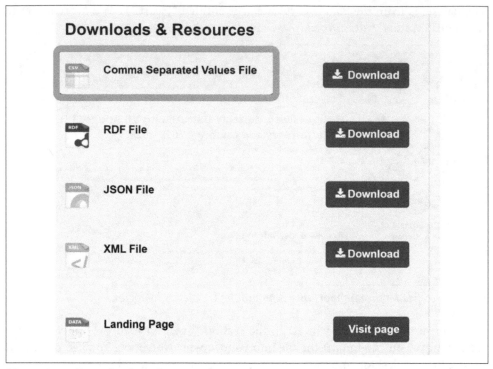

Figure 2-17. Downloads and resources page.

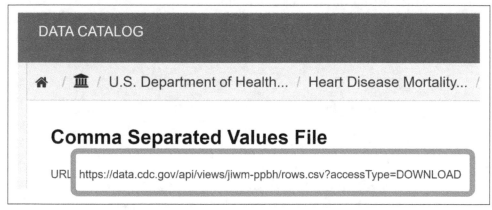

Figure 2-18. Comma separated values file URL link.

Copy the URL shown in Figure 2-18 from the website. Then, go to your Google Colab notebook and type in the code shown in Figure 2-19 into a new cell (A). Run the cell by clicking the arrow (B).

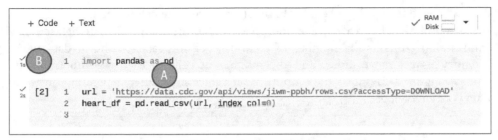

Figure 2-19. Code to read the URL into a Pandas DataFrame.

You have written code to import the dataset into a Pandas DataFrame. A Pandas DataFrame is a two-dimensional data structure that is used to store data in a table format. It is similar to a spreadsheet.

Now you add code to show the first five rows (or *head*) of the DataFrame. Add a new cell, type **heart_df.head()** into the cell, and run the cell. The code and output are shown in Figure 2-20.

```
heart_df.head()
```

GeographicLevel	DataSource	Class	Topic	Data_Value	Data_Value_Unit	Data_Value_Type
County	NVSS	Cardiovascular Diseases	Heart Disease Mortality	182.4	per 100,000 population	Age-adjusted, Spatially Smoothed, 3-year Avera...
County	NVSS	Cardiovascular Diseases	Heart Disease Mortality	172.6	per 100,000 population	Age-adjusted, Spatially Smoothed, 3-year Avera...
County	NVSS	Cardiovascular Diseases	Heart Disease Mortality	255.6	per 100,000 population	Age-adjusted, Spatially Smoothed, 3-year Avera...
County	NVSS	Cardiovascular Diseases	Heart Disease Mortality	343.4	per 100,000 population	Age-adjusted, Spatially Smoothed, 3-year Avera...
County	NVSS	Cardiovascular Diseases	Heart Disease Mortality	NaN	per 100,000 population	Age-adjusted, Spatially Smoothed, 3-year Avera...

Figure 2-20. First five rows of the DataFrame. Some columns were removed for the sake of readability.

Add a new code cell. Type **heart_df.info()** and run the cell to see information on the DataFrame. The .info() method gives you information on your dataset. The information contains the number of columns, column labels, column data types, memory usage, range index, and the number of cells in each column (non-null values). Figure 2-21 shows the output. Exact values may differ depending on when data is downloaded.

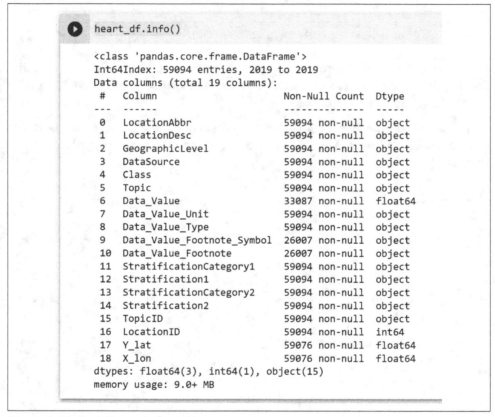

```
heart_df.info()

<class 'pandas.core.frame.DataFrame'>
Int64Index: 59094 entries, 2019 to 2019
Data columns (total 19 columns):
 #   Column                      Non-Null Count  Dtype
---  ------                      --------------  -----
 0   LocationAbbr                59094 non-null  object
 1   LocationDesc                59094 non-null  object
 2   GeographicLevel             59094 non-null  object
 3   DataSource                  59094 non-null  object
 4   Class                       59094 non-null  object
 5   Topic                       59094 non-null  object
 6   Data_Value                  33087 non-null  float64
 7   Data_Value_Unit             59094 non-null  object
 8   Data_Value_Type             59094 non-null  object
 9   Data_Value_Footnote_Symbol  26007 non-null  object
 10  Data_Value_Footnote         26007 non-null  object
 11  StratificationCategory1     59094 non-null  object
 12  Stratification1             59094 non-null  object
 13  StratificationCategory2     59094 non-null  object
 14  Stratification2             59094 non-null  object
 15  TopicID                     59094 non-null  object
 16  LocationID                  59094 non-null  int64
 17  Y_lat                       59076 non-null  float64
 18  X_lon                       59076 non-null  float64
dtypes: float64(3), int64(1), object(15)
memory usage: 9.0+ MB
```

Figure 2-21. DataFrame information output.

From what the .info() output shows, you have 15 string object columns (which is qualitative data) and 4 numeric columns (quantitative data). Think of int64 as a number without a decimal (for example, 25) and float64 as a number with a decimal (25.5).

3. Data validation

As a best practice, validate any data you import from a URL—especially if you have a CSV file format to compare it with. If the dataset page had listed more metadata about the data, such as the number of columns and the column names, you could have avoided the steps to follow. But alas, it is the nature of working with data!

Now, return to the *data.gov* page and download the CSV file to your computer. You are going to validate that the file you have downloaded matches the file you imported from the URL.

You do this by uploading the downloaded file to your Colab notebook and then reading that file into a Pandas DataFrame. Expand the table of contents in your Chapter 2 notebook by selecting the folder shown in Figure 2-22 (A). Then, to upload a file, select the up arrow folder (B).

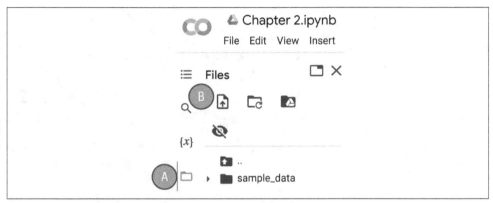

Figure 2-22. Upload file to your Colab notebook.

As you upload the file, you will see the warning message shown in Figure 2-23. This warning basically states that any file you upload will not be saved if the runtime is terminated (which can happen if you close out of Colab). Note that runtime provides the program with the environment it needs to run.

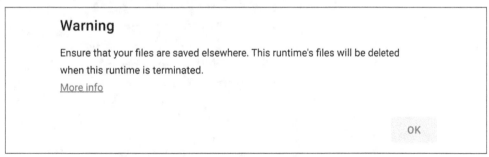

Figure 2-23. Warning message that any uploaded files are not permanently saved.

Refresh your notebook browser tab after the upload and expand it to see the table of contents. Your screen should look as shown in Figure 2-24.

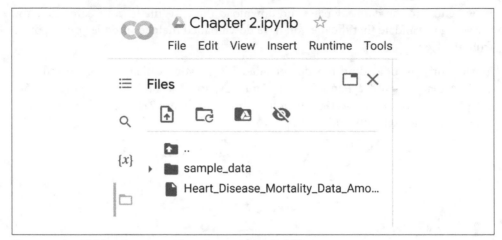

Figure 2-24. Table of contents that shows uploaded file.

Note how long the filename is—go ahead and rename it by right-clicking on the file and renaming it *heart.csv*. Your screen should look as shown in Figure 2-25.

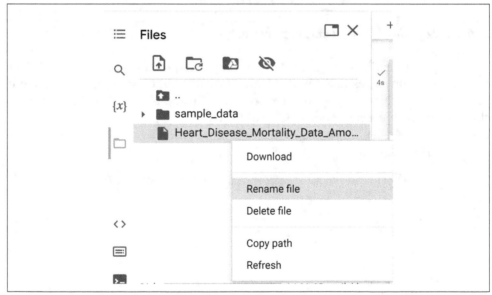

Figure 2-25. Select "Rename file" option.

Your screen should look as shown in Figure 2-26 after renaming the file.

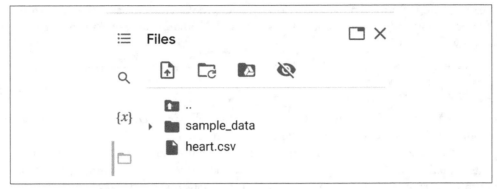

Figure 2-26. File renamed to heart.csv.

So, you've renamed your file to *heart.csv*. Now you need to copy the path of the file, as shown in Figure 2-27. Why? You will need the exact location to input as a parameter in the Pandas `read.csv` method. Right-click on the *heart.csv* file to get the path.

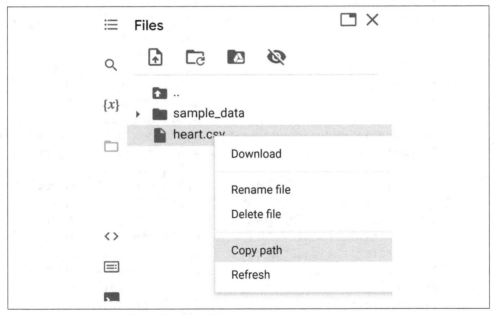

Figure 2-27. Copying the path of the file.

Add a code cell and type in the following code. Make sure to paste the path to the file between the two single quote marks around */content/heart.csv*. Run the cell and review the output:

```
heart_df = pd.read_csv('/content/heart.csv', error_bad_lines=False,
    engine="python")
heart_df.head()
```

Type **heart_df.info()** into a new cell. Run the cell to see DataFrame information. Compare the total columns from Figures 2-21 to 2-28. Figure 2-21 has 19 columns and Figure 2-28 has 20 columns. This means that by uploading the file, a Year column was added. The Year datatype is not a numeric value—it has numbers, but those numbers are meant to rank and order, not calculate on. Figure 2-28 indicates you have your first case of dirty data for our machine learning use case.

```
Data columns (total 20 columns):
 #   Column                     Non-Null Count   Dtype
---  ------                     --------------   -----
 0   Year                       41071 non-null   int64
 1   LocationAbbr               41071 non-null   object
 2   LocationDesc               41071 non-null   object
 3   GeographicLevel            41071 non-null   object
 4   DataSource                 41071 non-null   object
 5   Class                      41071 non-null   object
 6   Topic                      41071 non-null   object
 7   Data_Value                 23316 non-null   float64
 8   Data_Value_Unit            41071 non-null   object
 9   Data_Value_Type            41071 non-null   object
 10  Data_Value_Footnote_Symbol 17755 non-null   object
 11  Data_Value_Footnote        17755 non-null   object
 12  StratificationCategory1    41071 non-null   object
 13  Stratification1            41071 non-null   object
 14  StratificationCategory2    41071 non-null   object
 15  Stratification2            41071 non-null   object
 16  TopicID                    41071 non-null   object
 17  LocationID                 41071 non-null   int64
 18  Y_lat                      41071 non-null   float64
 19  X_lon                      41071 non-null   float64
dtypes: float64(3), int64(2), object(15)
```

Figure 2-28. Year column showing as int64.

Type **heart_df.isnull().sum()** into a new cell as shown in Figure 2-29. Run the cell. Are there any null values? A *null value* is a value that indicates the absence of a value. You have your second case of dirty data! Three of your columns have null values. You will learn how to deal with missing values in a subsequent chapter. Since you really don't have a use case yet, you may be wondering whether you really need all of these features. Note that features are the input data that is used to train a model. The model then uses the features to make predictions. You'll learn about feature selection in a subsequent chapter.

```
    ▶  heart_df.isnull().sum()

    ⟶  Year                                    0
       LocationAbbr                            0
       LocationDesc                            0
       GeographicLevel                         0
       DataSource                              0
       Class                                   0
       Topic                                   0
       Data_Value                          17755
       Data_Value_Unit                         0
       Data_Value_Type                         0
       Data_Value_Footnote_Symbol          23316
       Data_Value_Footnote                 23316
       StratificationCategory1                 0
       Stratification1                         0
       StratificationCategory2                 0
       Stratification2                         0
       TopicID                                 0
       LocationID                              0
       Y_lat                                   0
       X_lon                                   0
       dtype: int64
```

Figure 2-29. IsNull output showing the number of null cells in the three columns with null values.

What are your data quality issues?

Missing values

Most algorithms do not accept missing values. Therefore, when we see missing values in our dataset, there may be a tendency to just "drop all the rows" with missing values. However, there are various ways you can deal with missing values, as explained in the following note.

There are two main approaches to handling missing values in a dataset in ML: deletion or imputation.

Deletion involves removing the rows or columns with missing values from the dataset. This can be done by dropping all rows with missing values, dropping all columns with missing values, or dropping rows or columns with a certain threshold of missing values.

Imputation involves filling in the missing values with estimates. There are many different imputation techniques, including (1) mean imputation, which replaces missing values with the mean of the observed values for that variable; (2) median imputation, which replaces missing values with the median of the observed values for that variable; (3) mode imputation, which replaces missing values with the most frequent value of the variable; and (4) regression imputation, which uses a regression model to predict the missing values based on the observed values of other variables.

Although Pandas will fill in the blank space with *NaN (not a number)*, we should handle them in some way. More on that later in the book.

Data type incorrect

Year is shown as an int64 data type and should be a string object—where you would need to handle it as a qualitative, categorical feature.

Categorical columns

There are quite a number of string object features—which are not numeric. You cannot feed values like this into an ML model. These features need to be *one-hot encoded*. You'll see this in a subsequent chapter.

4. A little bit of exploratory data analysis

Before concluding this section, let's look at some simple ways to explore the data. Want to see all of the unique values in the feature Stratification2? Type **heart_df.Stratification2.unique()** into a new cell as shown in Figure 2-30. Run the cell.

```
heart_df.Stratification2.unique()

array(['Overall', 'White', 'Black', 'Hispanic',
       'Asian and Pacific Islander', 'American Indian and Alaskan Native'],
      dtype=object)
```

Figure 2-30. Code to show unique values of column `Stratification2`.

Let's use Seaborn's violin plot to visualize this feature. Seaborn is a Python library for making statistical graphics. You can write all of this in the same cell, as shown in Figure 2-31. This code uses the `Data_Value` feature as the *x* and the `Stratification2` as the *y*. Note that the `Data_Value` feature is the count of heart disease in each region and by group, as shown in Figure 2-32.

```
import seaborn as sns
sns.violinplot(x="Data_Value", y="Stratification2", data=heart_df)
```

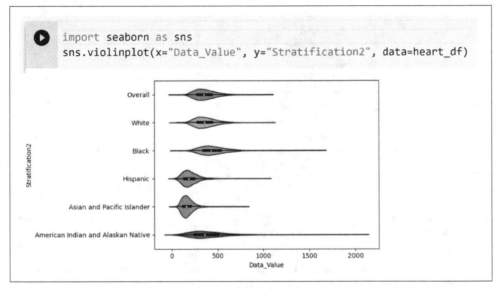

Figure 2-31. Violin plot of `Stratification2` column.

The "long tails" indicate there are more outliers in the data for that particular feature. The large shape of the violin body indicates how many heart disease cases are distributed by race.

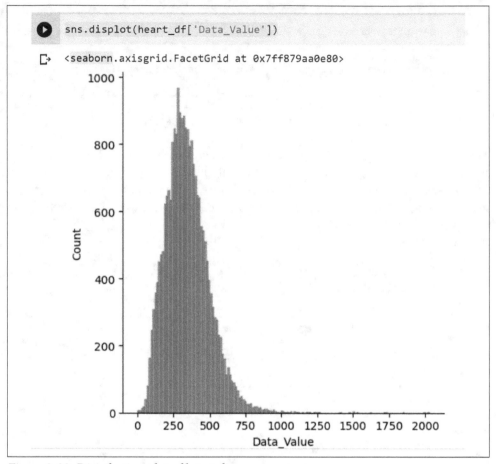

```
sns.displot(heart_df['Data_Value'])
```

<seaborn.axisgrid.FacetGrid at 0x7ff879aa0e80>

Figure 2-32. Distribution plot of heart disease count.

Seaborn's violin plot is a good way to visualize the distribution of a univariate set of data.

It is used to visualize the distribution of numerical data. Unlike a box plot that can only show summary statistics, violin plots depict summary statistics and the density of each variable.

In later chapters, you'll perform more data analysis and learn data preprocessing. For now, save your notebook to GitHub. On the Colab menu, click File > Save a copy in GitHub, as shown in Figure 2-33.

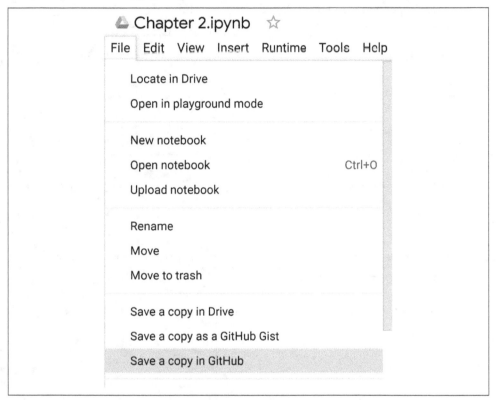

Figure 2-33. How to save a file copy of the notebook in GitHub.

Figure 2-34 shows the setup. From the drop-down under Repository, select the repo to save your notebook to. Under Branch, select Notebooks (you created this earlier). Keep the default "Include a link to Colaboratory." This will show a link in GitHub that allows you to open your notebook directly from GitHub.

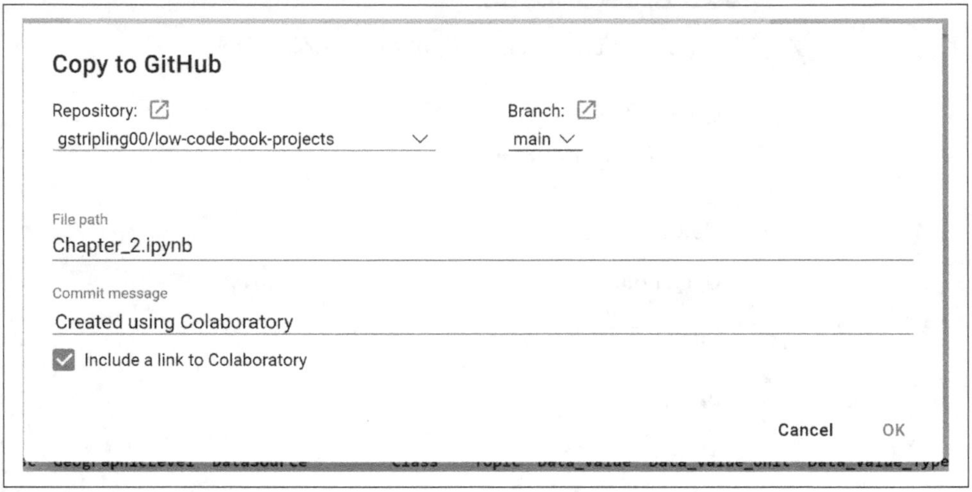

Figure 2-34. Colab's GitHub export window.

After Colab copies the notebook to GitHub, it takes you directly to GitHub, as shown in Figure 2-35.

Figure 2-35. Notebook copied to GitHub.

Refresh the screen in the repo. You should see your Colab Jupyter notebook, as shown in Figure 2-36.

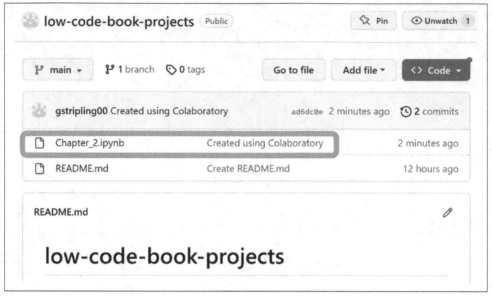

Figure 2-36. Copy of Colab Jupyter notebook in GitHub.

Summary

This chapter provided an overview of the use cases and datasets used in the book. You learned about data types and the difference between structured, semistructured, and unstructured and batch and streaming data. You got hands-on practice with a free browser-based Python Jupyter Notebook and GitHub. You discovered that dirty data is tricky and can impact data type and data ingestion into an ML model.

In the next chapter, you'll learn about ML frameworks and you'll get to work with AutoML. You are given a preprocessed dataset, and all you'll have to do is upload the dataset into the AutoML framework and you will be able to build and train a predictive model without writing a single line of code.

## CHAPTER 3

Machine Learning Libraries and Frameworks

This chapter introduces machine learning (ML) frameworks (*https://oreil.ly/IJbCu*) that simplify the development of ML models. Typically, you need to understand the underlying working principles of mathematics, statistics, and ML to build and train ML pipelines. These frameworks help you by automating many of the time-consuming ML workflow tasks such as feature selection, algorithm selection, code writing, pipeline development, performance tuning, and model deployment.

No-Code AutoML

Imagine you are a business analyst working for a utility company. You have a project that requires you to help the company develop marketing and outreach programs that target communities with high electrical energy consumption. The data is in a comma separated value (*CSV*) file format.

You do not have an ML background or any programming knowledge—but the team lead has asked you to take on this project because you have expressed an interest in ML and how it can be applied in the organization. Although you have no coding experience, the little research you have done has yielded a few observations:

- For noncoders like yourself, there are automated *no-code* ML frameworks with a graphical user interface (GUI) that you can use to build and train an ML model without writing a single line of code.

- For light coders, there are *low-code* ML frameworks that provide the ability to build and train an ML model by writing just a little bit of code.
- For seasoned coders, there are ML libraries that allow the flexibility and control to code every phase of the ML workflow.

Based on the data from your utility marketing outreach project and use case, you determine that your target is to predict total kilowatt-hours (kWh) based on multiple variables: zip code, month, year, and customer class (Residential, Commercial, Industrial, and Agricultural).

Let's assume you need to quickly get a baseline prediction. This is an excellent use case for AutoML. A GUI-based AutoML framework is the easiest to use. Figure 3-1 shows a high-level overview of the typical AutoML no-code workflow you can use for your business use case. This example uses Google's Vertex AI, which is an ML platform that helps you build, deploy, and scale ML models. Overall, Google AutoML, Microsoft Azure AutoML, and AWS SageMaker AutoML are all powerful AutoML solutions that can help you build and deploy ML models without writing any code. The best solution for you will depend on your specific needs and requirements.

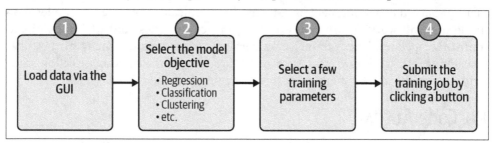

Figure 3-1. Typical Vertex AI AutoML no-code workflow.

Since the file format is CSV, you select the Tabular tab. Given that total kWh is the output and is the numeric value you want to predict, you note that this is a regression task—and since you have column names (or *labels*) for the multiple variables, it is a *supervised* ML problem. Data without labels require an unsupervised ML task, such as clustering. Figure 3-2 shows Regression/classification selected as the objective.

Vertex AI lets you create the following model types for tabular data:

Binary classification models
> These models predict a binary outcome (one of two classes). Use this type for yes or no questions.

Multi-class classification models
> These models predict one class from three or more discrete classes. Use this type for categorization.

Regression models
> These models predict a continuous value. Use this type to predict sales.

Forecasting models
> These models predict a sequence of values. Use this type to forecast daily demand.

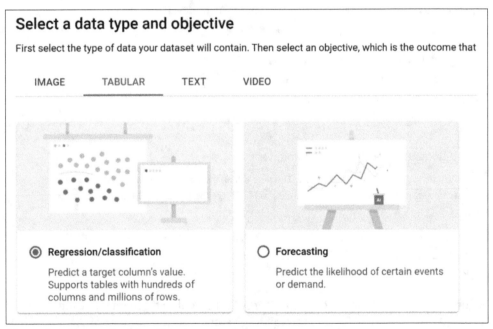

Figure 3-2. Regression/classification selection.

Some frameworks will generate statistics after the data loads. Other frameworks help minimize the need to manually clean data by automatically detecting and cleaning missing values, anomalous values, and duplicate rows and columns. Note that there are a few additional steps that you can employ, such as to review the data after it has loaded to check for missing values and view data statistics. Figure 3-3 shows the dataset upload options.

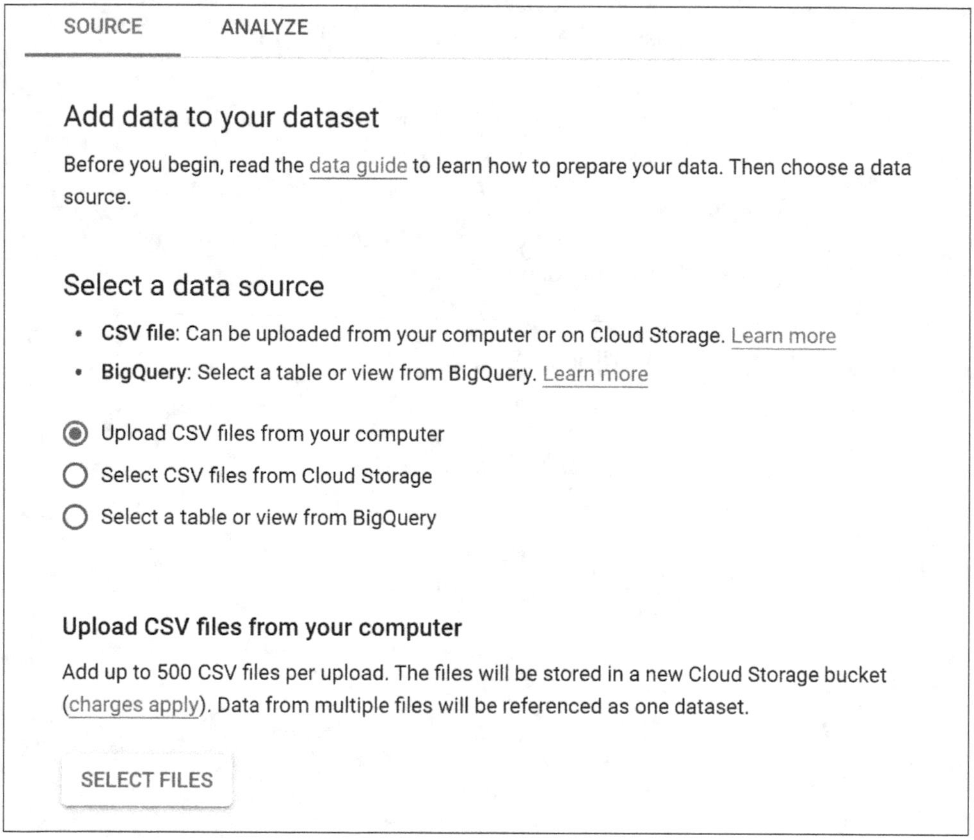

| SOURCE | ANALYZE |

Add data to your dataset

Before you begin, read the data guide to learn how to prepare your data. Then choose a data source.

Select a data source

- **CSV file**: Can be uploaded from your computer or on Cloud Storage. Learn more
- **BigQuery**: Select a table or view from BigQuery. Learn more

- ◉ Upload CSV files from your computer
- ○ Select CSV files from Cloud Storage
- ○ Select a table or view from BigQuery

Upload CSV files from your computer

Add up to 500 CSV files per upload. The files will be stored in a new Cloud Storage bucket (charges apply). Data from multiple files will be referenced as one dataset.

SELECT FILES

Figure 3-3. Data source options.

Figure 3-4 shows statistics of your energy utility dataset generated using Google's Vertex AI framework. There are no missing values, and the number of distinct values for each column is shown. For example, there are 145 zip codes. Because zip code is a number, the Transformation column shows it as "Numeric." However, zip code is a categorical feature, as each zip code is different from one another and can thus be put into its own "category." Changing ZipCode from numeric to categorical is as easy as selecting the drop-down to customize the transformation.

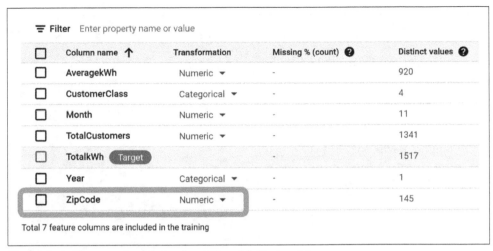

Column name ↑	Transformation	Missing % (count) ❓	Distinct values ❓
☐ AveragekWh	Numeric ▼	-	920
☐ CustomerClass	Categorical ▼	-	4
☐ Month	Numeric ▼	-	11
☐ TotalCustomers	Numeric ▼	-	1341
☐ TotalkWh (Target)		-	1517
☐ Year	Categorical ▼	-	1
☐ ZipCode	Numeric ▼	-	145

Total 7 feature columns are included in the training

Figure 3-4. Generated statistics from Google's Vertex AI.

Figure 3-5 shows `ZipCode` now as a categorical feature. Also note the far right column, where you can select or deselect a feature to be included for training.

GENERATE STATISTICS ▼

Column name ↑	Transformation	Missing % (count) ❓	Distinct values ❓	Correlation w/ targe	
☐ AveragekWh	Numeric ▼	-	920	-	⊖
☐ CustomerClass	Categorical ▼	-	4	-	⊖
☐ Month	Numeric ▼	-	11	-	⊖
☐ TotalCustomers	Numeric ▼	-	1341	-	⊖
☐ TotalkWh (Target)		-	1517	-	
☐ Year	Categorical ▼	-	1	-	⊕
☐ ZipCode	Categorical ▼	-	145	-	⊕

Total 5 feature columns are included in the training

Figure 3-5. `ZipCode` shown as categorical feature.

AutoML presents a data profile of each feature. Figure 3-6 shows zip code 92694 as the most common feature, which indicates more customers live in that zip code area. You can leverage this information for your marketing campaigns.

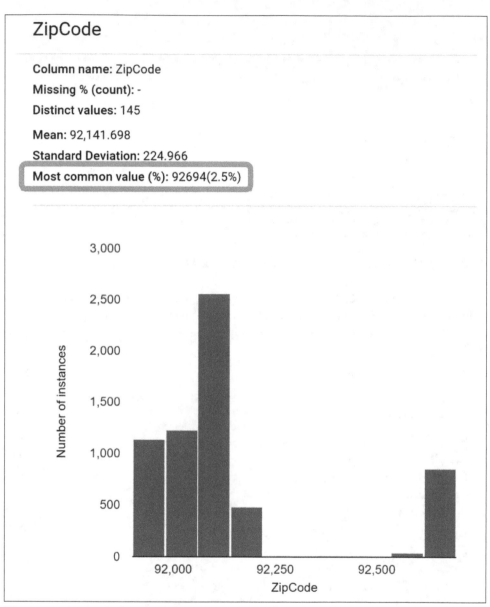

ZipCode

Column name: ZipCode

Missing % (count): -

Distinct values: 145

Mean: 92,141.698

Standard Deviation: 224.966

Most common value (%): 92694(2.5%)

Figure 3-6. Zip code shown as the most common feature.

In Step 3, you train a new model by selecting a few training parameters. Vertex AI's "Train new model" window lets you select the training method, model details, training options, and compute and pricing. Note the dataset and the objective (Regression) are shown as inputs in the "Training method" parameter. AutoML is selected by default. Figure 3-7 shows the "Train new model" window.

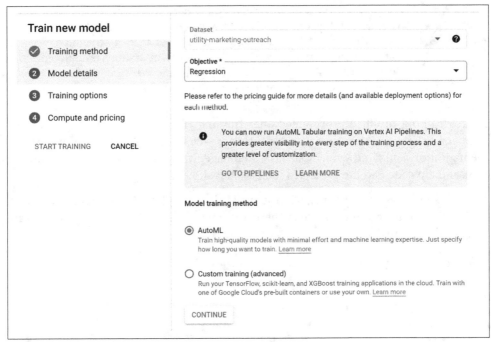

Figure 3-7. The "Train new model" window with compute and pricing selected.

Once all the parameters are entered, you start the training job. Figure 3-8 shows that it's ready to submit the training job for training.

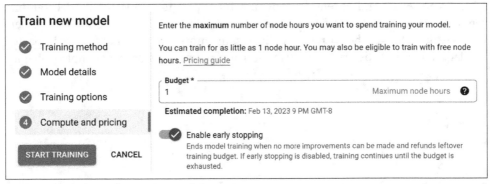

Figure 3-8. Submit the training job for training.

Training can take up to several hours, depending on the size of your data and type of model objective you choose. Image and video data types may take much longer to process than a structured data type such as a CSV file. The number of training samples also impacts training time. AutoML training is also time intensive because of the nature of AutoML and how it works.

Model training results are presented after training. You can now present your preliminary findings to the team before next steps—which could include more experimentation or deploying your model as a web page, where a user selects the customer class and zip code and the predicted total kWh is shown.

Figure 3-9 shows training results. You will see examples of a complete AutoML project in an upcoming chapter, where the metrics presented in Figure 3-9 are discussed in more detail.

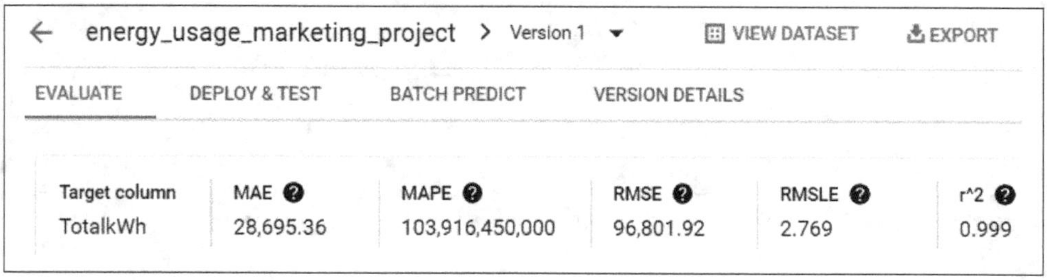

← energy_usage_marketing_project > Version 1 ▼				⊞ VIEW DATASET	⬇ EXPORT
EVALUATE	DEPLOY & TEST	BATCH PREDICT	VERSION DETAILS		

Target column	MAE ❷	MAPE ❷	RMSE ❷	RMSLE ❷	r^2 ❷
TotalkWh	28,695.36	103,916,450,000	96,801.92	2.769	0.999

Figure 3-9. Model training results.

Model feature attribution tells you how much each feature impacted model training. Figure 3-10 shows attribution values expressed as a percentage; the higher the percentage, the stronger the correlation—that is, the more strongly that feature impacted model training. Model feature attribution is expressed using the sampled Shapley method (see the glossary on GitHub (*https://oreil.ly/tVCwP*)).

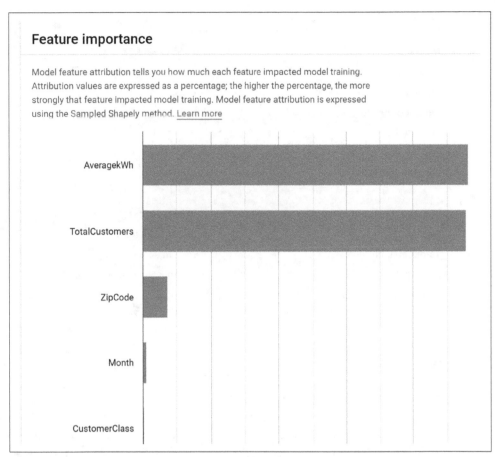

Figure 3-10. Attribution values are expressed as a percentage.

Figure 3-11 shows model metadata. You see various information about the model, from its ID, date created, and training time, to the dataset used, target column, data splitting percentage allocation, and the model evaluation metric used—in this case, root mean squared error (RMSE). Clicking on "Model" or "Trials" lets you retrieve info on which model has been used by AutoML.

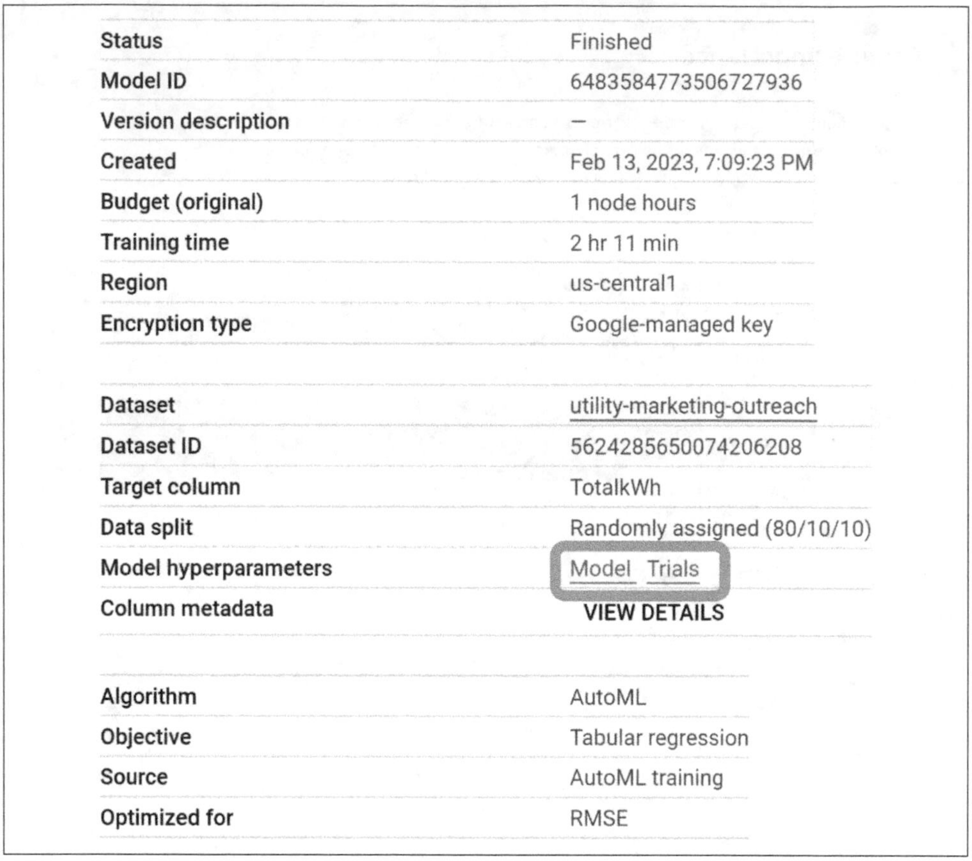

Status	Finished
Model ID	6483584773506727936
Version description	—
Created	Feb 13, 2023, 7:09:23 PM
Budget (original)	1 node hours
Training time	2 hr 11 min
Region	us-central1
Encryption type	Google-managed key
Dataset	utility-marketing-outreach
Dataset ID	5624285650074206208
Target column	TotalkWh
Data split	Randomly assigned (80/10/10)
Model hyperparameters	Model Trials
Column metadata	**VIEW DETAILS**
Algorithm	AutoML
Objective	Tabular regression
Source	AutoML training
Optimized for	RMSE

Figure 3-11. Model metadata.

How AutoML Works

Implementing an ML workflow is time-consuming. As you saw from the preceding marketing outreach use case, AutoML simplified the process of building an ML model for you—you did not have to write a single line of code—for any tasks. Figure 3-12 shows the workflow for the utility marketing outreach project. Phases 2, 3, and 4 required no coding.

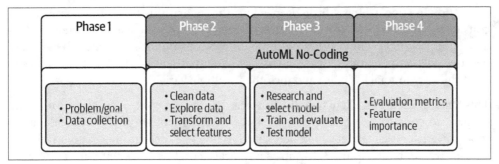

Figure 3-12. Workflow for the utility marketing outreach project.

To better understand how AutoML works, note what you did *not* have to do!

First, you did not have to set up an environment to run a Python Jupyter Notebook. There was no need to install any software libraries. In fact, there was nothing to install.

Once you uploaded the CSV data file into Vertex AI, the file was stored in the cloud. If you were using Python and Pandas, there was no need to write any code to load a dataset or even to split the dataset into training, validation, and testing files.

While the data was clean, there were two categorical features: zip code and customer class. If you had coded for those two features, you would have had to "one-hot encode" each one. *One-hot encoding* is the process of converting categorical data variables into numerical values. The following shows sample code for one-hot encoding for the feature zip code:

```
from sklearn.preprocessing import OneHotEncoder
one_hot = OneHotEncoder()
encoded = one_hot.fit_transform(df[[`zipcode`]])
df[one_hot.categories[0]] = encoded.toarray()
```

One-hot encoding is an example of feature *transformation* or engineering. You also had the ability to easily select the target (output) and/or deselect features—or *drop* them. You did not have to write code that resembled what is shown in the following, where the column "id" is being dropped from a Pandas DataFrame:

```
import pandas as pd
df = pd.read_csv(`/path/file.tsv`, header=0, delimiter=`\t`)
print df.drop(`id`, 1)
```

More features in your dataset lead to more complex relationships that may be nonlinear. Neural networks are perfect for working with nonlinear relationships. You may not have had any idea about any of this, so let's break it down a bit further.

As stated earlier, this is a prediction problem because you wanted to know whether future total kWh can be predicted based upon average KWh, customer class, month, year, and zip code. Going a little deeper into the theory, this type of use case can be considered complex due to the number of input features—it has multiple variables and is *multivariate*. These types of complex relationships are considered *nonlinear* because you cannot simply draw a "straight" line that will be the "best fit" between what the known total kWh are and the other multiple variables.

This dataset is an excellent candidate for a neural network. *Neural networks* are difficult to construct without prior ML knowledge. Although neural networks are a topic for a later chapter, let's look quickly at an image to determine what you did *not* have to think about. Figure 3-13 shows a typical neural network with an input layer, hidden layers, and an output layer.

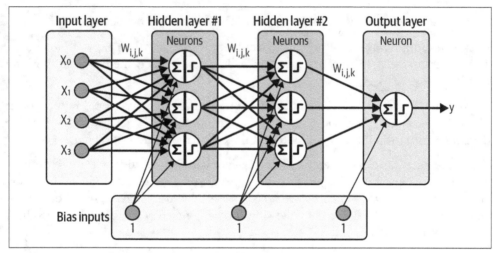

Figure 3-13. Four-layer neural network.

Coding a neural network in Python would look something like this:

```
# Create the 'Network' class and define its arguments:
# Set the number of neurons/nodes for each layer
# and initialize the weight matrices:
class Network:

    def __init__(self,
                no_of_in_nodes,
                no_of_out_nodes,
                no_of_hidden_nodes,
                learning_rate):
        self.no_of_in_nodes = no_of_in_nodes
        self.no_of_out_nodes = no_of_out_nodes
        self.no_of_hidden_nodes = no_of_hidden_nodes
        self.learning_rate = learning_rate
        self.create_weight_matrices()

    def create_weight_matrices(self):
```

```
""" A method to initialize the weight matrices of the neural network"""
rad = 1 / np.sqrt(self.no_of_in_nodes)
X = truncated_normal(mean=0, sd=1, low=-rad, upp=rad)
self.weights_in_hidden = X.rvs((self.no_of_hidden_nodes,
                                self.no_of_in_nodes))
rad = 1 / np.sqrt(self.no_of_hidden_nodes)
X = truncated_normal(mean=0, sd=1, low=-rad, upp=rad)
self.weights_hidden_out = X.rvs((self.no_of_out_nodes,
                                 self.no_of_hidden_nodes))

def train(self, input_vector, target_vector):
    pass # More work is needed to train the network

def run(self, input_vector):
    """
    running the network with an input vector 'input_vector'.
    'input_vector' can be tuple, list or ndarray
    """

    # Turn the input vector into a column vector:
    input_vector = np.array(input_vector, ndmin=2).T

    # activation_function() implements the expit function,
    # which is an implementation of the sigmoid function:
    input_hidden = activation_function(
        self.weights_in_hidden @ input_vector)
    output_vector = activation_function(
        self.weights_hidden_out @ input_hidden)
    return output_vector
```

Using Keras, the coding becomes somewhat easier. Coding a neural network would look something like this:

```
# Import python libraries required in this example:
from keras.layers import Dense, Activation
from keras.models import Sequential
import numpy as np

# Use numpy arrays to store inputs (x) and outputs (y):
x = np.array([[0, 0], [0, 1], [1, 0], [1, 1]])
y = np.array([[0], [1], [1], [0]])

# Define the network model and its arguments.
# Set the number of neurons/nodes for each layer:
model = Sequential()
model.add(Dense(2, input_shape=(2,)))
model.add(Activation('relu'))
model.add(Dense(1))
model.add(Activation('relu'))

# Compile the model and calculate its accuracy:
model.compile(
    loss='mean_squared_error', optimizer='rmse', metrics=['accuracy']
)
```

```
# Print a summary of the Keras model:
model.summary()
```

When you built your training job, you simply had to select a dataset and then select a few training parameters. There was no need for any of the following:

No need to understand what kind of regression algorithm to use
There are many types of regression analysis techniques, and the use of each method depends upon a number of factors. These factors include the type of target variable, shape of the regression line, and the number of independent variables.

No need to understand "classical machine learning" versus neural networks
There was no need to comprehend the commonly used neural-network building blocks such as layers, neurons (nodes), objectives, activation functions, or optimizers (see the glossary on GitHub (*https://oreil.ly/tVCwP*)).

No need to understand the training process or any model optimization strategies
During training, AutoML focuses on optimizing not only the model weights but also the architecture. Selecting the appropriate architecture is done by AutoML.

No need to understand or specify compute resources
When you chose "one node," AutoML selected the right machine type.

See the glossary on GitHub (*https://oreil.ly/tVCwP*) for definitions of the types of regression algorithms, such as linear regression, logistic regression, ridge regression, lasso regression, polynomial regression, and Bayesian linear regression.

Machine Learning as a Service

AutoML is part of the machine learning as a service (MLaaS) platform offered by cloud providers. The top three cloud providers are Google, Amazon, and Microsoft. If you are not familiar with cloud architecture and services, Figure 3-14 shows the typical cloud "platform pyramid."

Occupying the bottom of the pyramid is IaaS (infrastructure as a service). Think of this layer as the hardware and storage layer, with customers using the cloud provider's servers to handle the actual computation and storage services for storing dataset files, models, containers, and so on. The middle layer is PaaS (platform as a service). Think of this layer as providing the platform (operating systems such as Linux or Windows) that customers use to run their own software. The top layer is SaaS (software as a service). The best example of this is AutoML—you don't have to configure a server or write code, you just open a browser and use it.

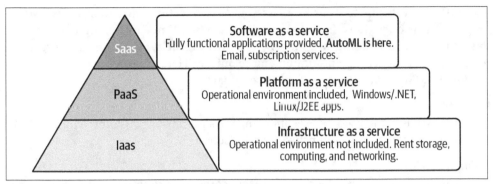

Figure 3-14. Typical cloud "platform pyramid."

Google, Amazon, and Microsoft offer services to support the entire ML workflow, including ML learning algorithm training and tuning, data visualization, data preprocessing, and deep learning (*https://oreil.ly/nD_w4*). They also provide managed Jupyter Notebooks for using frameworks such as scikit-learn, Keras, TensorFlow, and PyTorch. Table 3-1 shows the benefits of MLaaS.

Table 3-1. MLaaS benefits

Data extraction and exploration	• Extract and clean dataset using Jupyter Notebook or, in some cases, the cloud provider's own data visualization tools. • Apply data transformations and feature engineering to the model, and split the data into training, validation, and test sets. • Explore and visualize data using the GUI tool or Jupyter Notebook.
Model training	• Use AutoML for tabular, image, text, and video data. Automatic featurization and algorithm selection. • Shared notebooks, compute resources, data, and environments. • Custom training using open source platforms, such as PyTorch, TensorFlow, or scikit-learn. • Optimize hyperparameters. • Experiment by running different model versions using different techniques and compare results.
Distributed training	Offer multinode distributed training.
Model evaluation and iteration	Provide evaluation metrics so that you can make adjustments to your data and iterate on your model.
Model explainability	Understand how each feature contributes to model prediction (feature attribution).
Model serving	Deploy your model to production and get predictions.
Model monitoring	Monitors the performance of your deployed model for training-serving skew and prediction drift and sends you alerts when the incoming prediction data skews too far from the training baseline .

AutoML is a valuable tool for businesses and organizations that want to use ML to improve their operations. By automating many of the time-consuming and complex tasks involved in building ML models, AutoML can help businesses and organizations get their models up and running more quickly. Here are some specific examples of how AutoML is being used in businesses today:

Telecom
> AutoML is being used by telecom companies to improve customer churn prediction, fraud detection, and network optimization.

Manufacturing
> AutoML is being used by manufacturing companies to improve product quality, optimize production processes, and predict equipment failure.

Retail
> AutoML is being used by retailers to personalize customer experiences, recommend products, and optimize inventory levels.

Healthcare
> AutoML is being used by healthcare companies to diagnose diseases, predict patient outcomes, and personalize treatment plans.

These are just a few examples of how AutoML is being used in businesses today. As AutoML technology continues to mature, expect to see even more innovative applications of AutoML in the future. Table 3-2 shows the benefits of AutoML.

Table 3-2. AutoML benefits

Improved accuracy	AutoML can help businesses and organizations build more accurate ML models. This is because AutoML can experiment with a wider range of algorithms and hyperparameters than a human data scientist could.
Democratized ML	AutoML makes ML more accessible to nonexperts. This is because AutoML provides a simple, user-friendly interface for building and deploying ML models.
Reduced time to market	AutoML can help businesses and organizations get their ML models up and running more quickly. This is because AutoML automates many of the time-consuming tasks involved in building ML models, such as data cleaning, feature engineering, and model training.
Reduced risk	AutoML can help businesses and organizations reduce the risk of building ML models that are biased or inaccurate. This is because AutoML automates many of the steps involved in model validation and testing.

Figure 3-15 shows Google's Vertex AI solution, Figure 3-16 shows Microsoft's Azure ML Studio solution, and Figure 3-17 shows the AutoML for Amazon SageMaker solution.

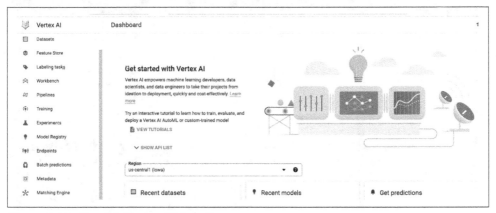

Figure 3-15. Google's Vertex AI interface.

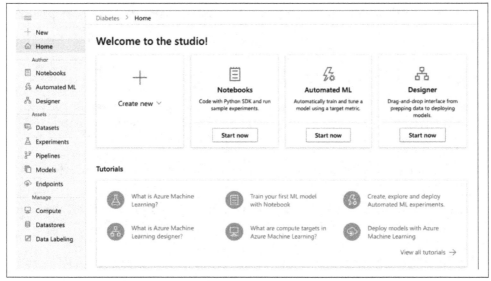

Figure 3-16. Microsoft's Azure ML Studio interface.

Figure 3-17. AutoML for Amazon SageMaker interface.

Low-Code ML Frameworks

Low-code AutoML requires installation and configuration of libraries, plus some knowledge of Python or some knowledge of Structured Query Language (SQL). *Low-code* is defined here as the following:

- ML frameworks that provide an "abstraction layer" on top of an existing ML framework.

- Databases that allow you to run ML models using SQL or databases that allow you to run Python code that includes ML code.

Table 3-3 shows some examples.

Table 3-3. ML framework examples

Cloud providers (SQL)		Open source
Google	BigQuery	AutoKeras
Amazon	Aurora, Redshift	Auto-sklearn
Microsoft	Azure SQL Server	Auto-PyTorch

SQL ML Frameworks

Data analysts and data scientists typically use SQL for data analysis. They can leverage their existing SQL skills and expertise and apply them to ML—without any ML programming backgrounds. If they know SQL but can't code in Python, Java, or R, they can work within a SQL-ML framework for their ML projects. This is why SQL-ML frameworks are considered low-code. There is not a lot of SQL coding required.

Benefits of using databases/data warehouses for SQL-ML:

Model building with large datasets
> When you can build the ML model where the data "lives," then the ML SQL code stays "close to the data" and reduces latency (data transmission times). This is especially crucial for large datasets using deep learning, where training requires iteration through a percentage of the data for training, validation, and testing.

Backend integration with existing ML systems
> Integrate with the cloud provider's backend ML framework (for example, Google's Vertex AI, Amazon's SageMaker, and Microsoft's Azure).

Common model build statements
> All use the `CREATE MODEL` SQL command and specify training data either as a table or `SELECT` statement. They then compile and import the trained model inside the data warehouse and prepare a SQL inference function that can be immediately used in SQL queries.

Use cases
> Typical use cases include fraud detection, product recommendations, and ad targeting due to low-latency, real-time requirements.

> A *database* is a collection of data or information. The term *database* is commonly used to reference both the database itself as well as the database management system (DBMS). *Data warehouses* store large amounts of current and historical data from various sources.

Google's BigQuery ML

Google's BigQuery (*https://oreil.ly/mQYE0*) is a data warehouse. It can provide decision-making guidance through predictive analytics by using its ML tool. You can create and train a model without ever exporting data out of BigQuery. Like Vertex AI, BigQuery ML does not require an environment and dependency setup. BigQuery ML is browser-based and serverless, meaning you don't need a server to run it. If you have data already residing in BigQuery's data warehouse, then you can use that data for your ML projects.

Amazon Aurora ML and Redshift ML

Amazon Aurora (*https://oreil.ly/2-Ngq*) is a relational database management system (RDBMS) built for the cloud with full MySQL and PostgreSQL compatibility. Amazon Aurora ML enables you to add ML-based predictions to applications using SQL. When you run an ML query, Aurora calls Amazon SageMaker for a wide variety of ML algorithms.

Redshift ML (*https://oreil.ly/hR0Lx*) is a data warehouse. You use SQL statements to create and train Amazon SageMaker ML models using Redshift data and then use these models to make predictions. Redshift ML makes the model available as a SQL function within the Redshift data warehouse.

Open Source ML Libraries

Open source AutoML refers to open source frameworks such as AutoKeras, Auto-sklearn (*https://oreil.ly/HtCyl*), and Auto-PyTorch (*https://oreil.ly/xoipb*) that add an additional layer of abstraction on top of existing open source libraries. Typically, you will need to code for the following using a Jupyter notebook:

1. Install the AutoML package.
2. Import the package.
3. Load a dataset.
4. Split the data.
5. Fit the model.
6. Predict.
7. Evaluate.
8. Export the model.

After Step 4, each open source framework has its own way to perform model fit, prediction, and evaluation. Figure 3-18 shows the first four steps.

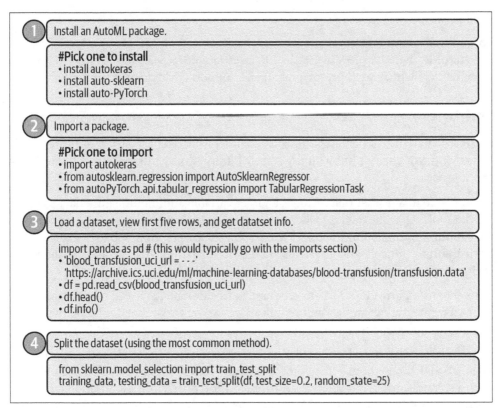

Figure 3-18. First four steps using open source libraries.

AutoKeras

AutoKeras, a Keras-based open source AutoML framework, was developed to allow nonexperts to quickly build neural networks with minimal code. When using Auto-Keras, you only need to specify the training data, and AutoKeras performs the data preprocessing independently. For example, if the data has categorical variables, it will convert them into one-hot encoding depending on whether it is a classification or regression task; if the input data contains text, AutoKeras transforms it into an embedding.

Auto-Sklearn

Auto-sklearn is an open source Python package based on the scikit-learn ML library. Auto-sklearn automatically searches for the right learning algorithm for a new ML dataset and optimizes its hyperparameters. This framework only supports sklearn-based models. Auto-sklearn was developed by labs at the University of Freiburg and the University of Hannover.

Auto-PyTorch

In addition to Auto-sklearn, the Freiburg-Hannover AutoML group also developed an AutoML based on PyTorch that focuses on deep learning. Auto-PyTorch is deemed excellent at rapid prototyping. It also supports distributed training.

Summary

Business analysts, data analysts, citizen data scientists, data scientists, software developers, and ML engineers can all use AutoML frameworks to streamline the development process.

First, you load a dataset that includes a target variable and input feature data used for predictions. After the data is loaded, a data profile is generated for each data column. To submit a training job, you select just a few parameters. AutoML then experiments with multiple models and performs model optimization. Results are presented, as well as feature attribution.

Cloud vendors provide MLaaS to accelerate and automate day-to-day ML workflows, tools for integrating models into applications or services, and tools for deploying models into production.

Low-code AutoML requires installation, configuration of libraries, and some knowledge of SQL or Python. Open source AutoML refers to open source frameworks such as AutoKeras, Auto-sklearn, and Auto-PyTorch that add an additional layer of abstraction on top of existing open source libraries.

In Chapter 4, you build an AutoML model to predict advertising media channel sales. First, you explore your data using Pandas. Then you learn how to use AutoML to build, train, and deploy an ML model to predict sales.

Use AutoML to Predict Advertising Media Channel Sales

In this chapter, you build an AutoML model to predict advertising media channel sales. First, you explore your data using Pandas. Then you learn how to use AutoML to build, train, and deploy an ML model to predict sales. You gain an overall understanding of the performance of your model using performance metrics and answer common business questions. Along the way, you'll learn about regression analysis, a common technique used for prediction use cases.

The Business Use Case: Media Channel Sales Prediction

Businesses use advertising media channels to promote their products, services, or brand. Marketers and media planners create marketing campaigns that may run on digital, TV, radio, or in the newspaper. In this scenario, you work as a media planner in the marketing department for a midsize solar energy company. Your firm has a modest media budget and needs to evaluate which channels offer the greatest number of benefits for the least cost. This is a spend optimization problem.

You have been asked to develop a marketing plan that will increase next year's product sales. To accomplish this goal, you need to understand the impact of the media channel product advertising budgets on overall sales. The advertising dataset captures the sales revenue generated with respect to advertisement costs across digital, TV, radio, and newspaper media channels.

Typically, this type of ask from the team lead would go to a data scientist or data analyst. But, although you do not have any coding experience, the marketing team lead has asked you to build a sales predictive model using AutoML, something they want to try for the first time on the team. The goal is to build an ML model to predict how much sales volume will be generated based on the money spent in each of the media channels.

Business questions include:

- Can the model predict how much sales volume will be generated based on the money spent in each media channel?
- Is there a relationship between advertising budget and sales?
- Which media channel contributes the most to sales?
- Can the model be used to forecast future sales based on the media channel's proposed budget?
- How accurately can the model predict future sales?

The use case is a simple regression problem with just five variables that you can use to answer the preceding five questions.

Project Workflow

Figure 4-1 shows the high-level overview of the typical AutoML no-code workflow from Chapter 3. This workflow is appropriate for your use case.

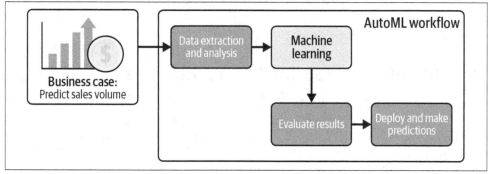

Figure 4-1. AutoML workflow for the business case.

Now that you understand the business use case and objective, you can proceed to data extraction and analysis. Note that this workflow does not include a data preprocessing step. You will get lots of hands-on experience with data preprocessing in later chapters. After data extraction and analysis, you will upload the dataset into the AutoML platform. The advertising budgets of digital, TV, newspaper, and radio data are then fed into the model. You'll then evaluate the AutoML results and then deploy the model to make predictions. After this chapter's hands-on exercise, you will be able to create a strategic marketing plan for your team.

Project Dataset

The dataset is composed of historical marketing channel data that can be leveraged to gain insights for spend allocation and to predict sales. The dataset being used for this chapter, the advertising_2023 dataset (*https://oreil.ly/JI6eL*), is based on data taken from *An Introduction to Statistical Learning with Applications in R* (*https://www.statlearning.com*) by Daniela Witten, Gareth M. James, Trevor Hastie, and Robert Tibshirani (Springer, 2021). The advertising dataset captures the sales revenue generated from advertising (in thousands of units) for particular product advertising budgets (in thousands of dollars) for TV, radio, and newspaper media.

For this book, the dataset has been updated to include a digital variable and modified to show the impact of digital budgets on sales. The number of markets has been increased from 200 to 1,200. Thus, the data consists of the advertising budgets for four media channels (digital, TV, radio, and newspapers) and the overall sales in 1,200 different markets. You should feel encouraged to look at other examples of how to work with this dataset to grow your knowledge after completing the exercises in this chapter.

The data is initially supplied in a CSV file, so you will need to spend some time loading the data into Pandas before you can explore it. The dataset contains only numeric variables.

There are five columns in the dataset. Table 4-1 gives the column names, data types, and some information about the possible values for these columns.

Table 4-1. Schema and field value information for the advertising dataset

Column name	Column type	Notes about field values
Digital	Numeric	Amount spent on advertisements in digital
Newspaper	Numeric	Amount spent on advertisements in newspapers
Radio	Numeric	Amount spent on advertisements in radio
TV	Numeric	Amount spent on advertisements in TV
Sales	Numeric	Total media channel sales

Exploring the Dataset Using Pandas, Matplotlib, and Seaborn

Before you begin using AutoML, you follow the workflow discussed in earlier chapters around understanding and preparing data for ML. This section shows you how to load data into a Google Colab notebook using Pandas, an open source Python package that is widely used for data science and data analysis. Once the data is loaded into a DataFrame, you will explore the data. Fortunately, the data has already been cleaned—there are no missing values or strange characters in the dataset. Your exploratory data analysis is to assist you in validating that the data is clean and to explore relationships between the variables to assist you in answering questions posed from the team. As noted in previous chapters, much of the ML work goes into understanding and preparing the training data—not training the model—because you are relying on AutoML to build the model.

All of the code in this section, including some additional examples, is included in a Jupyter notebook titled Chapter4_Media_Channel_Sales_Notebook in the low-code-ai repository on GitHub (*https://oreil.ly/supp-lcai*).

Load Data into a Pandas DataFrame in a Google Colab Notebook

First, go to *https://colab.research.google.com* and open a new notebook, following the process discussed in Chapter 2. You may rename this notebook to a more meaningful name by clicking on the name as shown in Figure 4-2 and replacing the current name with a new name, say *Advertising_Model.ipynb*.

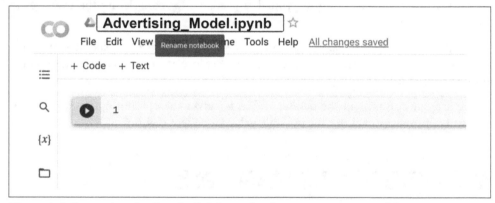

Figure 4-2. Renaming the Google Colab notebook to a more meaningful name.

Now type the following code into the first code block to import the packages needed to analyze and visualize the advertising dataset:

```
import pandas as pd
import numpy as np
import matplotlib.pyplot as plt
from scipy import stats
import seaborn as sns
%matplotlib inline
```

You saw some of these packages before in Chapter 2 when first exploring the use of Colab notebooks.

Now execute the cell containing the import statements to import the packages. To do this, you click the Run Cell button on the left side of the cell. You can also press Shift + Enter to run the cell.

Now you are ready to import your data. Using Pandas, you can directly import a CSV file into a DataFrame from a location on the internet without having to download the file first. To do this, copy the code from the solution notebook or type in the following code into a new cell and execute the cell:

```
url="https://github.com/maabel0712/low-code-ai/blob/main/advertising_2023.csv?raw=true"

advertising_df=pd.read_csv(url, index_col=0)
```

In general, it is a good idea to look at the first few rows of the DataFrame. Use `advertising_df.head()` to explore the first few rows of the DataFrame. The head Pandas method lets us see the first five rows of our data. By doing this, you can quickly see the features, some of their possible values, and whether they are numerical or not.

An example of a few of the columns is shown in Figure 4-3.

Out[4]:		digital	TV	radio	newspaper	sales
	1	345.15	156.0	37.8	69.2	22.1
	2	66.75	46.0	39.3	45.1	10.4
	3	25.80	18.3	45.9	69.3	9.3
	4	227.25	145.1	41.3	58.5	18.5
	5	271.20	165.2	10.8	58.4	12.9

Figure 4-3. A few columns of the first five rows of the DataFrame `advertising_df` printed using the `head()` method.

Explore the Advertising Dataset

Now that the data has been loaded into the DataFrame `advertising_df`, you can begin to explore and understand it. The immediate goal is to get an idea of where there could be issues with the data so that you may resolve those issues before moving forward.

Descriptive analysis: Check the data

First check the data using standard Python methods. To check the data types for your DataFrame, type **`advertising_df.info()`** into a new cell and execute the cell. The information contains the number of columns, column labels, column data types, memory usage, range index, and the number of cells in each column (non-null values).

Figure 4-4 shows an example of the `info()` method output.

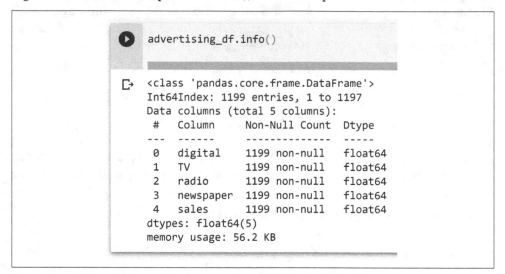

```
   advertising_df.info()


   <class 'pandas.core.frame.DataFrame'>
   Int64Index: 1199 entries, 1 to 1197
   Data columns (total 5 columns):
    #   Column     Non-Null Count   Dtype
   ---  ------     --------------   -----
    0   digital    1199 non-null    float64
    1   TV         1199 non-null    float64
    2   radio      1199 non-null    float64
    3   newspaper  1199 non-null    float64
    4   sales      1199 non-null    float64
   dtypes: float64(5)
   memory usage: 56.2 KB
```

Figure 4-4. Information on the dataset using the `info()` method.

Note that with information on the data type, you can check to make sure that the types inferred by Pandas match up with what was expected from Table 4-1.

Shown in Figure 4-5 is the `describe()` method, which computes and displays summary statistics for the dataset. The `describe` function shows information about the numerical variables of our dataset. You can see the mean, maximum, and minimum values of each of these variables, along with their standard deviation. Type **advertising_df.describe()** into a new cell and execute the cell.

```
advertising_df.describe()
```

	digital	TV	radio	newspaper	sales
count	1199.000000	1199.00000	1199.000000	1199.000000	1199.000000
mean	135.472394	146.61985	23.240617	30.529942	14.005505
std	135.730821	85.61047	14.820827	21.712507	5.202804
min	0.300000	0.70000	0.000000	0.300000	1.600000
25%	24.250000	73.40000	9.950000	12.800000	10.300000
50%	64.650000	149.70000	22.500000	25.600000	12.900000
75%	256.950000	218.50000	36.500000	45.100000	17.400000
max	444.600000	296.40000	49.600000	114.000000	27.000000

Figure 4-5. Summary statistics for all columns in the advertising dataset.

Shown in Figure 4-6 is the output of the .isnull() method. Type
advertising_df.isnull().sum() into a new cell and execute the cell. The output
shows all of the columns in the DataFrame with associated zeros. If there were null
values, the number of null values for the column would be shown.

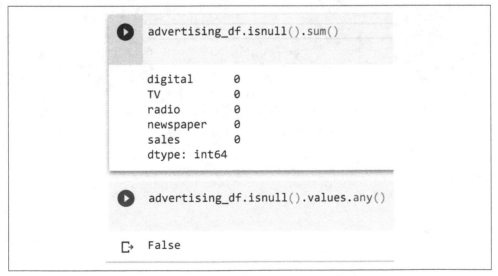

Figure 4-6. Determining null values using the isnull() method.

Explore the data

Exploratory data analysis (EDA) is the first step of any ML project. You need to explore your data before building any ML model. The goal is to take a look at the raw data, explore it, and gather relevant insights from the information derived from the data. Doing this also helps make models better, as you'll be able to spot any "dirty data" issues—such as missing values, strange characters in a column, etc.—that may impact performance.

Heat maps (correlations). A *heat map* is a way of representing the data visually. The data values are represented as colors in the graph. The goal of the heat map is to provide a colored visual summary of information. Heat maps show your relationships (correlations) between variables (features). *Correlation* is a statistical measure that shows the extent to which two or more variables move together. Shown in Figure 4-7 is the output of a correlation method that plots correlation values on the grid. Type the following code into a new cell and execute the cell:

```
plt.figure(figsize=(10,5))
sns.heatmap(advertising_df.corr(),annot=True,vmin=0,vmax=1,cmap='viridis')
```

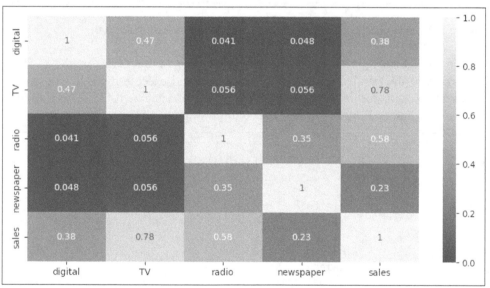

Figure 4-7. Correlation matrix for advertising media channels.

The results from a correlation matrix can be used in a variety of ways, including:

Identifying relationships between variables

The correlation coefficient between two variables can tell you how strongly they are related. A correlation coefficient of 0 means there is no relationship, whereas a correlation coefficient of 1 means there is a perfect positive relationship. A correlation coefficient of –1 means there is a perfect negative relationship. *Note that the stronger relationships are between sales and television (0.78), followed by sales and radio (0.58).* This information can be used to develop targeted marketing campaigns that are more likely to improve sales.

Selecting variables for inclusion in a model

When you are building a predictive model, you need to select the variables that are most likely to be predictive of the outcome. For example, should you include newspapers (with a 0.23 correlation to sales) as a feature for inclusion in the model to predict sales?

Detecting multicollinearity

Multicollinearity occurs when two or more predictor variables in a regression model are highly correlated. For example, if both TV and radio were highly correlated (meaning that both had a value >0.7 instead of 0.056 as shown in Figure 4-7), it would indicate multicollinearity. Since it is harder to numerically distinguish predictors with a strong collinear relationship from one another, it is more difficult for a regression algorithm to determine the degree of influence or weight one of them should have on sales.

As a warning, the results of a correlation matrix may change due to sample size or outliers in the dataset.

Scatterplots. Scatterplots are used to determine relationships between two numerical variables. They can help you see if there is a direct relationship (positive linear relationship or negative linear relationship, for example) between two variables. Also, they can help you detect if your data has outliers or not. Figure 4-8 shows a scatter of the digital feature and the sales target. Type the following code into a new cell and execute the cell:

```
advertising_df.plot(kind='scatter', x=['digital'], y='sales')
```

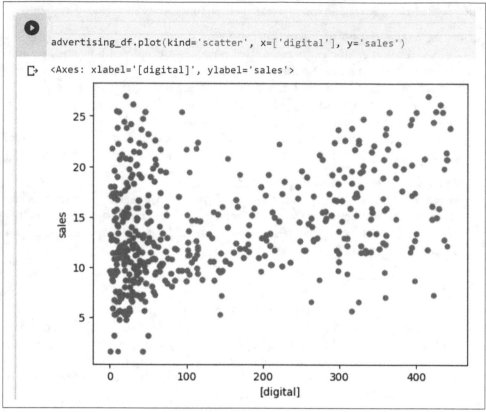

```
advertising_df.plot(kind='scatter', x=['digital'], y='sales')
```

```
<Axes: xlabel='[digital]', ylabel='sales'>
```

Figure 4-8. Scatterplot of digital and sales.

You want to explore the scatterplots for each variable with the predicted variable sales. You can plot each feature as a scatterplot separately (as you did earlier), or you can plot them so all of the relationships are shown in one plot. Type all of the following code into a new cell and execute the cell (Figure 4-9 shows the output):

```
plt.figure(figsize=(18, 18))

for i, col in enumerate(advertising_df.columns[0:13]):
    plt.subplot(5, 3, i+1) # each row three figure
    x = advertising_df[col] #x-axis
    y = advertising_df['sales'] #y-axis
    plt.plot(x, y, 'o')

    # Create regression line
    plt.plot(np.unique(x), np.poly1d(np.polyfit(x, y, 1)) (np.unique(x)),
        color='red')
    plt.xlabel(col) # x-label
    plt.ylabel('sales') # y-label
```

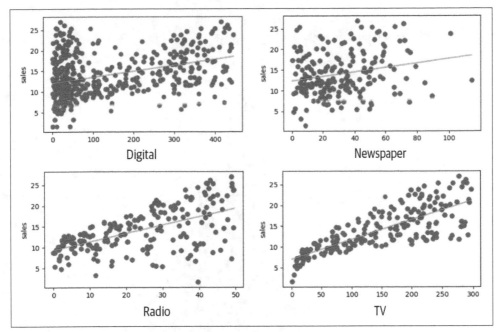

Figure 4-9. Scatterplots of all features and sales targets.

Note that TV and sales have a strong linear relationship—as it appears to show that for an increase in TV budget, there is a positive impact on sales volume. There does not appear to be a strong relationship between newspaper and sales. Recall the correlation values of 0.23 for this relationship. This is very different from the relationship between TV and sales (0.78).

Histogram distribution plot. A common approach to visualizing a distribution is the histogram. A *histogram* is a bar plot where the axis representing the target variable is divided into a set of discrete bins, and the count of observations falling within each bin is shown using the height of the corresponding bar.

Type this code into a new cell and run the cell:

```
sns.displot(advertising_df, x="sales")
```

Figure 4-10 shows the data values from the sales column. The plot looks somewhat like a bell curve that is slightly skewed to the left. The most common sales amount is $11,000 dollars.

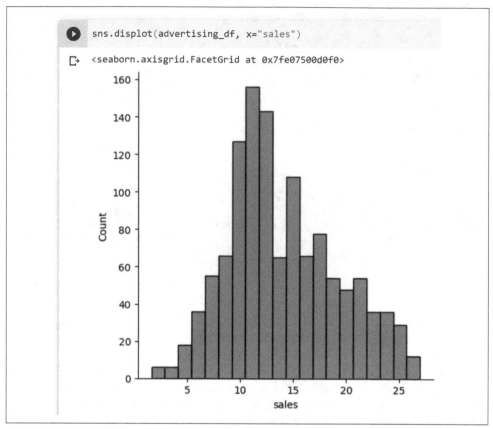

```
sns.displot(advertising_df, x="sales")
```

```
<seaborn.axisgrid.FacetGrid at 0x7fe07500d0f0>
```

Figure 4-10. Sales histogram that is slightly skewed to the left.

What about the other features—are they skewed left or right or do they have a "normal distribution," like a bell curve? You can type the preceding code for each individual feature or use the following code to see all of the features together. Type the following code into a new cell and execute the cell (Figure 4-11 shows the output):

```
lis = ['digital', 'newspaper', 'radio','TV']
plt.subplots(figsize=(15, 8))
index = 1
for i in lis:
    plt.subplot(2, 2, index)
    sns.distplot(advertising_df[i])
    index += 1
```

As you saw in Figure 4-10, sales have somewhat of a normal distribution. However, in Figure 4-11, digital appears to be skewed left, and TV, radio, and newspaper are not normally distributed. Standardizing these features so they are normally distributed before feeding them into your ML model would generate better results.

However, your role is not that of a data scientist. Do not worry about understanding these concepts. Discussing each transformation required for the features is beyond the scope of this chapter. Chapter 7 is where you perform transformations on a dataset.

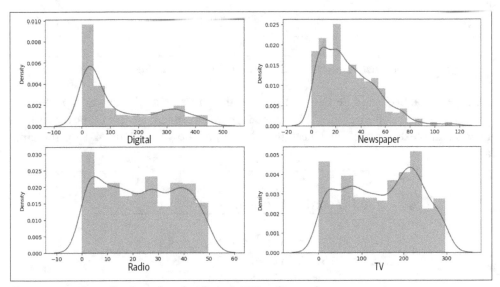

Figure 4-11. Distribution plots for digital, TV, radio, and newspaper.

Export the advertising dataset

After you have checked and explored the dataset, it is time to export the file so that it can be uploaded into your AutoML framework. Type the following code into a new cell and execute the cell. The first line imports the operating system that will allow you to make a directory called *data* (lines two and three):

```
import os
if not os.path.isdir("/content/data"):
    os.makedirs("/content/data")
```

After the directory has been created, type the following code into a new cell and execute the cell. The first line of code creates a CSV file format of the advertising DataFrame and places it in the *content/data* directory you made in the previous step:

```
advertising_df.to_csv('/content/data/advertising.csv',
    encoding='utf-8', index=False)
```

Figure 4-12 shows the newly created directory called *data* with the file *advertising.csv*.

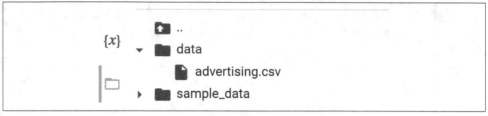

Figure 4-12. Newly created data directory with advertising.csv file.

As a best practice, validate that you can see the contents of the newly exported file in the newly created directory. Type **!head /content/data/advertising.csv** into a new cell and execute the cell. Check that the output shown in Figure 4-13 is the same as yours.

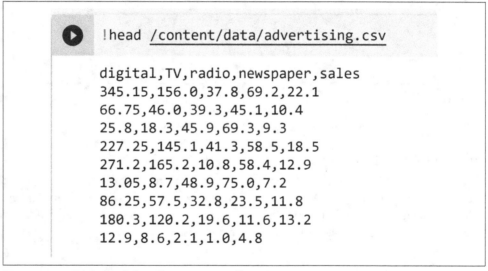

Figure 4-13. Output of the advertising.csv file.

Now that you have verified that the file has been properly exported, you can download it to your computer.

Right-click the *advertising.csv* file in the newly created *data* directory and select Download as shown in Figure 4-14. The file will download to your desktop. You are now ready to upload the file for AutoML use.

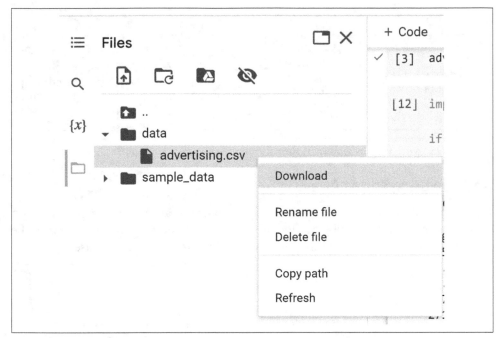

Figure 4-14. Validate advertising.csv in data directory.

In the next section, you build a code-free model based on the training data file you just exported.

Use AutoML to Train a Linear Regression Model

The AutoML projects for this book will be implemented using Google's Vertex AI, the GUI-based AutoML and custom training framework the authors are most familiar with. Note that the top three major cloud vendors (Google, Microsoft, and AWS) all offer AutoML tutorials. Each of these three major cloud vendor's guides can be found in their documentation. Many cloud vendors offer a trial period to explore their products without cost.

Given that Google offers a step-by-step tutorial on AutoML, some introductory steps are excluded.

Figure 4-15 shows a high-level overview of the AutoML no-code workflow for your business use case.

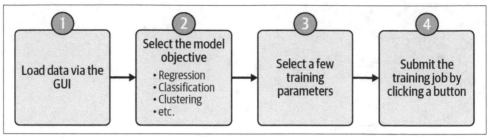

Figure 4-15. AutoML no-code workflow for your use case.

No-Code Using Vertex AI

Figure 4-16 shows the Vertex AI Dashboard. To create an AutoML model, turn on the Vertex AI API by clicking the Enable All Recommended APIs button. From the left-hand navigation menu, scroll down from Dashboard and select Datasets.

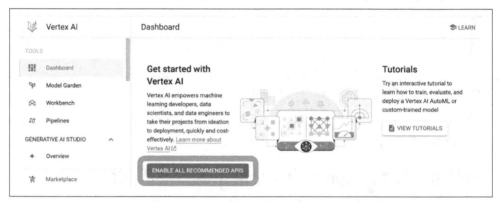

Figure 4-16. Vertex AI Dashboard showing the Enable All Recommended APIs button.

Create a Managed Dataset in Vertex AI

Vertex AI offers different AutoML models depending on data type and the objective you want to achieve with your model. When you create a dataset you pick an initial objective, but after a dataset is created you can use it to train models with different objectives. Keep the default region (us-central1), as shown in Figure 4-17.

Select the Create button at the top of the page and then enter a name for the dataset. For example, you can name the dataset *advertising_automl*.

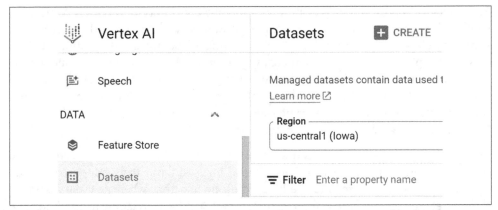

Figure 4-17. Vertex AI Dataset navigation that allows you to create a dataset.

Select the Model Objective

Figure 4-18 shows Regression/classification selected as the model objective under the Tabular tab. Given that you want to predict a target column's value (sales), this is the appropriate selection.

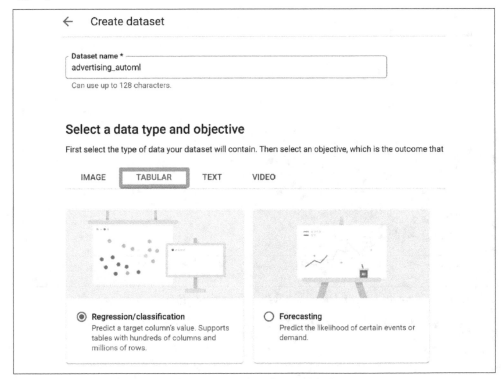

Figure 4-18. Regression/classification selection for model objective.

You selected Regression/classification as your objective. Let's cover some basic concepts to help you with future use cases. *Regression* is a supervised ML process. It is similar to classification, but rather than predicting a label for a classification, such as classifying spam from your email inbox, you try to predict a continuous value. *Linear* regression defines the relationship between a target variable (y) and a set of predictive features (x). If you need to predict a number, then use regression. In your use case, linear regression predicts a real value (sales) using some independent variables given in the dataset (digital, TV, radio, and newspaper).

Essentially, linear regression assumes a linear relationship with each feature. The predicted values are the data points on the line, and the true values are in the scatterplot. The goal is to find the best fitting line so that when new data is input the model can predict where the new data point will be in relation to the line. The "evaluation" of how good that fit is includes an evaluation criteria—which is covered in "Evaluate Model Performance" on page 98.

Figure 4-19 shows a "best-fit" line based on your dataset, where the model tries to fit the line to your data points, which are the dark scatters.

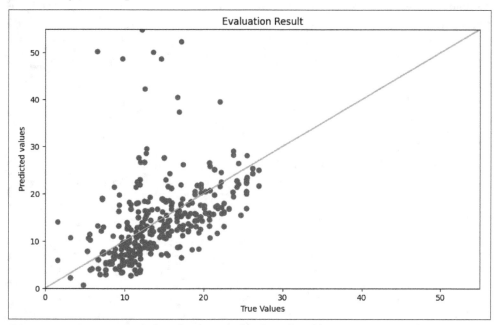

Figure 4-19. True and predicted values with a best-fitted line.

After making the Regression/classification selection, scroll down and click the Create button. You are now ready to add data to your dataset. Vertex AI–managed datasets are available for a variety of data types, including tabular, image, text, and video data.

Figure 4-20 shows the data source upload options—upload CSV from your computer, select CSV files from Cloud Storage, or select a table or view from BigQuery (Google's data warehouse).

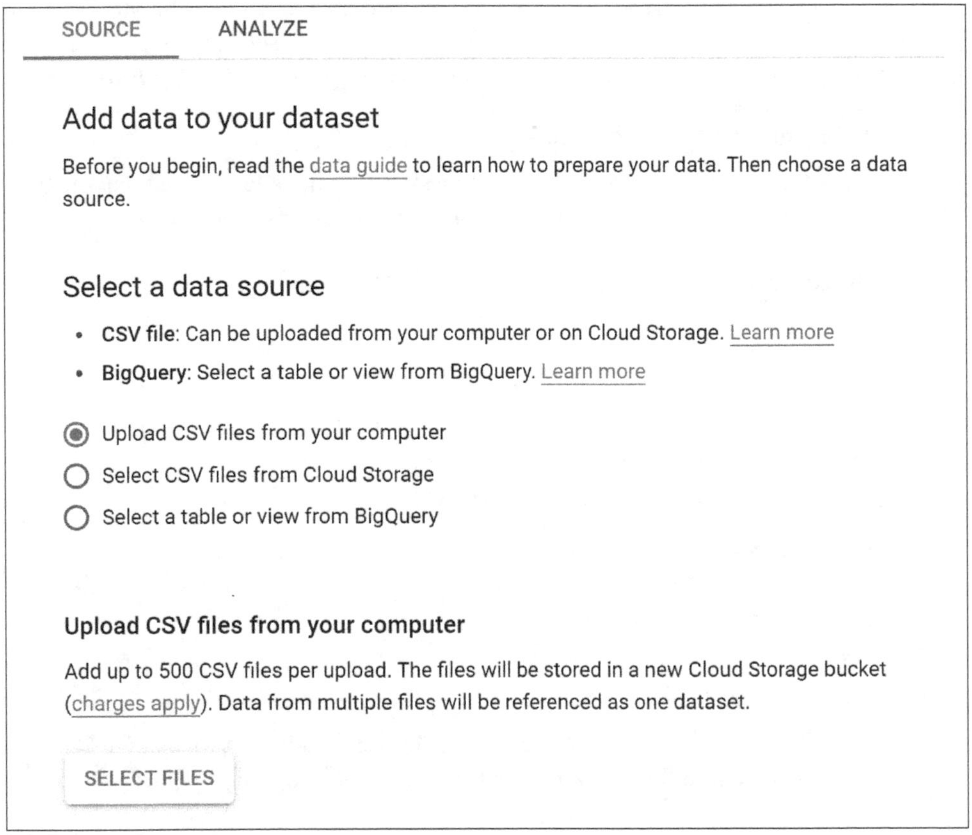

Figure 4-20. Data source upload options for your dataset file.

To upload your advertising dataset, select "Upload CSV files from your computer." Find the file on your local computer and load it.

Scroll down the page and review the Select a Cloud Storage Path section, which requires that you store the file in a cloud storage bucket. Why do you need to store the file in a cloud storage bucket? Two reasons: (1) when training a large-scale ML model, you may need to store terabytes or even petabytes of data; and (2) cloud storage buckets are scalable, reliable, and secure.

Figure 4-21 shows that the file *Advertising_automl.csv* has been uploaded and a cloud storage bucket has been created to store the uploaded file. To see the step-by-step process of creating the storage bucket and the entire exercise, see the PDF entitled *Chapter 4 AutoML Sales Prediction* in the repository (*https://oreil.ly/supp-lcai*).

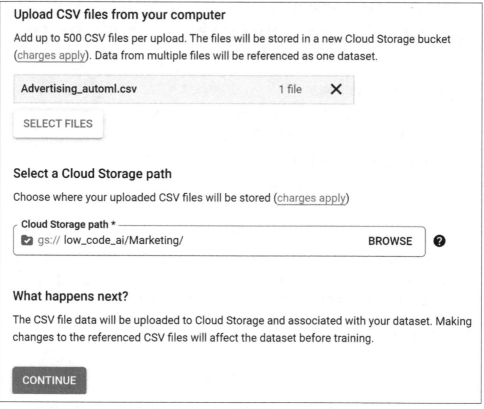

Figure 4-21. Data source options to load a CSV file and store it in a cloud storage bucket.

Some frameworks will generate statistics after the data loads. Other frameworks help minimize the need to manually clean data by automatically detecting and cleaning missing values, anomalous values, and duplicate rows and columns. Note that there are a few additional steps that you can employ, such as to review the data after it has loaded to check for missing values and view data statistics.

Figure 4-22 shows the output of the Generate Statistics window. Note there are no missing values and the number of distinct values for each column is shown.

☰ Filter	Enter property name or value	
Column name ↑	Missing % (count) ❓	Distinct values ❓
digital	-	190
newspaper	-	172
radio	-	167
sales	-	121
TV	-	190

Figure 4-22. The output of the Generate Statistics window.

AutoML presents a data profile of each feature. To analyze a feature, click the name of the feature. A page shows the feature distribution histograms for that feature.

Figure 4-23 shows the data profile for sales. Note that the mean is 14.014, which is very close to the numeric value you received when you typed in the `advertising_df.describe()` code earlier in the chapter as you were exploring the dataset.

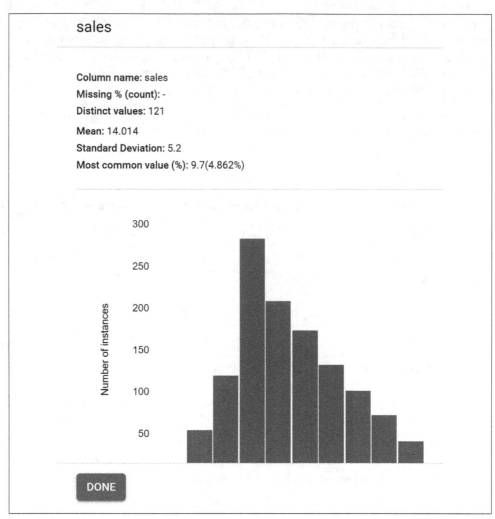

Figure 4-23. Feature profile for sales.

Build the Training Model

Figure 4-24 shows that the model is now ready to train. Select Train New Model under the "Training jobs and models" section. Select Other and not AutoML on Pipelines. AutoML on Pipelines is a feature that allows you to specify the type of ML model you want to build and other parameters. It is beyond the scope of the book.

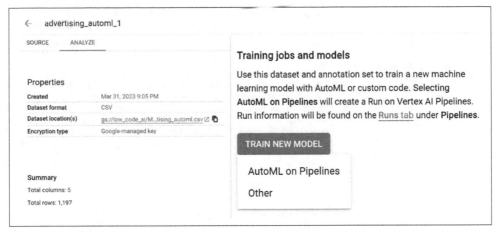

Figure 4-24. Model now ready for training.

The "Train new model" window appears. There are four steps:

1. Select the training method

2. Configure model details

3. Determine training options

4. Select compute and pricing

In Step 1, under the Objective, select the drop-down and choose Regression. Under "Model training method," select AutoML (as shown in Figure 4-25). Click Continue.

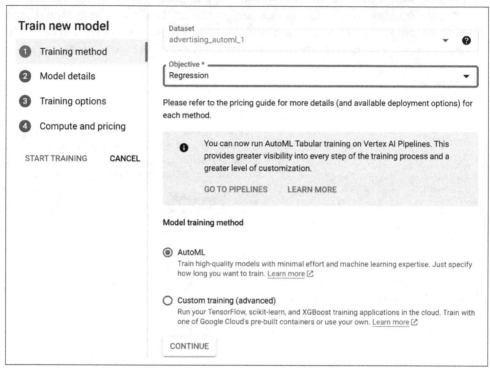

Figure 4-25. Configure the training method in Step 1.

In Step 2, under "Model details," name your model and give it a description. Under "Target column," select sales from the drop-down (as shown in Figure 4-26). Click Continue.

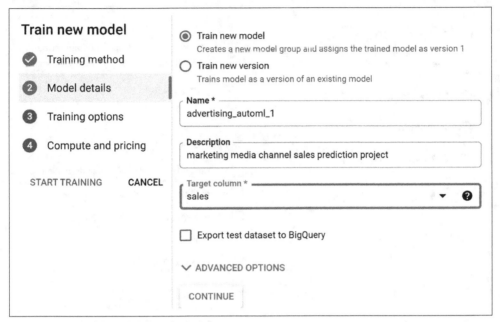

Figure 4-26. Add model details in Step 2.

In Step 3, review the training options. Note that any data transformations (or data processing) such as standardization are handled automatically (as shown in Figure 4-27). Click Continue.

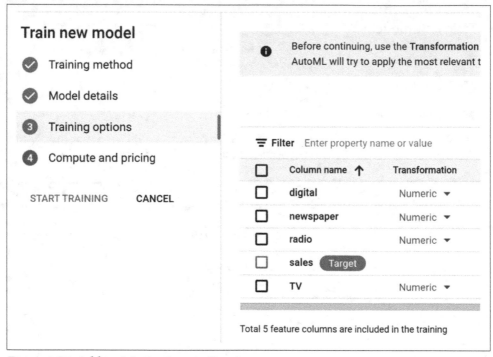

Figure 4-27. Add training options in Step 3.

In Step 4, you see "Compute and pricing" (*https://oreil.ly/x8C3f*) (as shown in Figure 4-28). The time required to train your model depends on the size and complexity of your training data. A *node hour* is one hour's usage of one node (think virtual machine) in the cloud, spread across all nodes. Enter the value **3** in the Budget field for maximum number of node hours—this is just an estimate. You pay only for compute hours used; if training fails for any reason other than a user-initiated cancellation, you are not billed for the time. You are charged for training time if you cancel the operation.

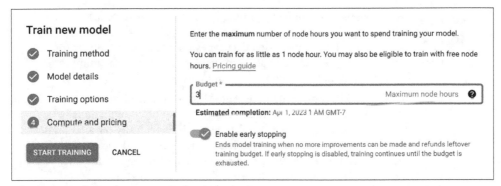

Figure 4-28. Select compute and pricing in Step 4.

Also under "Compute and pricing" is early stopping. When you enable this option, this means that training will end when AutoML determines that no more model improvements can be made. If you disable early stopping, AutoML will train the model until the budget hours are exhausted.

Once all the parameters are entered, you start the training job. Click Start Training.

After model training, the model is registered in the model registry (as shown in Figure 4-29).

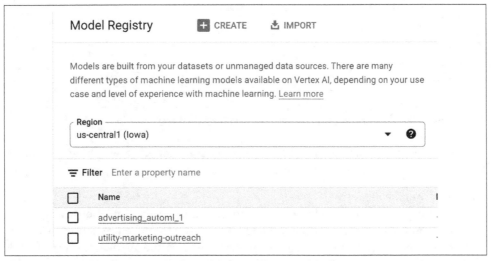

Figure 4-29. Advertising_automl model showing in model registry.

As previously mentioned, training can take up to several hours, depending on the size of your data and type of model objective you choose. Image and video data types may take much longer to process than a structured data type such as a CSV file. The number of training samples also impacts training time.

Also, AutoML is time intensive. AutoML algorithms need to train a variety of models, and this training process can be computationally expensive. This is because AutoML algorithms typically try a large number of different models and hyperparameters, and each model needs to be trained on the entire dataset. AutoML algorithms then need to select the best model from the set of trained models, and this selection process can also be time-consuming. This is because AutoML algorithms typically need to evaluate the performance of each model on a holdout dataset, and this evaluation process can be computationally expensive.

Evaluate Model Performance

Figure 4-30 shows the model training results.

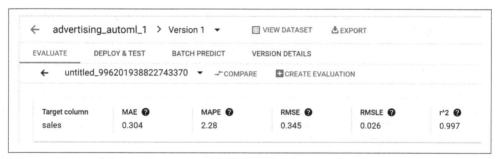

Figure 4-30. Model training results with five evaluation metrics.

There are a few factors that a practitioner should consider when weighing the importance of different linear regression evaluation metrics:

The purpose of the model
    The purpose of the model will determine which evaluation metrics are most important. For example, if the model is being used to make predictions, then the practitioner may want to focus on metrics such as mean squared error (MSE) or root mean squared error (RMSE). However, if the model is being used to understand the relationship between variables, then the practitioner may want to focus on metrics such as R-squared or adjusted R-squared.

The characteristics of the data

The characteristics of the data will also affect the importance of different evaluation metrics. For example, if the data is noisy (e.g., contains unwanted information or errors), then the practitioner may want to focus on metrics that are robust to noise, such as mean absolute error (MAE). However, if the data is not noisy, then the practitioner may be able to focus on metrics that are more sensitive to changes in the model, such as MSE.

The practitioner's preferences

Ultimately, the practitioner's preferences will also play a role in determining the importance of different evaluation metrics. Some practitioners may prefer metrics that are easy to understand, while others may prefer metrics that are more accurate. There is no right or wrong answer, and the practitioner should choose the metrics that are most important to them.

Here are common linear regression evaluation metrics:

R-squared

R-squared is a measure of how well the model fits the data. It is the square of the Pearson correlation coefficient between the observed and predicted values. It is calculated by dividing the sum of squared residuals (the difference between the predicted and the actual values) by the total sum of squares. A higher R-squared value indicates a better fit. R-squared ranges from 0 to 1, where a higher value indicates a higher-quality model. Your R^2 should be around 0.997.

Adjusted R-squared

Adjusted R-squared is a modified version of R-squared that takes into account the number of independent variables in the model. It is calculated by dividing the sum of squared residuals by the total sum of squares minus the degrees of freedom. A higher adjusted R-squared value indicates a better fit, but it is less sensitive to the number of independent variables than R-squared.

Mean squared error (MSE)

MSE is a measure of the average squared error between the predicted values and the actual values. A lower MSE value indicates a better fit. Figure 4-31 shows the loss visualized in a table and graph.

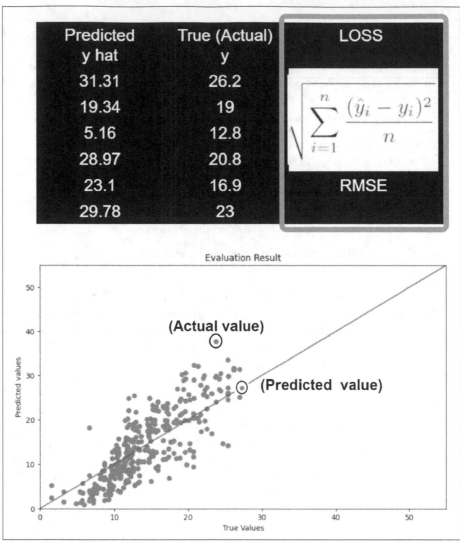

Predicted y hat	True (Actual) y
31.31	26.2
19.34	19
5.16	12.8
28.97	20.8
23.1	16.9
29.78	23

LOSS

$$\sqrt{\sum_{i=1}^{n} \frac{(\hat{y}_i - y_i)^2}{n}}$$

RMSE

Figure 4-31. Loss formula for RMSE of true and predicted values.

Root mean squared error (RMSE)

RMSE is the square root of MSE. It is a more interpretable version of MSE. A lower RMSE value indicates a better fit and a higher-quality model, where 0 means the model made no errors. Interpreting RMSE depends on the range of values in the series. Your RMSE should be around 0.345.

Root mean squared log error (RMSLE)

Interpreting RMSLE depends on the range of values in the series. RMSLE is less responsive to outliers than RMSE, and it tends to penalize underestimations slightly more than overestimations. Your RMSLE should be around 0.026.

Mean absolute error (MAE)

MAE is a measure of the average absolute error between the predicted values and the actual values. A lower MAE value indicates a better fit. Your MAE should be around 0.304.

Mean absolute percentage error (MAPE)

MAPE ranges from 0% to 100%, where a lower value indicates a higher-quality model. MAPE is the average of absolute percentage errors. Your MAPE should be around 2.28.

Model Feature Importance (Attribution)

Model feature importance tells you how much each feature impacted model training. Figure 4-32 shows attribution values expressed as a percentage; the higher the percentage, the more strongly the correlation—that is, the more strongly that feature impacted model training. Feature attribution allows you to see which features contributed most strongly to the resulting model training shown in Figure 4-32.

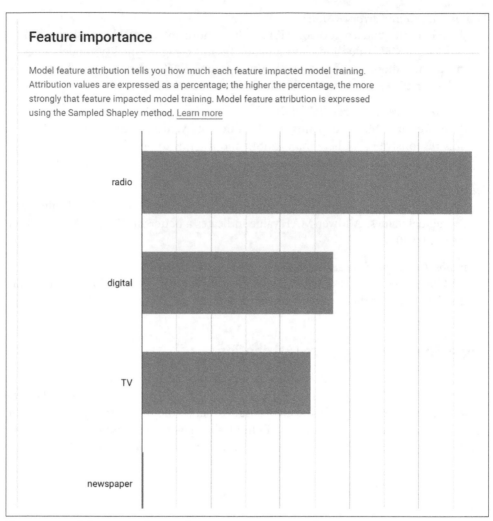

Feature importance

Model feature attribution tells you how much each feature impacted model training. Attribution values are expressed as a percentage; the higher the percentage, the more strongly that feature impacted model training. Model feature attribution is expressed using the Sampled Shapley method. Learn more

Figure 4-32. Advertising dataset feature importance results.

If you were to hover over the newspaper feature shown in Figure 4-32, you would see that its contribution to model training is 0.2%. This supports what you discovered during the EDA phase you completed earlier—the relationship between sales and newspaper advertising spend is the weakest. These results mean that advertising on *radio*, *digital*, and *TV* contribute the most in *sales*, and *newspaper* advertisements have little effect on *sales*.

Get Predictions from Your Model

To deploy your model, you will need to test it. You can deploy to your environment to test your model without building an application you would need to deploy to the cloud. After you train an ML model, you need to deploy the model so that others can use it to do inferencing. Inferencing in machine learning is the process of using a trained ML model to make predictions on new data.

There are four steps, but for this chapter you'll only need the first two. For this exercise, it is not necessary to configure model monitoring or model objectives. Model monitoring adds an additional charge for logging, while model objectives require you to choose from a variety of model objectives, depending on the type of model you are training and the application you are using it for. Here are the four steps:

1. Define your endpoint.
2. Configure model settings.
3. Configure model monitoring.
4. Configure model objectives.

What are endpoints and deployments? In ML, an *endpoint* is a service that exposes a model for online prediction. A *deployment* is the process of making a model available as an endpoint. An endpoint is an HTTPS path that provides an interface for clients to send requests (input data) and receive the inferencing (scoring) output of a trained model. Endpoints are typically used to make predictions in real time. For example, you could use an endpoint to predict the likelihood of a customer clicking on an ad or the risk of a loan defaulting.

Deployments are typically used to make a model available to a larger audience. For example, you could deploy a model to a production environment so that it can be used by your customers or employees.

Figure 4-33 shows the deploy and test page. To deploy your model, go to Model Registry, select Deploy and Test, and select your model.

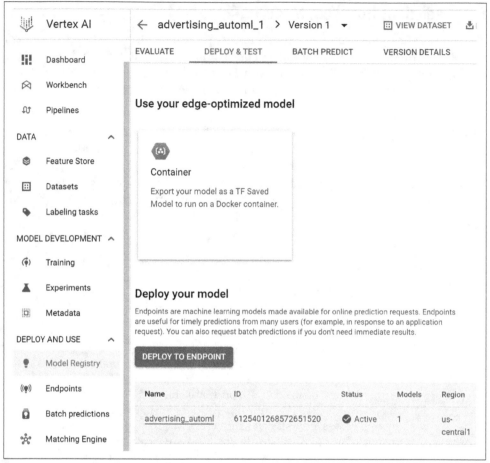

Figure 4-33. Deploy your model to an endpoint page.

In Step 1, you define your endpoint. You select a region and determine how your endpoint will be accessed.

In Step 2, you add the model and add traffic split. A *traffic split* in Vertex AI is a way to distribute traffic between multiple models that are deployed to the same endpoint. This can be useful for a variety of purposes, such as:

A/B testing
Traffic splitting can be used to A/B test different models to see which one performs better.

Canary deployments

Traffic splitting can be used to deploy a new model to a small percentage of users before deploying it to a larger audience. This can help to catch any problems with the new model before they affect too many users.

Rollouts

Traffic splitting can be used to roll out a new model to users gradually. This can help to mitigate the impact of any problems with the new model.

In Step 3, you choose how compute resources will serve the predictions to your model (shown in Figure 4-34). For this exercise, use the minimum number of compute nodes (virtual machine servers). Under "Machine type," select Standard.

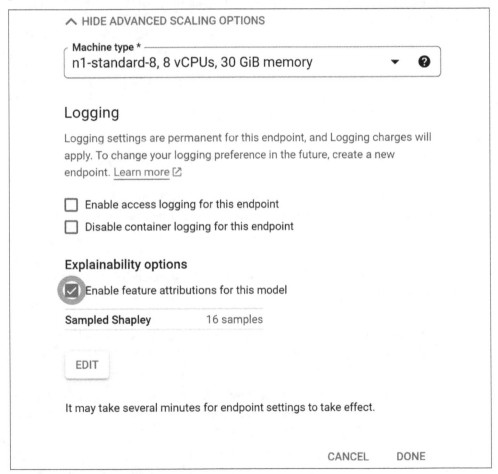

Figure 4-34. Select compute resources to train the model.

Note: "Machine types" differ in a few ways: (1) number of virtual central processing units (vCPUs) per node, (2) amount of memory per node, and (3) pricing (*https:// oreil.ly/x8C3f*).

There are a few factors to consider when choosing compute resources for a prediction model:

Size and complexity of the model
The larger and more complex the model, the more compute resources it will need. (This is more applicable to custom coding neural networks.)

Number of predictions that will be made
If you expect to make a large number of predictions, you will need to choose a compute resource that can handle the load.

Latency requirements
If you need to make predictions in real time or with very low latency, you will need to choose a compute resource that can provide the necessary performance. Note: low latency in machine learning refers to the time it takes for an ML model to make a prediction once it receives a new data point.

Cost
Compute resources can vary in price, so you will need to choose one that fits your budget.

Once you have considered these factors, you can start to narrow down your choices. Here are a few examples of compute resources that can be used to serve prediction models:

CPUs
Central processing units (CPUs) are the most common type of compute resource and are a good choice for models that are not too large or complex.

GPUs
Graphics processing units (GPUs) are more powerful than CPUs and can be used to speed up the training and inference of large and complex models.

TPUs
Tensor processing units (TPUs) are specialized hardware accelerators that are designed for ML workloads. They are the most powerful option and can be used to train and serve the most demanding models.

As part of Step 2 under "Model settings," there is a Logging setting. If you enable endpoint logging, charges will apply. Thus, for this exercise, please do not enable it.

The next setting is Explainability options, which do not carry a charge. Check "Enable feature attributions for this model."

Step 3 is "Model monitoring." Do not enable it for this project (as shown in Figure 4-35).

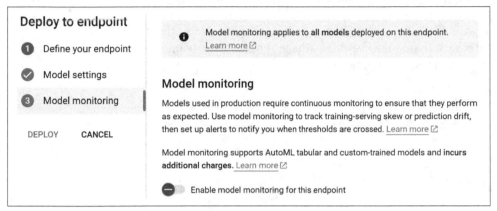

Figure 4-35. "Model monitoring" configuration window.

Now that all configurations are made, the Deploy button should be highlighted. Click Deploy to deploy your model to the endpoint (as shown in Figure 4-36).

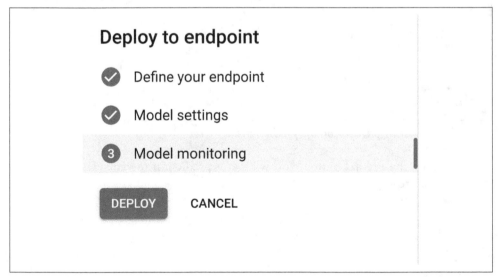

Figure 4-36. Deploy to the endpoint.

After the endpoint is created and the model deployed to the endpoint, you should receive an email regarding the endpoint deployment status. If deployment was successful, you can start making predictions. There are four steps:

1. Go to Model Registry.

2. Select your model.

3. Select the model's version.

4. Scroll down until you see the "Test your model" page.

Figure 4-37 shows the "Test your model" page. Note, this page could be an app or web page that looks like this—where you and your team input media channel values and predict sales volume.

Click the Predict button.

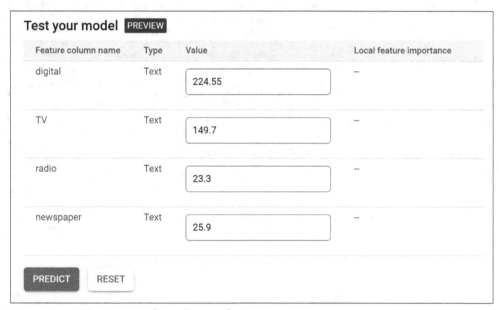

Figure 4-37. Testing page for online predictions.

After clicking the Predict button, you will get a prediction for your label (sales), as shown in Figure 4-38.

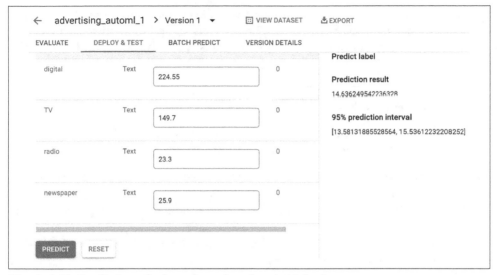

Figure 4-38. Prediction of sales volume based on initial values.

Regression models return a prediction value. Figure 4-38 shows a sales prediction result value of 14.63—which is very close to the mean from the sales histogram (shown in Figures 4-10 and 4-23). The prediction interval provides a range of values that the model has 95% confidence to contain the actual result. So, since the sales prediction result is 14.63, and the prediction interval is a range between 13.58 and 15.53, you can be 95% certain that any prediction result will fall within this range.

The Prediction Interval in Linear Regression

Prediction intervals are often used in regression analysis. A prediction interval is different from a confidence interval—though both are statistical measures that provide an estimate of the range of values within which a true value is likely to live. A *confidence interval* focuses on past or current events and is used to estimate a population parameter (e.g., standard deviation, mean).

A *prediction interval* is used to predict the value of a future observation, given what has already been observed. It provides an estimated range of values that may contain the value of a single new observation, based on previous data.

If you create a regression model, you can use it to develop a prediction interval that can determine where the next data point sampled may appear. Prediction intervals are wider than confidence intervals. This is because prediction intervals account for the uncertainty associated with predicting an individual value, as opposed to a population parameter.

Prediction intervals can be used to make decisions about future observations. For example, a company might use prediction intervals to decide whether to invest in a new product or service or to increase or decrease an advertising media channel budget.

Now, let's answer those business questions.

The goal was to build an ML model to predict how much sales volume will be generated based on the money spent in each of the media channels.

Can the model predict how much sales volume will be generated based on the money spent in each media channel?
Yes. Since Vertex AI allows you to input values for each media channel, you can now make decisions about future budget allocation. For example, your company's strategic media plan may now include increasing the digital channel budget based upon the results obtained from a prediction.

Is there a relationship between advertising spend and sales?
Yes. There is a positive linear relationship between advertising spend and sales for digital, TV, and radio. Newspaper spend has a weak relationship to sales.

Which media channel contributes the most to sales?
TV contributes more to sales than the other media channels. How? The scatterplot you built during the EDA section, and your review of the Vertex AI feature's attribution bar chart after the model was trained, show the contribution of TV to sales.

How accurately can the model predict future sales?
The regression model returns a prediction value when media channel values are input into the Predict window to predict sales volume. The prediction results showed a sales prediction value and prediction interval. Prediction intervals can be used to make decisions about future observations, so you can be 95% certain that any future sales prediction result will fall within that range.

 Do not forget to *undeploy* your model once you are finished with this chapter. Deployed models incur cost even when they are not being used so that they are always available to return quick predictions. To undeploy the model, go to Vertex AI Endpoints, click the endpoint name, then click the "More actions" three-dot menu, and finally click "Undeploy model from endpoint."

Summary

In this chapter, you built an AutoML model to predict advertising media channel sales. You explored your data using Pandas, creating heat maps, scatterplots, and histograms. After you exported the data file, you uploaded it into Google's Vertex AI framework. Then you learned how to use Google Cloud's AutoML to build, train, and deploy an ML model to predict sales. You gained an overall understanding of the performance of your model using performance metrics and answered common business questions. You used the model to make online predictions and do a bit of budget forecasting. You are now ready to present to your team!

## CHAPTER 5

Using AutoML to Detect Fraudulent Transactions

In this chapter, you build a Vertex AI AutoML model to predict whether a financial transaction is fraudulent or not. You will clean and explore the dataset in a Google Colab notebook environment before creating a managed dataset on Vertex AI as you did in Chapter 3. Once you have created a managed dataset, you will use AutoML to create a classification model to predict if a transaction is fraudulent or not. Along the way, the chapter discusses classification models in general and the corresponding metrics that are commonly used to evaluate them.

The overall workflow of this chapter is very similar to what you worked through in Chapter 4 for the problem of predicting advertising media channel sales. For this reason, in many places in this chapter you will see more concise details where the conversations would be very similar. If you get stuck in these sections, please refer back to Chapter 4 for more details.

The Business Use Case: Fraud Detection for Financial Transactions

Your task in this chapter, as mentioned, is to build a model to predict whether a financial transaction is fraudulent or legitimate. Your new company is a mobile payment service that serves hundreds of thousands of users. Fraudulent transactions are fairly rare and are usually caught by other protections. However, the unfortunate truth is that some of these are slipping through the cracks and negatively impacting your users. Your company can rectify these after the fact, but there is a fear of losing customers due to them having to report these transactions. The goal is to improve the fraud-detection software that your company is using by leveraging machine learning (ML) to build a bespoke model.

One complicating factor will be that the corresponding dataset will be highly unbalanced. The vast majority of transactions are going to be legitimate transactions, so a simple model that predicts that all transactions are legitimate would be equally accurate and useless. You will need to leverage other metrics to better understand your model's performance along the way.

This task might normally be one that is passed to a data scientist to create some sort of advanced model (such as an autoencoder), but you have been tasked to quickly get together a benchmark model that could be used to prototype other parts of the fraud-detection system. That may seem like a hopeless task, but remember in the previous project you were able to quickly create such a prototype using AutoML for media channel sales prediction. So, you should feel confident that you are up to the challenge!

Project Workflow

The project workflow in this chapter, illustrated in Figure 5-1, will be similar to that in the previous chapter. For this reason, some details of the process will be omitted to avoid repetition, but feel free to refer back to the previous chapter as needed.

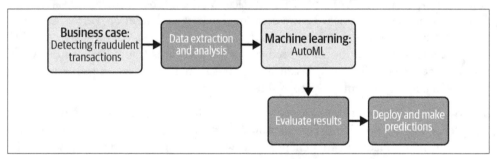

Figure 5-1. Overall workflow for the fraud-detection project.

Now that you understand the business use case and objective, you can proceed to data extraction and analysis as in your previous project. After the data extraction and analysis steps, you will upload the dataset into the AutoML platform. The various features (soon to be introduced) will be fed into the model. You'll evaluate the AutoML results and then deploy the model to make predictions. After this activity is completed, you will have the benchmark model ready for the engineering team to start developing a better fraud-detection pipeline. And who knows, this model may actually be the one that goes into production.

Project Dataset

The project dataset consists of transaction data that has been simulated to replicate user behavior and fraudulent transactions. This has been done using PaySim (*https://oreil.ly/VtIDP*). PaySim is an open source tool developed by a group of researchers who at the time were studying scalable resource-efficient systems for big data analytics.[1]

Since financial transaction data can be difficult to use without exposing user information, your company decided to use this simulated data. Data analysts at your company have confirmed that the dataset that has been shared is really similar in distribution to the actual data that your company sees in its application, so you can move forward assuming that the data is representative of the real-world data that your company wants to leverage at prediction time.

The dataset has been provided as a CSV file in Google Cloud Storage (download at *https://oreil.ly/n1y1X*). In your version of the dataset, there are 10 columns. Table 5-1 gives the column names, data types, and some information about the possible values for these columns.

Table 5-1. Schema and field value information for the customer churn dataset

Column name	Column type	Notes about field values
step	Integer	Represents number of hours since simulated data was generated
type	String	Type of transaction
amount	Float	Amount of transaction
nameOrig	String	Anonymized name of customer who originated transaction
oldbalanceOrg	Float	Initial balance before the transaction for the originator
newbalanceOrig	Float	New balance after the transaction for the originator
nameDest	String	Anonymized name of the customer who owns the destination account
oldbalanceDest	Float	Initial balance before the transaction for the destination account
newbalanceDest	Float	New balance after the transaction for the destination account
isFraud	Integer	1 if the transaction was fraudulent and 0 otherwise

---

[1] For more details, see "PaySim: A Financial Mobile Money Simulator for Fraud Detection" by E. A. Lopez-Rojas, A. Elmir, and S. Axelsson (in The 28th European Modeling and Simulation Symposium-EMSS, Larnaca, Cyprus, 2016).

Exploring the Dataset Using Pandas, Matplotlib, and Seaborn

All of the code in this section, including some additional examples, is included in a Jupyter notebook in the low-code-ai repository on GitHub (*https://oreil.ly/supp-lcai*). You will walk through how to create this notebook from the very beginning, but the notebook in GitHub is great to use as a resource for later independent work or in case you get stuck.

As in Chapter 4, you will be loading a CSV file into a Jupyter Notebook environment and analyzing and exploring your data using Pandas, Matplotlib, and Seaborn to get a better understanding of your features. You will use the information you gain from this process to select the best set of features for your model in AutoML.

Loading Data into a Pandas DataFrame in a Google Colab Notebook

First, go to *https://colab.research.google.com* and open a new notebook, following the process discussed in Chapters 2 and 4 for notebook creation in Google Colab. You may rename this notebook to a more meaningful name by clicking on the name and replacing the current name with a new one, say, *Fraud_Detection_Model.ipynb*.

Next, type the following code into the first code block to import the packages needed to analyze and visualize the financial transactions dataset and execute the cell:

```
import matplotlib.pyplot as plt
import numpy as np
import pandas as pd
import seaborn as sns

%matplotlib inline
```

Now that the packages are imported, the next step is to load the data into a Pandas DataFrame:

```
url = ('https://storage.googleapis.com/' +
'low-code-ai-book/financial_transactions.csv')

transaction_df = pd.read_csv(url)
```

Your data is now loaded into the DataFrame. It is always a good idea to take a peek at a few rows of data before moving forward. To look at the first few rows of data, add the following code to a new cell and execute that cell:

```
transaction_df.head()
```

Take a look now at the first five rows of data in the DataFrame. This will give you some insight into what the different columns look like. What do you notice about the data? Tables 5-2 and 5-3 show the output from this line of code.

Table 5-2. *The first six columns of output from the* `transaction_df.head()` *statement*

step	type	amount	nameOrig	oldbalanceOrg	newbalanceOrig
1	PAYMENT	9839.64	C1231006815	170136.0	160296.36
1	PAYMENT	1864.28	C1666544295	21249.0	19384.72
1	TRANSFER	181.00	C1305486145	181.0	0.00
1	CASH_OUT	181.00	C84003671	181.0	0.00
1	PAYMENT	11668.14	C2048537720	41554.0	29855.86

Table 5-3. *The last five columns of output from the* `transaction_df.head()` *statement*

nameDest	oldbalanceDest	newbalanceDest	isFraud	isFlaggedFraud
M1979787155	0.0	0.0	0	0
M204428225	0.0	0.0	0	0
C553264065	0.0	0.0	1	0
C38997010	21182.0	0.0	1	0
M1230701703	0.0	0.0	0	0

Note that so far the `step` column has a value of 1 for all of the rows you're looking at. There are many reasons this could be the case. For example, all rows could have the same value, the data could be grouped up in some way by step, or it could just be a coincidence since we are only looking at five rows. In this case, it is actually that the data is sorted by `step` in ascending order, though this is not clear at all from only five rows of data.

You may also notice a pattern with the `type` column with the `oldbalanceDest` and `newbalanceDest` columns. In these rows, whenever there is a PAYMENT or TRANSFER transaction type, the `oldbalanceDest` and `newbalanceDest` columns are both zero. This could be a coincidence, but it is something you should explore in the dataset later on.

In the last column in the DataFrame, you should notice something odd. There is a column, `isFlaggedFraud`, that you did not see in the original schema. There are a lot of reasons this could be the case, but this is another reason why basic data exploration can be useful. If you run across this sort of scenario in practice, you may have to reach back out to the person or team who shared the data so that you can validate whether the column should be there, and if so what it represents.

In this case, you learned that this was a column that gave the output of the previous model's prediction if the transaction was legitimate or fraudulent. Why would this be a bad feature for your model to use? Because you may not have `isFlaggedFraud` at prediction time. Ideally, this is coming from a model that you will deprecate once a new and better model has been deployed. However, this discovery is still useful. You can use the previous model as a benchmark to compare against to be sure that your new model shows improvement.

Exploring the Dataset

As you saw in Chapter 4, AutoML will do a lot of the work of describing your features and performing feature engineering before training your model, but it is important that you still take the time to understand the data you are using for training your model. ML is very sensitive to the quality of your data. If there are problems with your data, they will not magically go away in the process of using AutoML.

Descriptive analysis

First, use the `.info()` method on your DataFrame to get a quick understanding of the amount of data you are working with and the data types of the columns. Add the following code into a cell and execute it to do so:

```
transaction_df.info()
```

You should see that there are 6,362,620 rows of transaction data with the 11 columns that you expect. The data types all match the expected types (with the `object` type corresponding to the String data type in the Pandas DataFrame).

As before, the easiest way to get a quick look at the descriptive statistics of your dataset in Pandas is to use the `.describe()` method. Create a new cell in your notebook, add the following code, and execute the cell to see the descriptive statistics (as seen in Figure 5-2):

```
transaction_df.describe()
```

```
1   transaction_df.describe()
```

	step	amount	oldbalanceOrg	newbalanceOrig	oldbalanceDest	newbalanceDest	isFraud	isFlaggedFraud
count	6.362620e+06	6.362620e+06	6.362620e+06	6.362620e+06	6.362620e+06	6.362620e+06	6.362620e+06	6.362620e+06
mean	2.433972e+02	1.798619e+05	8.338831e+05	8.551137e+05	1.100702e+06	1.224996e+06	1.290820e-03	2.514687e-06
std	1.423320e+02	6.038582e+05	2.888243e+06	2.924049e+06	3.399180e+06	3.674129e+06	3.590480e-02	1.585775e-03
min	1.000000e+00	0.000000e+00	0.000000e+00	0.000000e+00	0.000000e+00	0.000000e+00	0.000000e+00	0.000000e+00
25%	1.560000e+02	1.338957e+04	0.000000e+00	0.000000e+00	0.000000e+00	0.000000e+00	0.000000e+00	0.000000e+00
50%	2.390000e+02	7.487194e+04	1.420800e+04	0.000000e+00	1.327057e+05	2.146614e+05	0.000000e+00	0.000000e+00
75%	3.350000e+02	2.087215e+05	1.073152e+05	1.442584e+05	9.430367e+05	1.111909e+06	0.000000e+00	0.000000e+00
max	7.430000e+02	9.244552e+07	5.958504e+07	4.958504e+07	3.560159e+08	3.561793e+08	1.000000e+00	1.000000e+00

Figure 5-2. Rendered output of `transaction_df.describe()`.

It seems like there are no null values by looking at the count for each row. The `step` field varies between 1 and 743 fairly uniformly. The `amount`, `oldbalanceOrg`, `newbalanceOrig`, `oldbalanceDest`, and `newbalanceDest` vary over a large range, but this is reasonably to be expected of financial transactions.

The isFraud column shows an interesting feature of the dataset. The mean of a field with values of only 0 and 1 corresponds to the proportion of values that are equal to 1. In this case, about 0.129% of transactions were indeed fraudulent, or about 1 in every 800 transactions. This represents a fairly unbalanced dataset that can cause issues when attempting to build a classification model. You will explore these issues and possible solutions in later sections, but for now continue to explore the data.

The isFlaggedFraud column has about double the number of rows flagged as fraudulent transactions compared with the actual amount of fraudulent transactions. Is this a bad thing? Not necessarily. You want to be sure you are catching the fraudulent transactions, and if you flag a few extra transactions and recognize them as legitimate transactions upon further consideration, then it is a small price to pay for capturing fraudulent transactions. However, if you flag too many additional transactions, then you will be wasting a significant amount of time and resources exploring legitimate transactions. These are both things you will need to consider when evaluating models in the near future.

There are a few columns missing from your descriptive analysis, though. Notice that you only have statistics for the numeric features (the columns of type integer and float), but you're missing data from the type, nameOrig, and nameDest columns. The describe() method will only return the statistics for numerical features if there is a mix of numerical and categorical features. To see descriptive statistics for categorical features, limit the scope to just those columns. To do that, add the following code to a new cell and execute that cell:

```
cols = ['type', 'nameOrig', 'nameDest']
transaction_df[cols].describe()
```

You are defining a list of columns you want to see the descriptive statistics for, and then using the notation transaction_df[cols], only considering those columns for the .describe() method (Figure 5-3).

```
1   cols = ['type','nameOrig', 'nameDest']
2   transaction_df[cols].describe()
```

	type	nameOrig	nameDest
count	6362620	6362620	6362620
unique	5	6353307	2722362
top	CASH_OUT	C1902386530	C1286084959
freq	2237500	3	113

Figure 5-3. Code and output of the describe() method for categorical columns.

Once again, we see that there is a value for every row for each of these columns by comparing the count with the number of rows in the DataFrame. As expected, there are five unique values for the type column, but notice that the nameOrig column is almost in a one-to-one relationship with the transactions. In particular, there are 6,353,307 values for nameOrig and 6,362,620 total transactions. This is not a good sign for this being a useful feature for building a good model. Why? Because if there is a feature that identifies a row, or nearly identifies a row, then you risk the model only looking at that value and not learning more complex relationships between the features. This seems to be less of an issue for the nameDest column, but it's still a risk given the large number of unique values.

 AutoML will perform feature engineering and selection for you, but if you can give it a better set of features to start with, you will still see better performance. For example, you could re-create the nameOrig and nameDest features as a Boolean-valued column where the value is True if the value is repeated more than once and False otherwise. Is this the right approach? Maybe. To verify this, you should reach out to domain experts and experiment with different feature transformations to see what works best. You will learn more about feature engineering as a whole when working through upcoming chapters.

Exploratory analysis

Before visualizing certain features of the data, it is worth exploring how well the previous model is performing. One easy way to do this is by creating a new column, which you will call isCorrect, which is a simple 1 if isFraud and isFlaggedFraud are the same and 0 otherwise. To compute this new column and count the number of times that the old model correctly predicted fraudulent transactions, execute the following code in a new cell:

```
transaction_df['isCorrect'] = (
    transaction_df['isFraud'] == transaction_df['isFlaggedFraud']
)
transaction_df['isCorrect'].sum()
```

You should see the result of 6354423, but what does that actually mean? In Python, the Boolean data type has two possible values: True and False. When you use the sum function, it treats the True value as 1 and the False value as 0. The result that you see then is the number of True values from the statement transaction_df['isFraud'] == transaction_df['isFlaggedFraud']. This statement returns True when the columns have the same value and False otherwise. Recall that there were 6362620 rows of data total, which means that 99.87% of transactions were correctly flagged.

So, the old model was a really good model, right? Most of the transactions are not fraudulent, and those are the ones that you are most worried about. But consider another related question: How many fraudulent transactions did it correctly predict? You can figure that out by asking where the isFraud column has a value of 1 and the isCorrect column also has a value of 1. Execute the following code in a new cell to see the results:

```
(transaction_df['isFraud']*transaction_df['isCorrect']).sum()
```

Why does that line of code tell you the number of fraudulent transactions that were successfully flagged? The isFraud column has a value of 1 only if the transaction was fraudulent, and the isCorrect column is True (which is treated as 1 for arithmetic) if the prediction was correct. So, multiplying the values of these columns will only give 1 if both columns have a value of 1—otherwise that product will be 0. Adding up the number of 1s gives the total number of correctly flagged fraudulent transactions.

The number of correctly marked fraudulent transactions was 16. By using the code transaction_df['isFraud'].sum(), you see that the total number of fraudulent transactions was 8,213. That means only 0.19% of fraudulent transactions were successfully flagged. This model, which looked great when we saw the overall accuracy, did very poorly when we asked a slightly different, maybe more relevant question. This is an example of a metric known as *recall*. When selecting the model objective and considering evaluation metrics later in the chapter, you will explore how to interpret the different available metrics in AutoML.

The next way that you can visualize the data is to create a bar chart for categorical features to understand the percentage of fraudulent transactions by value. For example, for the type feature, there are five values. To create such a bar chart, use the following code in a new cell to create the visualization:

```
transaction_df.groupby('type')['isFraud'].mean().plot.bar()
```

This line of code groups the rows by the value of type and takes the mean of the isFraud column. Recall that since isFraud has a value of 1 or 0, this is equivalent to the percentage of values that are 1. You then use the plot.bar() method to plot the results as a bar graph, as shown in Figure 5-4.

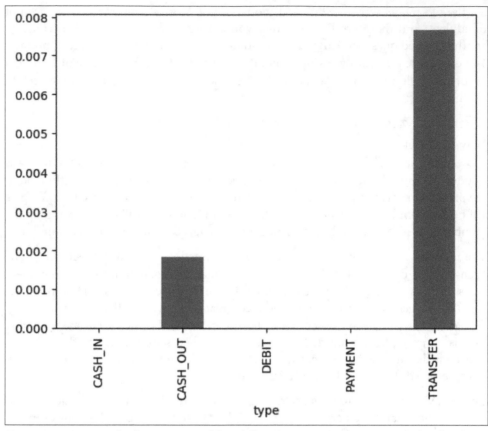

Figure 5-4. Bar graph of percentage of fraudulent transactions versus type of transaction.

You should notice something interesting immediately. There are only two transaction types in your dataset that have fraudulent transactions: CASH_OUT and TRANSFER. You can confirm this with the following line of code:

```
transaction_df.groupby('type')['isFraud'].value_counts()
```

That outputs the number of times each value combination appears. The output you should see will be similar to Table 5-4.

Table 5-4. Output from the `value_counts()` function

type	isFraud	
CASH_IN	0	1399284
CASH_OUT	0	2233384
	1	4116
DEBIT	0	41432
PAYMENT	0	2151495
TRANSFER	0	528812
	1	4097

In this case you can confirm that fraudulent transactions only appear for the transaction types mentioned. That means—as long as this dataset is really representative of the transactions your company sees—this could be a very useful feature. However, if fraudulent transactions of new types start appearing, your model will almost certainly miss them because it never saw such an example.

 It will be important to monitor the transaction types for fraudulent transactions over time and consider retraining the model as needed. This conversation around model monitoring and continuous training is beyond the scope of this book, but it's certainly a concept worth being aware of.

Another useful way to visualize data with categorical labels is to bucketize the numeric features and see for each bucket what percentage of rows is fraudulent versus legitimate. *Bucketization*, or *discretization*, is the process of splitting a numeric variable into value ranges or "buckets" and assigning each element to one of the buckets. You did this in Chapter 4 when you created histograms as well. You can do this for exploring the amount of the transaction and the new and old balance features for the originator and destination accounts.

For example, suppose you want to visualize the percentage of different ranges of the amount feature:

```
transaction_df['amountBkts'] = pd.qcut(transaction_df['amount'], 10)
transaction_df.groupby('amountBkts')['isFraud'].mean().plot.bar()
```

Before looking at the output, take a moment to parse that first line of code. You are creating a new column, amountBkts, in your DataFrame that will contain the bucket information. The pd.qcut() function assigns buckets based on quantiles. You are bucketizing the amount column into 10 buckets. The first bucket contains the data from the 0th to the 10th percentile, the second contains the data from the 10th to the 20th percentile, and so on (see Figure 5-5).

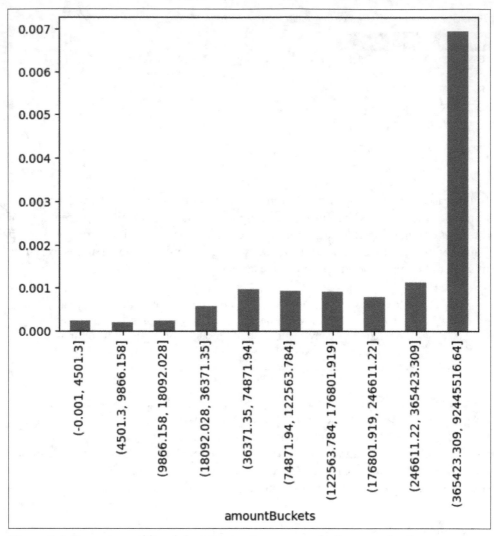

Figure 5-5. Percentage of fraudulent transactions versus decile ranges for the amount column.

You can see a general trend here that hints at something you may have intuitively considered. The larger the transaction amount, the more likely it is that the transaction is fraudulent. In particular, you see that there is a sevenfold jump in the fraudulent transaction rate for transactions with an amount above the 90th percentile.

To look at the same visualization for the oldbalanceOrg column, add the following code into a new cell and execute that cell:

```
transaction_df['oldbalanceOrgBkts'] = pd.qcut(transaction_df['oldbalanceOrg'],
                                        10, duplicates='drop')
transaction_df.groupby('oldbalanceOrgBkts')['isFraud'].mean().plot.bar()
```

There is a new argument, duplicates='drop', in the pd.qcut() function. This argument is here to merge duplicate buckets into a single bucket. In this case, the 30th percentile of the oldbalanceOrg column is 0, so the first three buckets would be identical. These buckets are merged into the 30th to 40th percentile bucket instead.

As you can see in Figure 5-6, there is definitely some sort of relationship between oldbalanceOrg and isFraud. The overall trend is that the higher the old balance in the originator account, the higher the chance of fraud—but only up to a certain point. This chance of fraud decreases once the value is in the 90th to 100th percentile bucket.

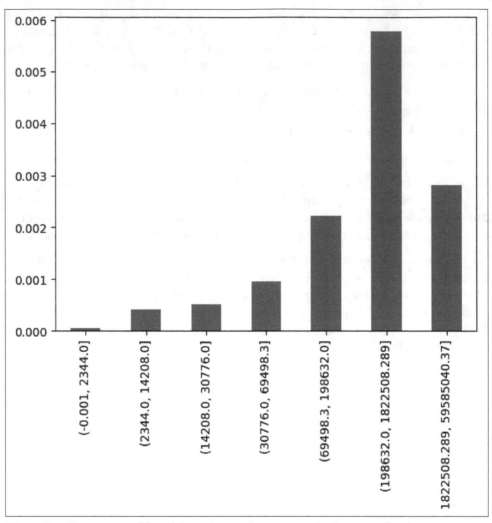

Figure 5-6. Percentage of fraudulent transactions versus decile ranges for the oldbalanceOrg *column.*

As an exercise, explore the relationship between the other numeric features and the label in a similar fashion. The code for these examples is available in the GitHub notebook, and the corresponding visualizations can be found in Figures 5-7, 5-8, and 5-9.

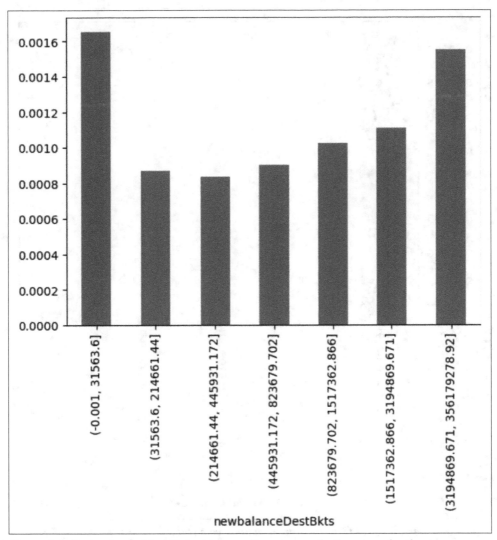

Figure 5-7. Percentage of fraudulent transactions versus decile ranges for the `newbalanceDest` *column.*

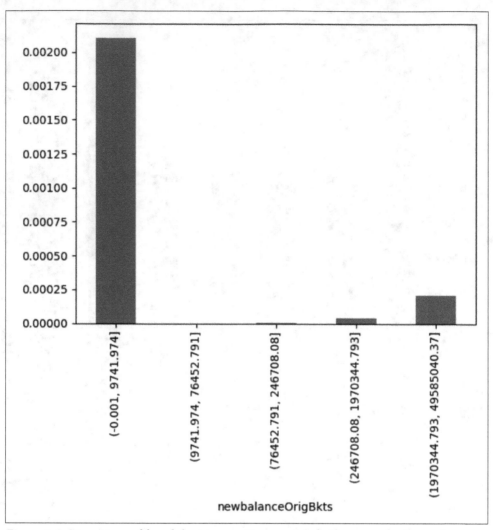

Figure 5-8. Percentage of fraudulent transactions versus decile ranges for the newbalanceOrig column.

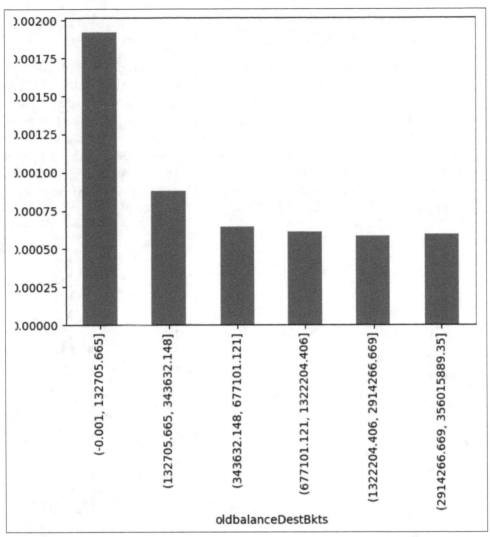

Figure 5-9. *Percentage of fraudulent transactions versus decile ranges for the* oldbalanceDest *column.*

There are other ways to explore transactions. For example, you know that only two types of transactions historically have been fraudulent. You can create a scatterplot for one of these types, say CASH_OUT, where you plot the newbalanceDest versus the oldbalanceDest and then color the points depending on whether they were fraudulent or not. Use the following code to create this visualization:

```
cashout_df = transaction_df.query("type == 'CASH_OUT' & newbalanceDest < 1e8")
cashout_df.plot.scatter(x='oldbalanceDest',
                        y='newbalanceDest',
```

```
c='isFraud',
colormap='YlOrRd',
alpha=0.1)
```

The first line applies two filters. The first filter pulls rows with the `type` of `CASH_OUT` and all transactions where the `newbalanceDest` is less than `1e8` or 100,000,000. The second line is about building the scatterplot. We set the x and y columns, the column for coloring the points (`isFraud`), and a color map `YlOrRd` to make it easier to see the points. This specific color map assigns a darker color (red) to `isFraud=1` and a lighter color (yellow) to `isFraud=0`. For other color maps, see the documentation for Matplotlib (*https://oreil.ly/oDW76*). Finally, since you are plotting many points, you set `alpha=0.1` to add a little bit of transparency to the points. This makes the visualization easier to parse (see Figure 5-10).

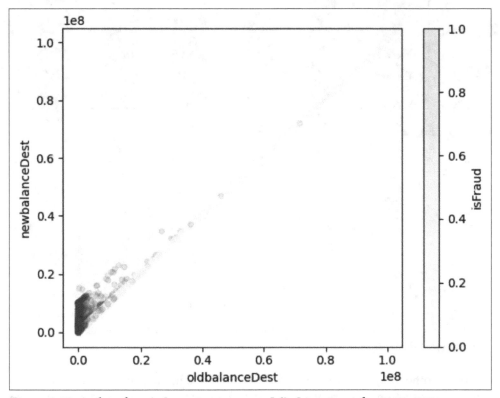

Figure 5-10. A plot of `newbalanceDest` versus `oldbalanceDest` for CASH_OUT transaction type colored by the value of `isFraud`.

There seems to be a region where the points are closer to red than yellow, or where there are more fraudulent transactions than legitimate transactions. This is a good sign that there is some sort of cross-correlation between these two columns. This relationship can be captured in a few different ways, such as *feature crossing*, which

AutoML will use as part of the feature selection and engineering process. Feature crossing is the process of creating synthetic features by concatenating, or crossing, two or more preexisting categorical features. You will explore manually performing this process in Chapter 8 when working with custom code models.

As an exercise, continue to visually explore the dataset using the tools you have learned about in this chapter and the previous chapter. See if you can find any interesting new insights that you may have not expected.

Exporting the Dataset

After exploring the dataset, you are ready to export it into a form that will ultimately be usable by Vertex AI AutoML. You will see a reminder here of how to do this, but note that the data is already stored in a CSV file in Google Cloud Storage and stored in a table on BigQuery, so for the next section you don't need to load the exported dataset. If you are interested in learning more about loading data into BigQuery, this will be one of the steps in the project you work through in Chapter 6.

To export data from a Pandas DataFrame to a CSV file, you can use the following code:

```
transaction_df.to_csv('transactions.csv', encoding='utf-8', index=False)
```

It is always a good practice to check the contents of the CSV file after it has been written, and you can use the !head command to do this:

```
!head transactions.csv
```

To download the file, follow the process from Chapter 4. Additionally, Google Colab has a function in the google.colab package that can also download the file for you. To use this function, import the function from the google.colab package and download the file to your local machine:

```
from google.colab import files
files.download('transactions.csv')
```

 Though downloading files programmatically is a very convenient capability of Google Colab, this is also why it is extremely important to go through any notebook that you are running and be sure that you understand what code is being run in the notebook. You do not want to have unexpected files downloaded to your machine that could be malicious in nature, and the easiest way to avoid this is to carefully read through the code being executed.

Classification Models and Metrics

Before you begin to train the model, let's ask what exactly classification models are and how to properly evaluate them. More mathematical details will be found later in Chapter 7, but with at least a basic understanding of classification models, you can comprehend results and detect troublesome behavior from your model.

A *classification model* is a model that returns a categorical output, like *cat, dog, fish*, or *fraudulent*. In a classification model, you know up front which classes you are trying to distinguish. These classes can be numbers as well; for example, a rating or a problem where numeric labels have been used in place of categorical labels. In the case of your problem in this chapter, those classes are 0 and 1, representing *legitimate* and *fraudulent* transactions respectively.

In practice, classification models do not return the predicted class per se, but rather return a probability for all of the possible classes. Usually, the predicted class is simply the most likely class. In the case of binary classification, where there are two possible classes, that may not be the case. For example, suppose you only classify a transaction as *fraudulent* if there is at least a 50% chance of the transaction being fraudulent from the output of the model. You may be missing cases of fraud. On the other hand, if you set that *threshold* too low, say 5%, then you may end up flagging way too many transactions as fraudulent and thus spending too many resources exploring those transactions further. As you may guess, figuring out where exactly to place the threshold is both a modeling problem and a business problem.

To help determine where to place this threshold, you can leverage different evaluation metrics to make the decision based on your business needs. Accuracy is a simple and easy-to-understand metric that is commonly used for classification models. However, you have already seen the danger in using accuracy as your main evaluation metric. After all, the original model was highly accurate, over 99%, but barely caught any of the fraudulent transactions. Accuracy is an important metric nonetheless, but it does not always give the complete picture.

These sorts of issues tend to arise when you have unbalanced classes, that is, when one class is much more common than other classes. In your case here, recall that only 0.129% of transactions were fraudulent. The ratio of fraudulent to legitimate is nearly 1:800. This scenario means that certain issues can easily be masked by metrics like accuracy. In scenarios such as fraud detection, where the *positive* class is very rare, accuracy quickly becomes unreliable on its own.

You can use metrics like recall and precision together with accuracy to get a clearer picture of your model's performance. *Recall* can be thought of as the true positive rate. In this example of fraudulent transactions, the recall represents the percentage of fraudulent transactions that the model successfully predicts. *Precision* can be thought of as the probability the model is right when it predicts a positive case. In the case of the fraudulent transactions problem, precision represents the percentage of the predicted fraudulent transactions that were indeed fraudulent. If your goal is to proactively flag fraudulent transactions for review, recall would be a very important metric to consider. You would likely be willing to sacrifice a little bit of accuracy or precision to improve recall. Of course, this is still something you want to balance, as there is a resource cost to reviewing a large number of transactions.

Often, recall and precision are computed in terms of the confusion matrix. The *confusion matrix* breaks down the predictions into a table based on the predicted class and the actual class. An example of this is shown in Table 5-5.

Table 5-5. Confusion matrix for a general problem

	Predicted positives	Predicted negatives
Actual positives	True positives (TP)	False negatives (FN)
Actual negatives	False positives (FP)	True negatives (TN)

Recall is defined as $\frac{TP}{(FN + TP)}$, or the percentage of actual positives that was predicted as positive. Precision is defined as $\frac{TP}{(FP + TP)}$, or the percentage of predicted positives that was actually positive. As you may expect, there is a balancing act between precision and recall in practice. Having a lower threshold for the positive class (say, *fraudulent transaction*) will lead to more false positives and fewer false negatives, thus lower precision and higher recall. On the other hand, having a higher threshold for the positive class will lead to more false negatives and fewer false positives, thus higher precision and lower recall.

 Which is more important: precision or recall? Many times, the answer to this question comes down to a business decision. What are your priorities? For example, if your company wants to capture fraudulent transactions as much as possible but is willing to check some legitimate transactions as well, you will likely want to favor recall as your evaluation metric.

How do you know you are finding the right balance between precision and recall? One metric is known as the *F1-score*, which is the *harmonic mean* of precision and recall. In general, harmonic means are often considered the "best average" for ratios. For two numbers it is easy to write down. Let P be the precision and R be the recall. Then the F1-score can be computed using the following formula:

$$\text{F1-score} = \frac{2(P \times R)}{P + R}$$

The F1-score tends to be skewed more toward the smaller of precision and recall. For that reason, this can be a good metric for ensuring that you don't sacrifice too much of one metric to optimize another.

Precision and recall heavily depend on the set threshold, but also on the underlying model as well. How do you decide on the underlying model when your metrics (including accuracy) depend so heavily on the threshold? There are metrics that depend only on the underlying model, such as the area under the receiver operator characteristic curve (ROC AUC) and the area under the precision-recall curve (PR AUC). Both of these metrics vary between 0 and 1. The closer in value to 1 your metric is, the better the model. A deep discussion on these metrics is beyond the scope of this chapter, but an intuitive understanding will be helpful in practice.

The ROC curve plots the recall (or the true positive rate) versus the false positive rate, which is defined as the percentage of negative examples that were classified as positive. The different points on this curve correspond to different thresholds, thus the curve as a whole sees all of the different possible thresholds. The area under this curve, the ROC AUC, can be thought of as the chance that the model (independent of threshold) gives a higher probability that a positive example is indeed positive, versus a negative example. This is a really useful metric for classification problems, but often it is not as useful for situations where the dataset is unbalanced or there is a bigger cost to a false negative than a false positive. One could reasonably argue that this is the situation that you are in here, where missing a fraudulent transaction will likely be more costly than having to check a legitimate one.

Another metric is the PR curve. The idea is the same as the ROC curve, but here you plot precision versus recall instead. The PR curve tends to be a stronger metric in the case of unbalanced datasets. Why is this? Well, both the precision and recall are focused on the positive class, and if you set the positive class to be the rarer class, then your metrics are based on the success of predicting this class rather than the dataset as a whole.

In the following section, when evaluating the model that you train in AutoML, you will see examples of both the ROC curve and the PR curve.

Using AutoML to Train a Classification Model

Now that you have explored your data, you are ready to train a model using AutoML. Similarly to Chapter 4, you will create a managed dataset on Vertex AI and then explore the dataset statistics. Then you will train the model and check model performance. Since classification metrics in general may be newer to you, you will spend some time studying those before moving on to understanding feature importances and serving predictions with your model.

Many of these steps were covered in detail in Chapter 4 for a regression problem. For that reason you will see a lighter treatment of some topics in this chapter and be referred back to Chapter 4 for more details.

Creating a Managed Dataset and Selecting the Model Objective

Go to *console.cloud.google.com* (*https://console.cloud.google.com*) and then go to Vertex AI (either using the side menu or the search bar). From there, select Datasets, and once on the Datasets page click the Create button. Replace the autogenerated name with `fraud_detection`. Similarly to the project from Chapter 4, you first need to choose a data type and objective. Since you are working with tabular data and want to solve a classification problem, you should choose Tabular and then "Regression/classification" as shown in Figure 5-11.

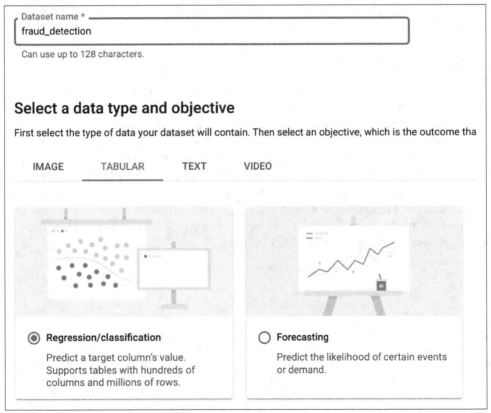

Figure 5-11. The required options for your new `fraud_detection` dataset.

Click the Create button and you will be taken to the next page, where you can specify the source data. Here you have two choices: the CSV file in Google Cloud Storage, which you used in your notebook exploration, or a table in BigQuery that contains the exact same data that was prepared for you in advance. The data stored in BigQuery will come with additional schema information—for example, the data types of each column—that the CSV does not contain, so you will use this approach.

Under "Select a data source," click the radio button for "Select a table or view from BigQuery" and then type in the following BigQuery path and hit the Continue button:

```
ma-low-code-ai.low_code_ai.financial_transactions
```

It will take around 15–20 minutes to load and preprocess the data. AutoML does a lot of additional preprocessing to analyze and prepare the data for the upcoming training job. Afterward you will be ready to explore the data in the Vertex AI Datasets UI.

Exploring Dataset Statistics

Once the data has been loaded and prepared, you can move on to analyzing the dataset. Click the Generate Statistics button. It will take a few minutes to generate the statistics. Once they are generated, you can click on the various columns and explore the statistics. Based on your analysis from before, there should not be any surprises, but it is always worth taking an additional look before moving forward. For example, if you click the type column you will see the statistics shown in Figure 5-12. You will see that there are no missing values; there are the five distinct values that you saw before and the breakdown of the number of times each value appears. The new part here should be the nice visualization to be able to quickly visually parse the portion of the total number of values each value comprises.

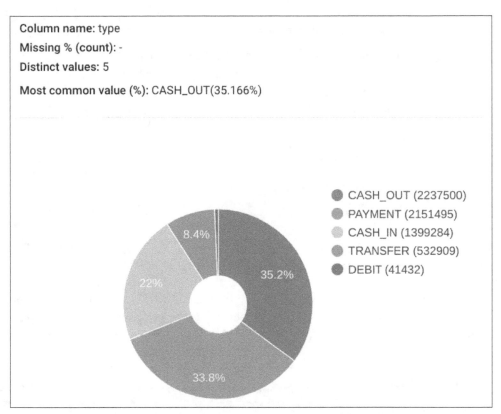

Column name: type

Missing % (count): -

Distinct values: 5

Most common value (%): CASH_OUT(35.166%)

- CASH_OUT (2237500)
- PAYMENT (2151495)
- CASH_IN (1399284)
- TRANSFER (532909)
- DEBIT (41432)

8.4%

22%

35.2%

33.8%

Figure 5-12. Column statistics for the type column generated by Vertex AI.

Before moving on to the next section, go through each column and ensure that everything looks how you expect based on the analysis you did before. Pay attention to the data types and the statistics and ensure that there are no surprises. You will not find any such surprises this time around, but developing this habit is good, and it is a best practice to be sure before you begin any training using AutoML.

Training the Model

To train your model, click the Train New Model button and select the Other option (as shown in Figure 5-13). Be sure that Classification is chosen as the objective and AutoML is selected as the model training method, and hit the Continue button.

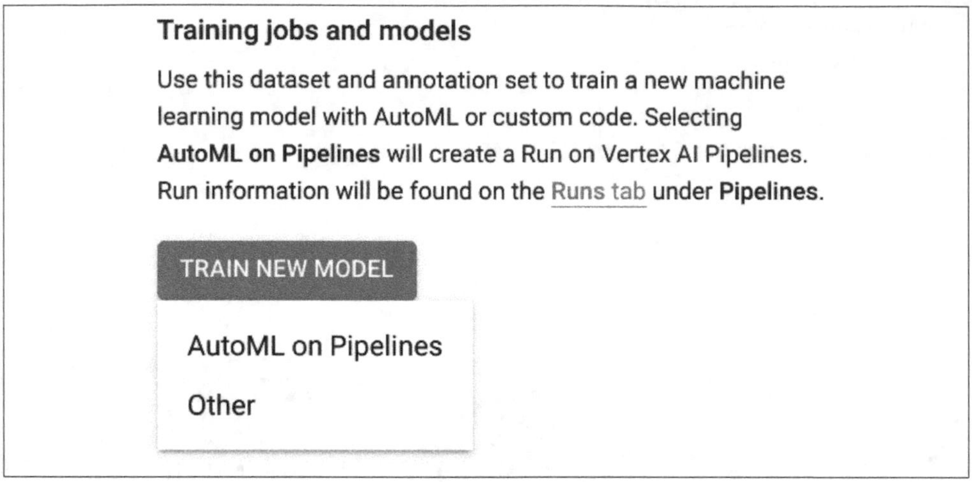

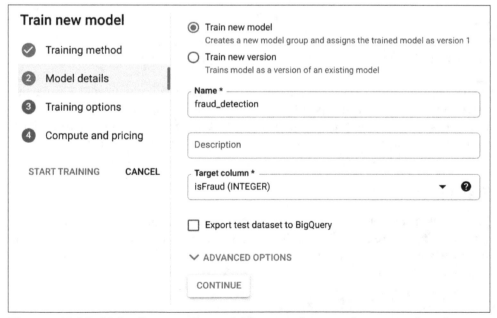

Training jobs and models

Use this dataset and annotation set to train a new machine learning model with AutoML or custom code. Selecting **AutoML on Pipelines** will create a Run on Vertex AI Pipelines. Run information will be found on the Runs tab under **Pipelines**.

TRAIN NEW MODEL

AutoML on Pipelines

Other

Figure 5-13. Options for training a new model in Vertex AI AutoML.

Next, on the "Model details" page, select "Train new model" and set the name of the model as fraud_detection. Also, choose isFraud as the target column. Your inputs should look like those shown in Figure 5-14. Hit the Continue button to go to the next page.

Train new model

- ✓ Training method
- ② Model details
- ③ Training options
- ④ Compute and pricing

START TRAINING   CANCEL

◉ Train new model
Creates a new model group and assigns the trained model as version 1

○ Train new version
Trains model as a version of an existing model

Name *
fraud_detection

Description

Target column *
isFraud (INTEGER)

☐ Export test dataset to BigQuery

∨ ADVANCED OPTIONS

CONTINUE

Figure 5-14. Model details page after model name and target column are selected.

On the "Training options" page, choose which features to use to train and ensure that the features are treated correctly as either categorical or numeric. On the right side of the screen, click the minus signs beside the `isFlaggedFraud`, `nameDest`, and `nameOrig` features. This will remove these features from the training process. Ensure that the `step` feature is treated as categorical as well. This will be important because this represents a time period and not a numeric value. In particular, `step` being 10 should not be counted as twice as influential on the model as `step` being 5. See Figure 5-15 to see what your page should look like before hitting the Continue button.

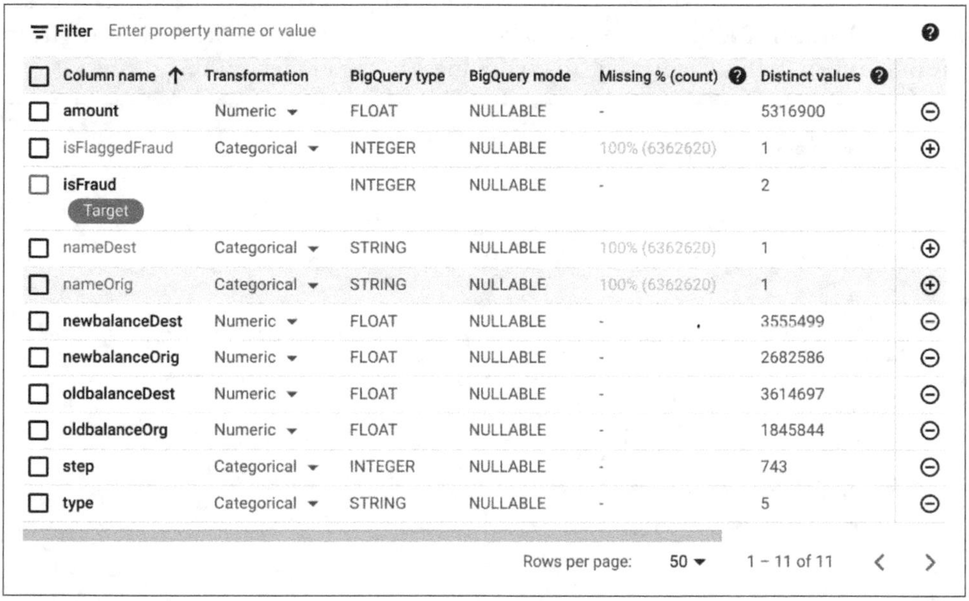

Column name ↑	Transformation	BigQuery type	BigQuery mode	Missing % (count) ❷	Distinct values ❷	
☐ amount	Numeric ▾	FLOAT	NULLABLE	-	5316900	⊖
☐ isFlaggedFraud	Categorical ▾	INTEGER	NULLABLE	100% (6362620)	1	⊕
☐ isFraud Target		INTEGER	NULLABLE	-	2	
☐ nameDest	Categorical ▾	STRING	NULLABLE	100% (6362620)	1	⊕
☐ nameOrig	Categorical ▾	STRING	NULLABLE	100% (6362620)	1	⊕
☐ newbalanceDest	Numeric ▾	FLOAT	NULLABLE	- .	3555499	⊖
☐ newbalanceOrig	Numeric ▾	FLOAT	NULLABLE	-	2682586	⊖
☐ oldbalanceDest	Numeric ▾	FLOAT	NULLABLE	-	3614697	⊖
☐ oldbalanceOrg	Numeric ▾	FLOAT	NULLABLE	-	1845844	⊖
☐ step	Categorical ▾	INTEGER	NULLABLE	-	743	⊖
☐ type	Categorical ▾	STRING	NULLABLE	-	5	⊖

Rows per page: 50 ▾   1 – 11 of 11   ‹   ›

Figure 5-15. Training options page after options are selected.

On the final "Compute and pricing" page, you will set the training budget. As a note, the pricing is computed per hour of training performed. For up-to-date pricing, please see the Vertex AI documentation (*https://oreil.ly/x8C3f*). With this in mind, set the budget to one hour. Be sure Early Stopping is selected since it will terminate the model training process once improvement is no longer being seen. This is very useful if you set a higher budget but ultimately end up not needing that time. Once you are done, click Start Training.

After model training is completed, you will receive an email notification, and the model is registered in the model registry.

Evaluating Model Performance

Once your model has completed the training process, you are ready to view the evaluation metrics. Navigate, either via the side menu or the search bar, to Vertex AI Model Registry. Click on your model, fraud_detection, and then click the corresponding version you want to view. If you are following this chapter, that will be version 1.

Since you care most about trying to predict fraudulent transactions, click the 1 class (highlighted in Figure 5-16) to see how your model performed on the test dataset set aside by AutoML. Note that the evaluation metrics for your model may differ from the one shown in this chapter due to randomness in the model training process.

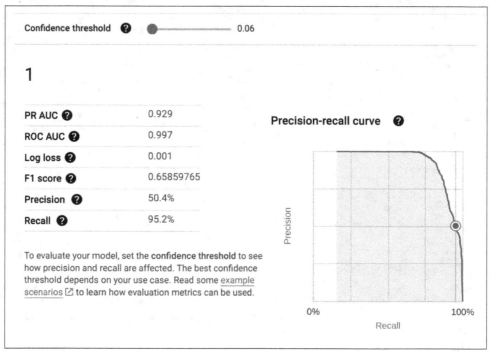

Figure 5-16. Model evaluation metrics for the fraud_detection *model.*

Note the slider for Confidence threshold. You can move this around to see how it affects the precision and recall. Suppose, for example, your company is willing to have up to 50% of flagged transactions be legitimate so that they can capture as much fraud as possible while still being able to have the resources to check the flagged transactions. For the model represented in Figure 5-16, the threshold that corresponds to 50% precision is 0.06. That is, if the model predicts that there is more than a 6% chance of fraud, you would want to flag it as fraud and check it out. Note that the recall in this scenario is 95.2%—in other words, only 1 in 20 fraudulent transactions would be expected to be missed in this scenario.

The best confidence threshold will depend on your business needs and goals, so there is no single correct answer here.

Model Feature Importances

If you click "All labels" on the side of the UI and then scroll down to the bottom of the page, you can see the feature importances for your model. Recall from Chapter 4 that feature importances measure features' impact on model predictions. Note that, as with the evaluation metrics, the exact importances you see for your model may differ from the importances that are shown in this chapter.

The feature importances for this model are shown in Figure 5-17. The oldbalanceOrg and newbalanceOrig features were the most important features, and amount and type were the third and fourth, respectively. Recall, when you were exploring your data in the notebook environment, these features seemed to have the clearest patterns between the feature value and the percentage of fraudulent transactions. In general, these are good to check to be sure that nothing is possibly odd with what your model learned. It is not uncommon for a model to notice patterns that you may not have noticed, but it should be a red flag if your model seems to have learned something nonsensical. For example, if a model to predict taxi fare learned that the distance of the ride was the least important feature, in some circumstances this could be a reason to explore your data more closely. Feature importances are very useful both to stakeholders, to understand how a model makes predictions, and to data scientists and ML engineers, to understand how to debug models in the case that surprising or nonsensical predictions are being made.

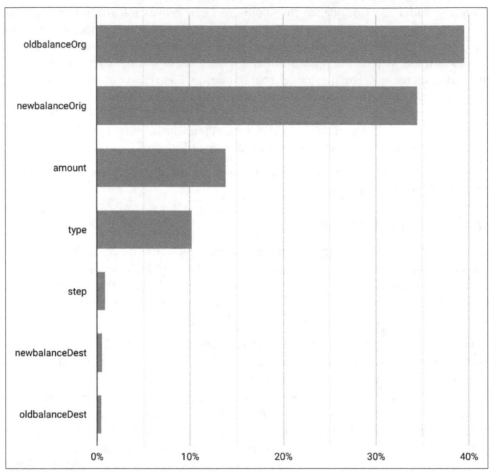

Figure 5-17. Feature importances for the `fraud_detection` *model.*

Getting Predictions from Your Model

Now that you have seen the evaluation metrics for your model, you are ready to deploy the model for prediction. If you get stuck in the process for deploying your model, refer back to Chapter 4, as the process in this chapter will be identical.

Complete the following steps to deploy your model, leaving all unmentioned options as the default value:

1. On the "Define your endpoint" page, name the endpoint fraud_endpoint.

2. On the "Model settings" page, select n1-standard-2, 2vCPUs, 7.5GiB memory as the Machine type. Using a smaller machine type will lower the cost of the deployed model and meet your needs in this example.

3. On the "Model settings" page, under Explainability options, click the checkbox for "Enable feature attributions for this model."

4. On the "Model monitoring" page, disable model monitoring, as you will not need it here.

After completing these steps, click Deploy. The model will take a few minutes to deploy. Once the model has finished deploying, you can test the model on the bottom of the page.

Use the following values to test your model, noting that once again, your exact results will vary from the model being shown in Figure 5-18:

step	14
type	CASH_OUT
amount	1000000
oldbalanceOrg	1000000
newbalanceOrig	0
oldbalanceDest	0
newbalanceDest	0

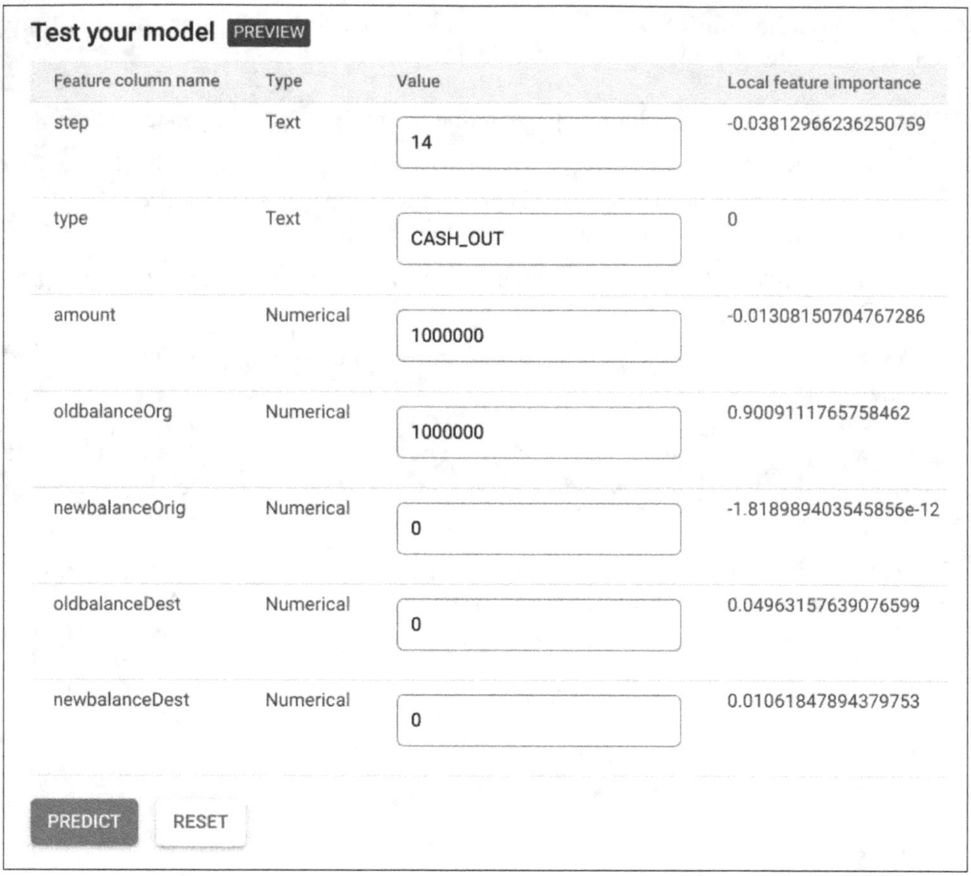

Test your model `PREVIEW`

Feature column name	Type	Value	Local feature importance
step	Text	14	-0.03812966236250759
type	Text	CASH_OUT	0
amount	Numerical	1000000	-0.01308150704767286
oldbalanceOrg	Numerical	1000000	0.9009111765758462
newbalanceOrig	Numerical	0	-1.818989403545856e-12
oldbalanceDest	Numerical	0	0.04963157639076599
newbalanceDest	Numerical	0	0.01061847894379753

`PREDICT`   `RESET`

Figure 5-18. Model testing with predictions and local feature importances.

Once you are done, click the Predict button. To see the predicted probability of a fraudulent transaction from your model, change the "Selected label" to 1.

For the model shown in Figure 5-18, the "Confidence score" is the predicted probability. In this case, it gives a 91% chance of the transaction being fraudulent. Based on the conversation from before around evaluation metrics and thresholds, this transaction would be marked as fraudulent. You can also see the local feature importances. The highest feature importance value corresponds to the oldbalanceOrg feature. In this case, there is a CASH_OUT transaction for the exact balance of the account with 1,000,000 dollars in it. Based on your model, there is a high chance that this transaction is fraudulent.

As an exercise, explore different combinations of feature values and see what the predicted probabilities and corresponding feature attributions are.

Do not forget to *undeploy* your model once you are finished with this chapter. Deployed models incur cost even when they are not being used so that they are always available to return quick predictions. To undeploy the model, go to Vertex AI Endpoints, click the endpoint name `fraud_endpoint`, click the "More actions" three-dot menu (as shown in Figure 5-19), and finally click "Undeploy model from endpoint."

Figure 5-19. The location of the "Undeploy model from endpoint" option.

Summary

You have now trained both a regression model and a classification model over the past two chapters using AutoML! In this chapter you explored your data in a Google Colab environment, then uploaded that data to a Vertex AI managed dataset before training the classification model using AutoML. The recall of the original model was significantly lower than the recall of the new model, meaning that this new model will ultimately lead to better flagging of transactions and saving your customers' accounts.

This is just the beginning of your ML journey, though. In many cases, you will want the ability to have more control over your model training process. In practice, this means moving toward more low-code and custom code solutions. The next chapter covers how to explore data using SQL in BigQuery and train ML models using SQL in BigQuery ML.

## CHAPTER 6

Using BigQuery ML to Train a Linear Regression Model

In this chapter you learn how to build a linear regression model and a neural network model from scratch to forecast power plant production. You perform this task using SQL for data analysis, Jupyter Notebook for data exploration, and BigQuery Machine Learning (BigQuery ML) for training the ML model. Along the way, you learn new techniques for understanding your data in preparation for ML and how to apply this knowledge in improving your model performance.

The Business Use Case: Power Plant Production

Your goal in this project will be to predict the net hourly electrical energy output for a combined cycle power plant (CCPP) given the weather conditions near the plant at the time.

A CCPP is composed of gas turbines, steam turbines, and heat recovery steam generators. The electricity is generated by gas and steam turbines, which are combined in one cycle, and is transferred from one turbine to another. While the vacuum is collected from the steam turbine, the other three ambient variables (temperature, ambient pressure, and relative humidity) affect the gas turbine performance.

The dataset in this section contains data points collected from a CCPP over a six-year period (2006–2011) when the power plant was set to work with a full load. The data is aggregated per hour, though the exact hour for the recorded weather conditions and energy production is not supplied in the dataset. From a practical viewpoint, this means that you will not be able to treat the data as sequence or time-series data, where you use information from previous records to predict future records.

The data is initially supplied in a CSV file,[1] so you will need to spend some time loading the data into BigQuery before you can explore it and ultimately use it to create the ML model. As you will see momentarily, there are five columns in our dataset, as shown in Table 6-1, and 9,590 rows.

Table 6-1. The five columns in the dataset: the target variable, Energy Production, is shown in bold

Column name	Minimum value	Maximum value
Temperature	1.81°C	37.11°C
Ambient pressure	992.89 millibar	1,033.30 millibar
Relative humidity	25.56%	100.16%
Exhaust vacuum	25.36 cm Hg	81.56 cm Hg
Energy production	420.26 MW	495.76 MW

These expected value ranges are well documented by the power plant engineers and have been shared with you (say, via a technical report). This will be helpful when exploring the data to ensure that there are no issues, such as null values or magic numbers, as discussed in Chapter 4.

Cleaning the Dataset Using SQL in BigQuery

As discussed before, it is important that you understand your dataset before beginning the processing of building ML models. Recall that the quality of any ML model you train will rely heavily on the quality of the dataset being used to train the model. If the dataset is filled with erroneous data or missing values, then the ML model will not be able to learn the proper insights.

In this section, you will use SQL as the tool of choice and BigQuery as the platform. All of the SQL code from this chapter is also available in the low-code-ai repository (*https://oreil.ly/supp-lcai*). BigQuery is Google Cloud's solution for a serverless data warehouse. Here, *serverless* will mean that you can quickly load the data into Big-Query and begin SQL data analysis without having to provision any servers. If you are not familiar with SQL, then the "Prepare Data for Exploration" course (*https://oreil.ly/zWLKA*) by Google on Coursera is a great free starting point. *Learning SQL* (3rd edition) by Alan Beaulieu (O'Reilly, 2020) is a good resource for those wanting to dive deeper into using SQL.

---

1 This dataset (*https://oreil.ly/_EvWy*) was created using the Combined Cycle Power Plant dataset from UC Irvine's Machine Learning Repository. Some small changes were made to better demonstrate concepts in this chapter.

If you're not already using BigQuery, it has a free tier that will cover the activities within this chapter for linear regression. The first 1 TB of data processed by SQL queries per month and 10 GB of storage each month are free. Additionally, the first 10 GB of data processed for creating certain types of ML models, such as linear regression, are free. If you are interested in doing ML on your data stored in BigQuery, then you can use BigQuery ML. BigQuery ML uses resources in Vertex AI for training neural network models. If you wish to follow this section to train a neural network model in BigQuery ML, you will incur charges against a free trial or billing account.

Loading a Dataset into BigQuery

The CCPP dataset is not already available in BigQuery. The first thing that you will need to do is load the data into BigQuery. For your convenience, we have placed the data into a public Google Cloud Storage bucket (download at *https://oreil.ly/zY85-*).

To load the data into BigQuery, first open the Google Cloud Console and return to the BigQuery SQL workspace. On the left side of the UI, select your project name and then click the "View actions" button, the three vertical dots, to the right of the project name. Select "Create dataset" as shown in Figure 6-1.

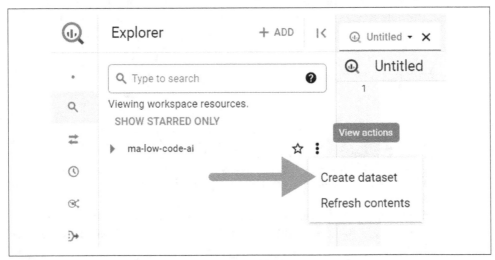

Figure 6-1. The "Create dataset" button in the BigQuery console.

Ensure that your project is selected under Project ID. For Dataset ID, type **data_driven_ml** into the box. Select US as the data location. We make this choice since the data we will be loading into BigQuery is located in a US-based Cloud Storage bucket. Now click Create Dataset. Enter the data into the fields as shown in Figure 6-2.

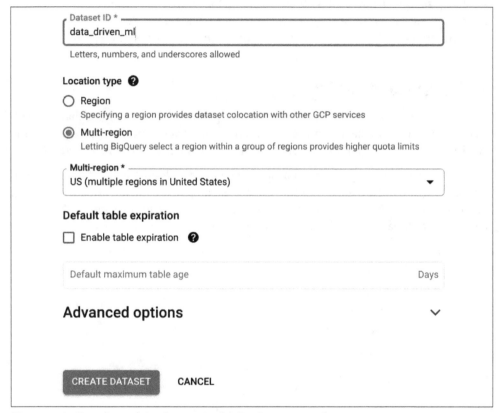

Figure 6-2. Creating a new dataset in the BigQuery console.

Once the dataset is created, you can use the "View actions" button, as shown in Figure 6-3, to create a BigQuery table. Select the dataset, click "View actions," then select "Create table."

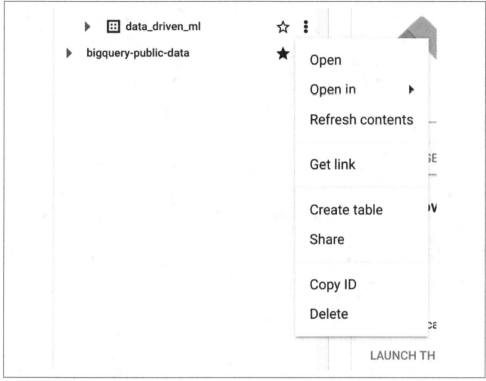

Figure 6-3. The "View actions" and "Create table" buttons.

You will need to specify where you will load the data from, the file format, and the name of the table to be created. These choices are summarized in Table 6-2.

Table 6-2. Summary of choices for creating a table

Field	Value
Create table from	Google Cloud Storage
Select file from GCS bucket or use a URI pattern	low-code-ai-book/ccpp.csv
File format	CSV
Table	ccpp_raw
Schema	Auto detect

Figure 6-4 shows the completed "Create table" window with all the required values completed. In your case, the CSV has a header and all of the values are floating-point numbers, so you can have BigQuery detect the schema from this information.

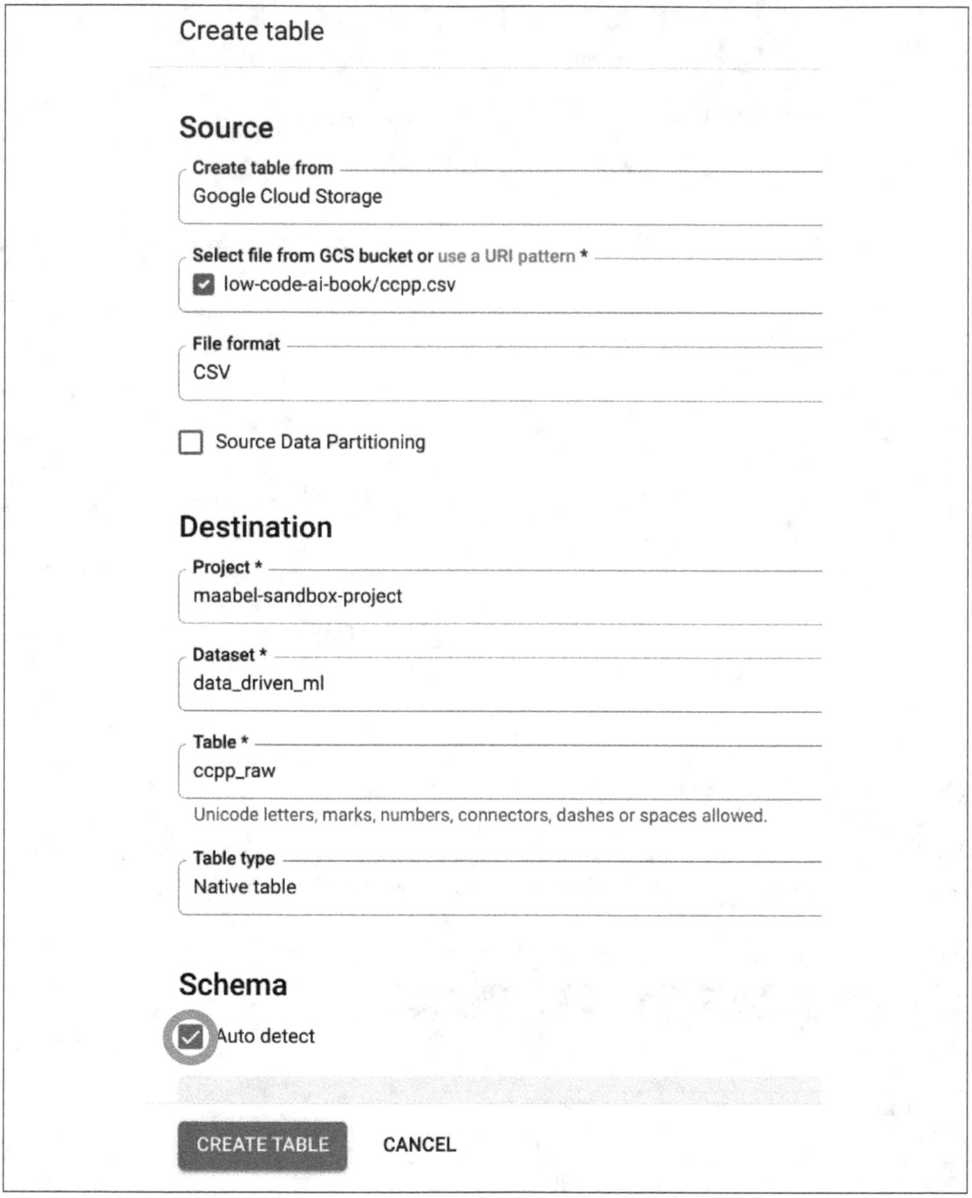

Create table

Source

Create table from
Google Cloud Storage

Select file from GCS bucket or use a URI pattern *
☑ low-code-ai-book/ccpp.csv

File format
CSV

☐ Source Data Partitioning

Destination

Project *
maabel-sandbox-project

Dataset *
data_driven_ml

Table *
ccpp_raw

Unicode letters, marks, numbers, connectors, dashes or spaces allowed.

Table type
Native table

Schema

☑ Auto detect

[CREATE TABLE] CANCEL

Figure 6-4. The "Create table" window with specified values.

Leave the default values for "Table type," "Table partitioning," and "Clustering." Click the Create Table button to start the load job and create the table for your raw data.

Table partitioning is a method to break larger tables into "smaller tables," or *partitions*, that can be accessed separately via filters. Any partitions that are not referenced in a query will not be read, lowering the cost of the query and improving the performance. Likewise, clustered tables in BigQuery are tables that have a user-defined column sort order using clustered columns. Clustered tables can improve query performance and reduce query costs by storing data close in the sort order in the same physical location.

After the table is created, you can see the schema for the table by selecting the table and selecting the Schema tab. You can also preview the data in the table by selecting the Preview tab. Figures 6-5 and 6-6 show what you should see in the BigQuery console for these steps.

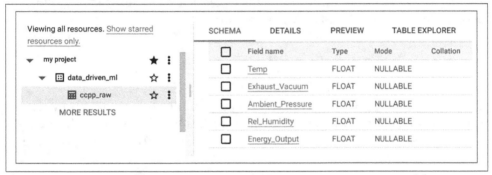

Figure 6-5. Schema for the newly created ccpp_raw table.

Row	Temp	Exhaust_Va...	Ambient_Pr...	Rel_Humidity	Energy_Out...
1	12.85	40.0	1015.89	68.85	463.74
2	10.12	40.0	1021.15	91.67	479.62
3	15.28	40.0	1016.65	65.0	458.76
4	15.52	40.0	1017.0	66.27	454.14
5	10.45	40.0	1019.01	89.01	465.43
6	9.05	40.0	1015.48	80.91	472.41
7	13.79	40.0	1016.02	70.17	461.16
8	6.79	40.0	1019.01	81.83	480.83

Figure 6-6. Preview of the ccpp_raw table.

Exploring Data in BigQuery Using SQL

Now that the data is loaded into BigQuery, it is time to start exploring the data. First check to see if there are any null values. The easiest way to do this is using the IF function in BigQuery. The IF statement, IF(expr, true_result, else_result), takes three arguments. The expr statement returns a Boolean value that determines if it is the true_result or the else_result. As you may expect, if expr returns TRUE then the true_result is returned, else the else_result is returned.

Using the Null function to check for null values

What if you wanted to see if the Temp column had any null values? You could use the following statement: IF(Temp IS NULL, 1, 0). This will return 1 if Temp is NULL and 0 if Temp is not NULL. Run the following query, replacing your-project-id with your Google Cloud project ID, and look at the results:

```
SELECT
  IF(Temp IS NULL, 1, 0) AS is_temp_null
FROM
  `your-project-id.data_driven_ml.ccpp_raw`
```

If you scroll through the results, you will find two 1s in our column of over 9,000 values. This approach works, but it's not too efficient, is it (Figure 6-7)? Instead, let's take advantage of the fact that the choice of the true_result and else_result is 1 and 0 respectively.

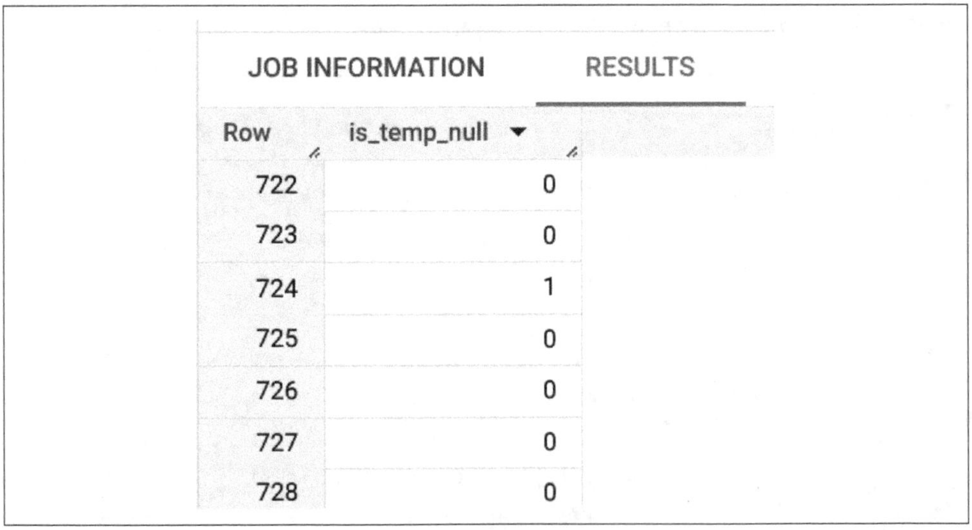

JOB INFORMATION		RESULTS
Row	is_temp_null ▼	
722	0	
723	0	
724	1	
725	0	
726	0	
727	0	
728	0	

Figure 6-7. It is inefficient to scroll through the results to find two 1s in our column of over 9,000 values.

You can easily compute the number of null values by simply using the SUM() function instead of scrolling through the list. Run the following query, replacing your-project-id with your Google Cloud project ID, to compute the number of nulls for every column:

```
SELECT
  SUM(IF(Temp IS NULL, 1, 0)) AS no_temp_nulls,
  SUM(IF(Exhaust_Vacuum IS NULL, 1, 0)) AS no_ev_nulls,
  SUM(IF(Ambient_Pressure IS NULL, 1, 0)) AS no_ap_nulls,
  SUM(IF(Relative_Humidity IS NULL, 1, 0)) AS no_rh_nulls,
  SUM(IF(Energy_Production IS NULL, 1, 0)) AS no_ep_nulls
FROM
  `your-project-id.data_driven_ml.ccpp_raw`
```

After running this query, you should see that all columns except Ambient_Pressure have null values. Compare your results to the results in Figure 6-8.

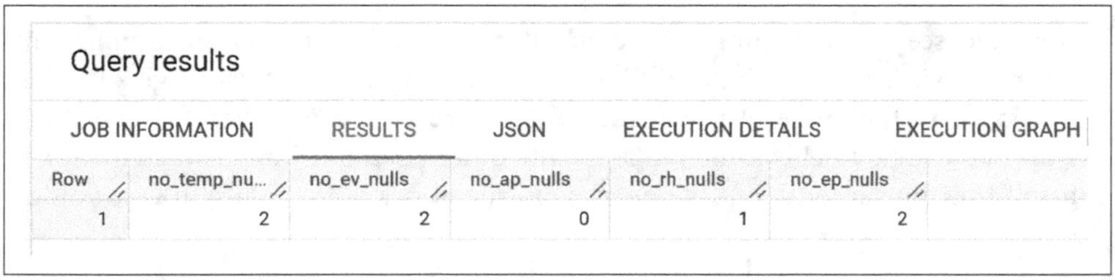

Figure 6-8. Results from query counting null values. All columns except for Ambient_Pressure have null values.

What should be done with the rows containing null values? The easiest approach is to simply omit these rows. Another option, explored in Chapter 7, is to follow an imputation strategy. *Imputation* is the process of replacing missing data with substituted values, often done in such a way that the substituted values are realistic within the specific context. In this case, you may not be an expert on CCPPs. In the worst-case scenario, the rows containing null values will make up around 0.1% of the data. For this reason, simply omitting those rows is a very reasonable strategy.

When would you want to impute instead of throwing out data? If you have a small dataset or if the rows with missing values are a significant percentage of your dataset, then throwing out the rows in question could greatly affect your model performance. Another issue with removing data that is more subtle is around *bias*. Statistical bias refers to a systematic difference in the distribution of your data versus the real distribution of the data. If the null values show up for a specific subset of examples (say, certain demographics in a marketing dataset), then removing the rows with missing values will keep the model from learning important information.

Using the Min and Max functions to determine acceptable data ranges

Next, check to be sure that all of the values are within the expected ranges. The easiest way to do this quickly is by using the MIN and MAX functions. Like the SUM function, MIN and MAX are examples of aggregate functions. An *aggregate* function is a function that takes in a column, or subset of a column, and returns a single value. The MIN and MAX functions return the minimum and maximum values respectively for the column they are applied to. Go ahead and apply these functions to the Temp column by running the following SQL query, once again replacing your-project-id with your Google Cloud project ID:

```
SELECT
  MIN(Temp) as min_temp,
  MAX(Temp) as max_temp
FROM
  `your-project-id.data_driven_ml.ccpp_raw`
```

You should see that the minimum temperature is 1.81°C, and the maximum temperature is 37.11°C (see Figure 6-9). The good news is that this range of values corresponds to the range of values for temperature specified earlier. Go ahead and use the same logic to check the range for the other columns. Try to write the query yourself this time around, but the query is included below the figure in case you get stuck.

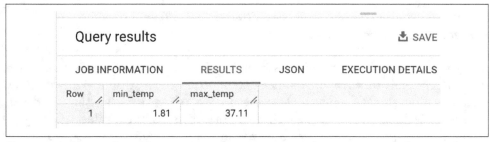

Figure 6-9. The results of the previous query computing the minimum and maximum values of temperature in our dataset.

```
SELECT
  MIN(Temp) as min_temp,
  MAX(Temp) as max_temp,
  MIN(Exhaust_Vacuum) as min_ev,
  MAX(Exhaust_Vacuum) as max_ev,
  MIN(Ambient_Pressure) as min_ap,
  MAX(Ambient_Pressure) as max_ap,
  MIN(Relative_Humidity) as min_rh,
  MAX(Relative_Humidity) as max_rh,
  MIN(Energy_Production) as min_ep,
  MAX(Energy_Production) as max_ep
FROM
  `your-project-id.data_driven_ml.ccpp_raw`
```

You can present the results in BigQuery in the JavaScript Object Notation, or JSON, format. JSON is a programming language–independent data format that is used in many different web applications and products, including BigQuery, for exchanging information. An advantage of the JSON format is that it is human-readable and stored in text format, so it is easy to work with. An example is shown in Figure 6-10.

Query results

JOB INFORMATION   RESULTS   JSON

```
[{
    "min_temp": "1.81",
    "max_temp": "37.11",
    "min_ev": "25.36",
    "max_ev": "81.56",
    "min_ap": "0.0",
    "max_ap": "1033.3",
    "min_rh": "25.56",
    "max_rh": "100.16",
    "min_ep": "-1.0",
    "max_ep": "495.76"
}]
```

Figure 6-10. The minimum and maximum values of all columns in the `ccpp_raw` *table presented in JSON format. Note the anomalous values.*

If you look carefully, you will see a couple of suspicious values. The minimum ambient pressure is 0.0, and the minimum energy production is –1.0. Based on the communicated range of values, and likely common sense, we know that neither of these two values make sense. Likely, the –1.0 value is an example of a magic number. *Magic numbers* are distinctive unique values that are meant to represent something different than a standard meaning. Since –1.0 does not make sense as an energy production value, this is likely a magic number to represent missing data. Likewise, the value of 0.0 for the minimum ambient pressure is likely an example of a default value. *Default values* are often present in applications as a way to record a value when none are reported. This is used to avoid some issues that can arise with NULL values.

Knowing the ranges of expected values from the technical report, the easiest way to ensure that you are avoiding these unrealistic values is to filter based on the expected ranges. Note that this will also eliminate the NULL values that you detected earlier, since those values will also not be inside of the ranges.

Saving query results using a DDL statement in BigQuery

Before writing the query to filter out NULL and other unwanted values, it is important to think through how the results of that query will be stored for use in training an ML model. This can be done by executing a DDL statement in BigQuery. DDL stands for *data definition language* and is a syntax for creating and modifying objects in datasets such as tables. You will use the CREATE TABLE statement to create a new table. The basic syntax for the CREATE TABLE statement in BigQuery is as follows:

```
CREATE TABLE
  table_name
AS
  query_statement
```

This query will create a new table with the name table_name and save the results of the query_statement as this table. Note that with this statement, if the table already exists, it will not be overwritten. If you want to do that, you would replace CREATE TABLE with CREATE OR REPLACE TABLE.

Now that you know how to save the results of a query using a CREATE TABLE statement, you can write the query to clean your raw power plant data and save the data into a new table—say, ccpp_cleaned—for the purpose of training an ML model.

The query is straightforward, but it can be fairly verbose if written in terms of inequalities. However, the operator BETWEEN can be leveraged to simplify the query. To use BETWEEN, you specify a minimum and maximum value by writing the following:

```
Field_name BETWEEN min_value AND max_value
```

If the value you are checking is in the range between min_value and max_value, the statement will return TRUE; otherwise, the statement will return FALSE. For example, here you are looking for Energy_Production values between 420.26 and 495.76. The value of −1.0 that was discussed earlier is not in this range, so it will be filtered out. In particular, we want to only keep values that match the ranges shared with us in the technical report.

As before, try to write the query yourself and run it in BigQuery, but if you need help, here it is:

```
CREATE TABLE
  `data_driven_ml.ccpp_cleaned`
AS
  SELECT
    *
  FROM
    `your-project-id.data_driven_ml.ccpp_raw`
  WHERE
    Temp BETWEEN 1.81 AND 37.11 AND
```

```
Ambient_Pressure BETWEEN 992.89 AND 1033.30 AND
Relative_Humidity BETWEEN 25.56 AND 100.16 AND
Exhaust_Vacuum BETWEEN 25.36 AND 81.56 AND
Energy_Production BETWEEN 420.26 AND 495.76
```

After executing the query, you can view the metadata for the new table we created by going to your project name in the pane on the left side of the BigQuery UI, then clicking on the dataset name (`data_driven_ml`), and finally selecting the table `ccpp_cleaned`. After opening a tab corresponding to the table, click on the Details tab to see the table metadata (see Figure 6-11).

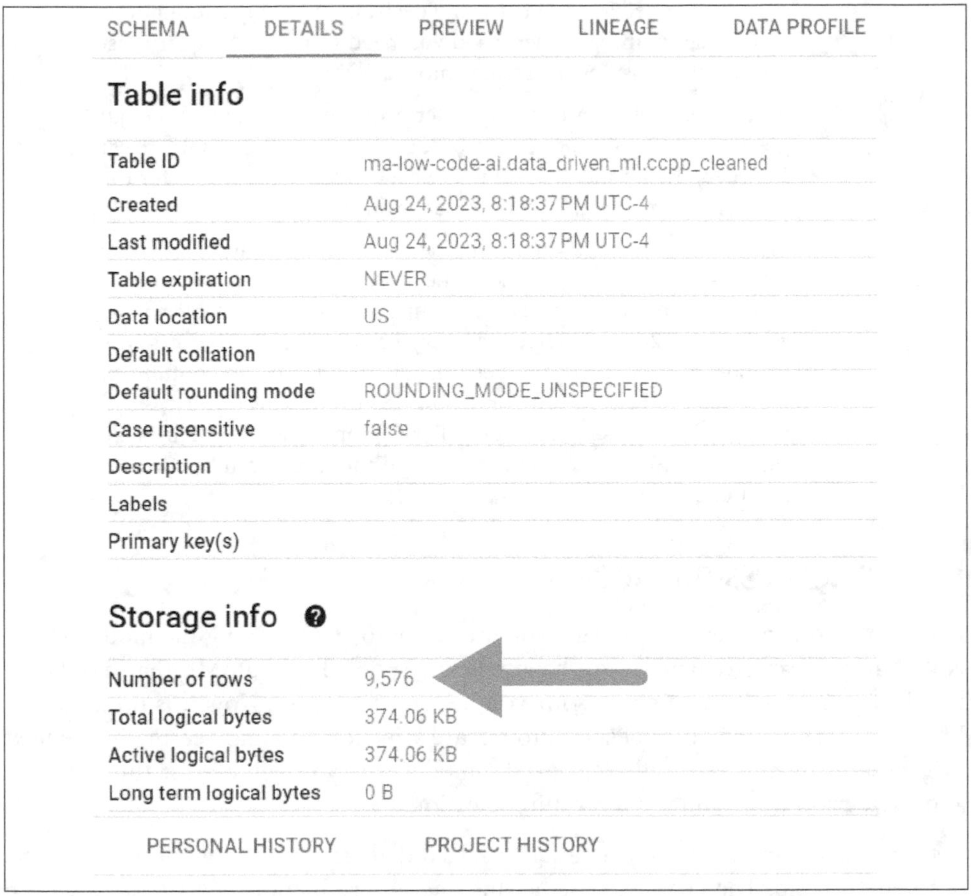

Figure 6-11. Metadata for the newly created ccpp_cleaned table. Compare the number of rows in this table to the number of rows in ccpp_raw to see how many rows were removed.

The newly created `ccpp_cleaned` table has 9,576 rows. If you follow the same process for the original `ccpp_raw` table, you can see that it has 9,590 rows. So that means you filtered out 14 rows from our dataset, or about 0.15% of all data. Very little data was lost due to cleaning here! However, a few incorrect values, especially if they lead to extreme outliers, can greatly harm model performance. So it is a good thing to go through this process.

In the preceding example, you knew in advance that you wanted to save the results of the query and used a DDL statement to create the table immediately. What if the decision to save the results was made after running a query? Do you need to rerun the query just for the sake of saving the results into a table?

Fortunately, the answer is no. After a query is executed, you can go to Save Results on the web console above the result, select BigQuery Table, and then fill in the dataset and table names for the table you want to create from these results.

What if you realize later on that you should have saved the results—are you out of luck? When you execute a query in Big-Query, the results are stored in a temporary table. This table will be retained for 24 hours after the query has completed. To access the temporary table, go to the Personal History tab on the bottom of the console, click the job corresponding to the query you wish to retrieve the results for, and then click "Temporary table." This table can be queried like any other table, and the results can be saved as mentioned.

Linear Regression Models

Now that you have cleaned the data, you are ready to start training the model, right? Not quite. In earlier chapters you have relied on tools like AutoML that handled a lot of the feature-selection process for you behind the scenes. Now it is up to you in BigQuery ML. You will dive deeper into feature selection and engineering in the next project, but for now you will focus on the model type you will use for this problem and what criteria you will use for feature selection.

Before you go any further, take a step back and think a little bit more about the problem at hand. The goal is to predict the energy production of a CCPP based on the temperature, ambient pressure, relative humidity, and exhaust vacuum pressure, as you can see in Figure 6-12.

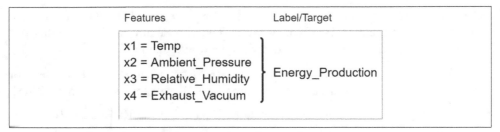

Features	Label/Target
x1 = Temp x2 = Ambient_Pressure x3 = Relative_Humidity x4 = Exhaust_Vacuum	Energy_Production

Figure 6-12. The goal is to predict energy production based on temperature, ambient pressure, relative humidity, and exhaust vacuum pressure.

This is an example of a *regression* problem, since the goal is to predict a real number: the energy production of the power plant in megawatts (MW). Though BigQuery ML supports many different model types, often the best starting point is the simplest one, a linear regression model, where you seek to find the line of best fit.

In Chapter 4, you saw a simplified example of linear regression. In this chapter, the discussion will go a little deeper so that you better understand how the model works (see Figure 6-13). This way, you will be better informed when selecting which of our features we want to use in training an ML model later in the chapter.

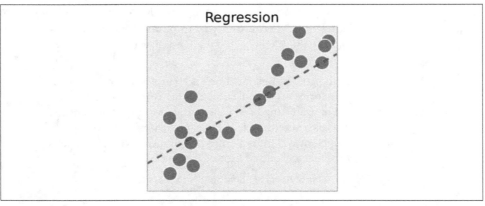

Figure 6-13. A simple example of linear regression. The dots correspond to examples with the x value being a feature and the y value being the label. The dotted line represents the line of best fit.

Suppose you have some number of numeric features, $x_1, \ldots, x_n$, and you want to predict some real number y based on the feature values. Often, $\vec{x}$ is used as a shorthand notation to represent the list of features $x_1, \ldots, x_n$. A *linear regression* model is a function of the form:

$$f\left(\vec{x}\right) = w_0 + w_1 \times x_1 + \ldots + w_n \times x_n$$

Where $w_0, w_1, \ldots, w_n$ are also real numbers, they are called *weights*; w_0 is often called the *bias* of the model. Of course, you could choose any random weights you want and get a function, but how good of a model would that be?

Recall that you used *root mean squared error* (RMSE) in Chapter 4 to evaluate your regression models, and you can do the same here. Recall the definition of RMSE before moving forward. Suppose your dataset D has N examples $\left(\vec{x}^{(i)}, y^{(i)}\right)$, that is, for feature values $\vec{x}^{(i)}$, the corresponding label is $y^{(i)}$. The superscript (i) denotes that we are looking at the ith example in your dataset.

Given a model $f\left(\vec{x}\right)$, the RMSE of the model is the expression:

$$L(f, D) = \frac{1}{N}\sqrt{\Sigma_i \left(f\left(\vec{x}^{(i)}\right) - y^{(i)}\right)^2}$$

where the sum is over all examples in the dataset D. The argument D is included here as a reminder that the RMSE depends on the dataset that is being used to compute it, just as much as the model that we are evaluating.

If you just choose some weights $w_0, \ldots, w_n$, then how do you know you have the weights that give you the best model? Another way to phrase this question is that you want to make the *loss function*, the RMSE $L(f, D)$, as small as possible.

Recall that the goal of loss functions is to measure how well your algorithm performs on your dataset. In other words, a loss function is a method of evaluating how well your algorithm (*https://oreil.ly/CJqzM*) models your dataset. If your predictions are totally off, your loss function will output a higher number. If the predictions are pretty good, it will output a lower number.

See Chapter 4 for a visual explanation of the loss function.

There are two commonly used approaches to determine the appropriate weights for a linear regression model. The first is called the *normal equation*. Using a dataset and the corresponding labels, solving the normal equation gives an exact analytical solution to which weights give the best model for the features that have been selected. Many analytics packages and products (including BigQuery) include this approach in their toolkits.

If there is a nice method to always find the best weights, why is it not always used? Well, there are a few reasons. The first is *computational complexity*, or how much effort it is to compute. Technically speaking, we say that the computational complexity of solving the normal equation is slightly less than $O(n^3)$. What does that actually mean? Suppose a dataset is increased from 1,000 to 10,000 examples, or tenfold. The amount of work that would need to be done to solve the normal equation would increase by roughly a factor of $10^3 = 1,000$! You can see with larger and larger datasets this quickly gets out of hand.

Another reason that is a little bit more mathematically subtle is that the computation could involve very large numbers. Due to how arithmetic is handled on computers (floating-point arithmetic), these large numbers could create an issue in solving the normal equation. The technical term for this situation is that the system is *ill-conditioned*.

Regardless of the situation, if you have a large number of examples or run into issues solving the normal equation, there's a second approach you can take called *gradient descent*. We don't cover that in detail here, but know that most (if not all) ML frameworks have gradient descent and variations of it available for use to train your models. To learn more about the basics of gradient descent, see the corresponding section in the "Machine Learning Crash Course" (*https://oreil.ly/oSW8e*) by Google.

 If you have a little background working with matrices, then the normal equation is not too bad to describe once the notation is set up. The derivation is not covered here, but it is a common topic in calculus and linear algebra texts. For an example of the derivation using techniques from calculus, see this blog post (*https://oreil.ly/uX9tp*).

Feature Selection and Correlation

Now that the model type being used (linear regression) has been identified, it is time to select the features to be used. Recall that there are four columns in your prepared dataset in BigQuery that could be used to predict the energy production: `Temp`, `Ambient_Pressure`, `Relative_Humidity`, and `Exhaust_Vacuum`. How do you decide which of these features to use?

In general, when selecting features there are three basic guidelines that you can follow:

- The feature should be related to the problem objective.
- The feature should be known at prediction time.
- The feature should be numeric, or can be transformed into a numeric value.

These are by no means the only considerations, and you will look at more considerations throughout this chapter and later chapters, but they are a great place to get started. The third condition is important due to the nature of a linear regression model, and most other model types used in practice. When all is said and done, an ML model is a mathematical function that takes numeric features as inputs and outputs some real number, which then is interpreted depending on the model objective. So, either having numeric features or being able to transform the chosen features to numeric features is critical from the computational point of view.

 Features with numeric values that do not have meaningful magnitudes need to be treated differently than those with meaningful magnitudes. Consider a feature that records the color of a car as a number, say 0 for red, 1 for blue, 2 for silver, etc. It does not make sense to say that silver has twice the value as blue. You will see techniques in later chapters, such as one-hot encoding, to properly encode features of this type as numeric features with meaningful magnitude.

Are your features related to the problem objective? Well, this can be a tricky question to answer in general. You have to have some level of domain knowledge to be able to address this question properly, and even then the answer can be rather subtle in certain cases. There are a couple different ways to address this issue:

- You can leverage either your own or another expert's domain expertise.
- You can use statistical methods such as correlation to understand the relationship between a feature and an objective.

As for the first approach, for the sake of simplicity, assume that, in the report, domain experts communicated that these features were indeed related to the objective. This may be an unsatisfying answer, but often as an ML practitioner, you have to rely on those who truly understand the domain to guide you toward possible features. This should not dissuade you from trying to research the problem domains your models address, though! As you work on more problems in a domain, you will learn more about the domain and will be able to really gain an intuitive understanding of key concepts in that domain. This intuition is another way of bringing human insight to your models. This is not only a useful tool, but often a necessary component in building robust models for your problems.

Now to the second approach. Yes, you know that all the features should relate to the model objective, but how do you understand this relationship? When you are building a model, this "how" is very important in understanding how to utilize and transform your features. This process, often called *feature engineering*, tends to be one of the most powerful tools you have in improving model performance beyond improving the quality and quantity of your data.

For linear models, one simple tool that you can use is called *Pearson correlation*. Given two (numeric) variables, *X* and *Y*, the Pearson correlation coefficient, *Corr(X, Y)*, is a number between −1 and 1 that measures how close the relationship between the two variables is to being linear. In particular, if the coefficient is exactly 1, then *X* and *Y* have a perfectly linear relationship. That is, $Y = m \times X + b$ for some positive number *m* and *b*. If the coefficient is exactly −1, it is the same idea, but now *m* is negative. What about in between? The closer the absolute value of the coefficient is to 0, the further away the variables are from having a linear relationship. There are several methods available to determine the correlation between features. Some examples of scatterplots with the corresponding correlation coefficients are shown in Figure 6-14.

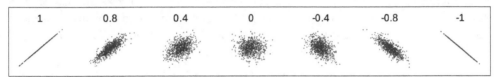

Figure 6-14. Examples of scatterplots and their corresponding Pearson correlation coefficients; image from Wikipedia (https://oreil.ly/Demk9) (CC0 license).

The first method is to compute the correlation coefficient for each pair of variables. For example, to compute the correlation coefficient in BigQuery between the `Temp` column and the `Exhaust_Vacuum` columns, you can use the `CORR` function as shown in the following query:

```
SELECT
    CORR(Temp, Exhaust_Vacuum)
FROM
    `your-project-id.data_driven_ml.ccpp_cleaned`
```

You will see that the correlation coefficient between the `Temp` and `Exhaust_Vacuum` is about 0.844. How should you interpret this? This says that there is a moderate to strong (positive) linear relationship between the two features. From the physical perspective, this makes sense, as pressure increases with an increase in temperature (assuming all other variables are constant).

You could be a bit more efficient and do one column correlated to multiple columns at once—but that will still take time to write the query. For example:

```
SELECT
    CORR(Temp, Ambient_Pressure) AS corr_t_ap,
    CORR(Temp, Relative_Humidity) AS corr_t_rh,
    CORR(Temp, Exhaust_Vacuum) AS corr_t_ev
FROM
    `your-project-id.data_driven_ml.ccpp_cleaned`
```

For a low number of columns, this is not an unreasonable approach. Here we have 5 columns including our label, so we would need to compute 10 correlation coefficients total. This number grows quickly, though, with the number of columns. Of course, you could go a step further and create more advanced queries with automation to compute all of the correlation coefficients, but this approach is beyond the scope of this book.

Google Colaboratory

Another method is to take advantage of Google Colaboratory, or Google Colab for short, to create, plot, and visualize a correlation matrix. In later chapters, when introducing ML packages in Python, you will use Colaboratory as an easy way to run Python code without having to set up an environment in advance. For now, you will see how to bring query results from BigQuery to Google Colab to perform exploratory data analysis (EDA) using some basic Python.

The easiest way to load the data you want from BigQuery is to use built-in connectors in Google Colab. BigQuery has a feature to create a templated notebook to load the results of a query into the notebook environment. Now you will walk through the steps of setting up this environment.

First, you need to run the query whose results you want to load into the notebook environment. In this case, write and run a query that will return the entire cleaned dataset. As before, here's the query in case you need a little help:

```
SELECT
  *
FROM
  `your-project-id.data_driven_ml.ccpp_cleaned`
```

Next, in the same window as the query you just ran, select Explore Data in the console (under the Query Editor) and then Explore with Python notebook, as shown in Figure 6-15.

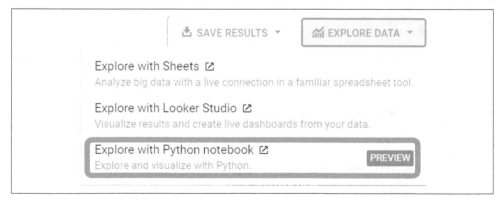

Figure 6-15. The Explore with Python notebook option for exploring query results.

When you select Explore with Python notebook, a templated notebook is created in Google Colab that enables you to explore with visualizations or create descriptive statistics using boilerplate Python. For creating visualizations, you simply add two `import` statements to the first cell (Setup):

```
import matplotlib.pyplot as plt
import seaborn as sns
```

After these two lines, the first cell should look like the following:

```
# @title Setup
from google.colab import auth
from google.cloud import bigquery
from google.colab import data_table
import matplotlib.pyplot as plt
import seaborn as sns

project = 'your-project-id'
location = 'US'
client = bigquery.Client(project=project, location=location)
data_table.enable_dataframe_formatter()
auth.authenticate_user()
```

Now you are ready to run all of the cells that currently exist in the notebook. To do so, click the cell and then click the Run Cell button on the left side of the cell. You can also press Ctrl+Enter (or Cmd+Enter if you're using macOS X) to execute the cell. Go through the cells one by one and run the cells in order. It is important to be sure to run the cells in order and not skip cells to ensure that everything runs without issue.

The last cell is precoded to show descriptive statistics, such as `results.describe()`. Note that `results` is the DataFrame shown in Figure 6-16.

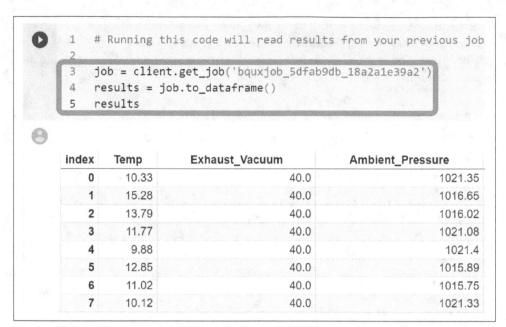

```
1  # Running this code will read results from your previous job
2
3  job = client.get_job('bquxjob_5dfab9db_18a2a1e39a2')
4  results = job.to_dataframe()
5  results
```

index	Temp	Exhaust_Vacuum	Ambient_Pressure
0	10.33	40.0	1021.35
1	15.28	40.0	1016.65
2	13.79	40.0	1016.02
3	11.77	40.0	1021.08
4	9.88	40.0	1021.4
5	12.85	40.0	1015.89
6	11.02	40.0	1015.75
7	10.12	40.0	1021.33

Figure 6-16. An example of the cell of a generated notebook to retrieve the results and the first five rows of results. Only the first three columns are shown for the sake of readability.

Now you can easily create a *correlation matrix*—an array of the different correlation coefficients for every pair of features.

To create this matrix, create a new cell by clicking the + Code button above the notebook and type in the code **results.corr().round(2)**. The round method is used to round the correlations to two decimal places for improved readability. Run the cell as before and compare your results with those in Figure 6-17.

```
[5]  1  results.corr().round(2)
```

	Temp	Exhaust_Vacuum	Ambient_Pressure	Relative_Humidity	Energy_Production
Temp	1.00	0.84	-0.51	-0.54	-0.95
Exhaust_Vacuum	0.84	1.00	-0.41	-0.31	-0.87
Ambient_Pressure	-0.51	-0.41	1.00	0.10	0.52
Relative_Humidity	-0.54	-0.31	0.10	1.00	0.39
Energy_Production	-0.95	-0.87	0.52	0.39	1.00

Figure 6-17. The new code cell to compute the correlation matrix and the corresponding results.

The correlation matrix is easy to read. To find the correlation between two features—say, `Temp` and `Ambient_Pressure`—go to the column for `Temp` and the row for `Ambient_Pressure` (or vice versa) to find the value. In this case, that value is –0.508 (rounded to the nearest thousandth). This means that there is a moderate negative correlation between these two features, where decreasing the temperature will increase the ambient pressure or vice versa.

You can also visualize this matrix with a heat map. To do so, type the following code into a new cell and run the cell as before. Note that the two `import` statements you added to the first cell of the notebook earlier are needed to run these lines of code. The results are shown in Figure 6-18:

```
plt.figure(figsize=(10,6))
sns.heatmap(results.corr());
```

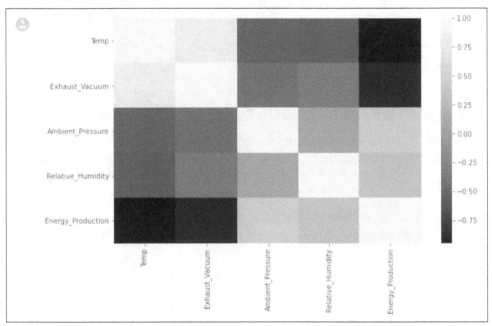

Figure 6-18. A correlation heat map for our features. Darker colors correspond to larger negative correlations, and lighter colors to larger positive correlations.

Work through the following knowledge check on the data you are given before moving forward:

- Which features have a strong correlation to `Energy_Production`? Why?
- Which features have a weak correlation to `Energy_Production`? Why?
- Which features have a moderate correlation to `Energy_Production`? Why?

 Collinearity or *multicollinearity* exists when two or more of the predictors in a regression model are moderately or highly correlated, for example, meaning predictor variables are correlated with each other, making it harder to determine the role each of the correlated variables is playing. This means that, mathematically, the standard errors are increased. Multicollinearity occurs when there are high correlations among predictor variables, leading to unreliable and unstable estimates of regression coefficients. Multicollinearity can limit the research conclusions that can be drawn, especially when using linear models such as linear regression.

Plotting Feature Relationships to the Label

Performing EDA to visualize the relationship between the features and the label is also a great way to understand which features will be most useful for the model. You can continue visualizing your data in the same Google Colab notebook you were using before.

First, visualize the relationship between the `Temp` feature and the label, `Energy_Production`, by adding the following code to a new cell and running the cell. Check your results against the visualization in Figure 6-19:

```
ax = sns.regplot(
    x='Temp', y='Energy_Production',
    fit_reg=False, ci=None, truncate=True, data=results)
ax.figure.set_size_inches(10,8)
```

```
ax = sns.regplot(
    x="Temp", y="Energy_Production",
    fit_reg=False, ci=None, truncate=True, data=results)
ax.figure.set_size_inches(10, 8)
```

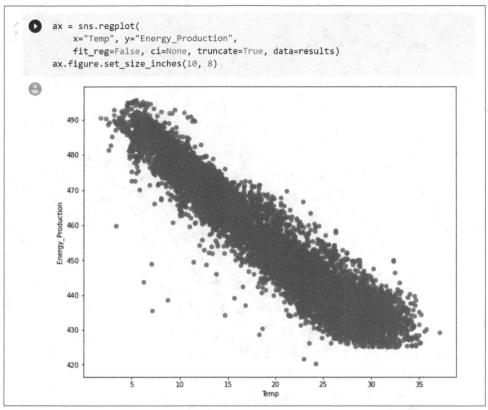

Figure 6-19. A scatterplot visualizing the relationship between `Temp` *and* `Energy_Produc tion`*. The relationship looks like a negative linear relationship.*

Now visualize the relationship between the `Ambient_Pressure` feature and the label, `Energy_Production`. Try to write the code yourself first, but the solution follows in case you need help. Check your results against the visualization in Figure 6-20:

```
ax = sns.regplot(
    x='Ambient_Pressure', y='Energy_Production',
    fit_reg=False, ci=None, truncate=True, data=results)
ax.figure.set_size_inches(10,8)
```

```
ax = sns.regplot(
    x="Ambient_Pressure", y="Energy_Production",
    fit_reg=False, ci=None, truncate=True, data=results)
ax.figure.set_size_inches(10, 8)
```

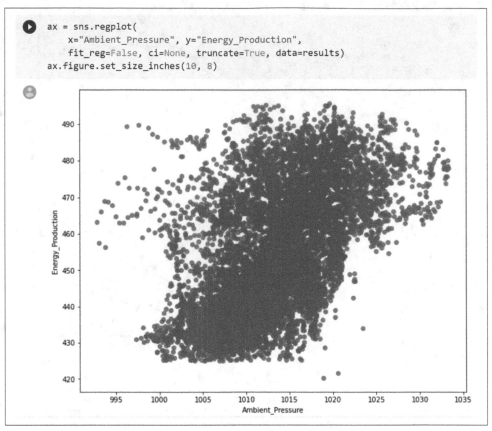

Figure 6-20. A scatterplot visualizing the relationship between `Ambient_Pressure` and `Energy_Production`. The relationship seems to be vaguely positive, but this is not as clear as it was for the `Temp` feature.

Finally, repeat this process for both the `Relative_Humidity` and the `Exhaust_Vacuum` features. As before, the solution code is visualized next, and you should compare your results with the visualizations in Figures 6-21 and 6-22:

```
ax = sns.regplot(
    x='Relative_Humidity', y='Energy_Production',
    fit_reg=False, ci=None, truncate=True, data=results)
ax.figure.set_size_inches(10,8)
```

```
ax = sns.regplot(
    x="Relative_Humidity", y="Energy_Production",
    fit_reg=False, ci=None, truncate=True, data=results)
ax.figure.set_size_inches(10, 8)
```

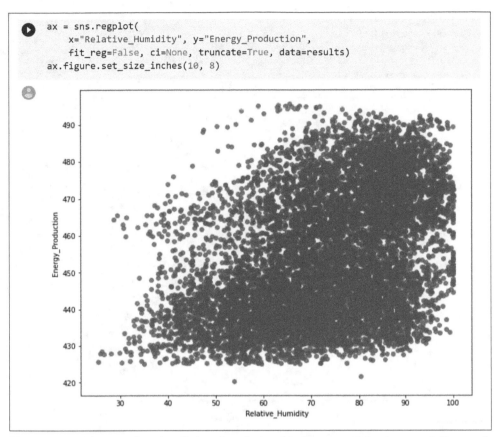

Figure 6-21. A scatterplot visualizing the relationship between `Relative_Humidity` *and* `Energy_Production`. *The relationship seems to be weakly positive, but it is not very clear from this visualization.*

```
ax = sns.regplot(
    x='Vacuum_Pressure', y='Energy_Production',
    fit_reg=False, ci=None, truncate=True, data=results)
ax.figure.set_size_inches(10,8)
```

```
   ax = sns.regplot(
       x="Exhaust_Vacuum", y="Energy_Production",
       fit_reg=False, ci=None, truncate=True, data=results)
   ax.figure.set_size_inches(10, 8)
```

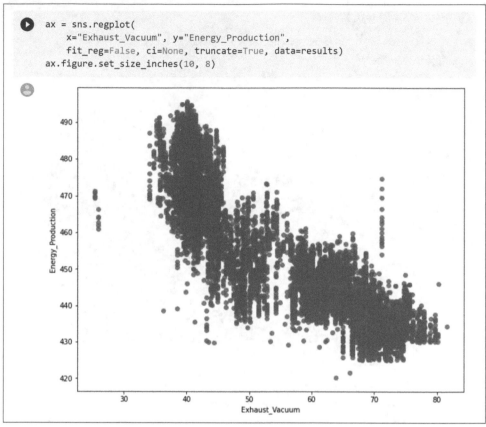

Figure 6-22. A scatterplot visualizing the relationship between Vacuum_Pressure *and* Energy_Production. *The relationship seems to be a negative linear relationship.*

To summarize, it appears that there is a strong "inverse" relationship between Temp and Energy_Production—the lower the temperature, the higher the energy output. If you refer to your previous correlation matrix in Figure 6-17, the correlation between Temp and Energy_Production is –0.948. This corresponds to what you see in Figure 6-19 about expecting a negative linear relationship.

Recall that your goal is to predict energy production based on temperature, ambient pressure, relative humidity, and exhaust vacuum pressure. Should you discard the features with weak correlations? This would move you from a multivariate model to a univariate model. In essence, you would have one feature (Temp) that you would use to predict the label (Energy_Production). Would this model be generalizable? Is there additional data you could collect to determine feature importance to energy production? These are questions that you need to ask yourself when presented with this scenario. Utilize Chapter 1's business decision model to assist you.

The CREATE MODEL Statement in BigQuery ML

In this section you will use BigQuery ML to create a linear regression model that uses all of the features in your power plant dataset. As you will see, now that you have prepared your data the process is very straightforward.

Using the CREATE MODEL statement

Return to the BigQuery console. Enter the following SQL statements in the BigQuery Editor window to create a linear regression model:

```
CREATE OR REPLACE MODEL data_driven_ml.energy_production OPTIONS
  (model_type='linear_reg',
   input_label_cols=['Energy_Production']) AS
SELECT
  Temp,
  Ambient_Pressure,
  Relative_Humidity,
  Exhaust_Vacuum,
  Energy_Production
FROM
  `your-project-id.data_driven_ml.ccpp_cleaned`
```

A few things to note about the notation before executing the query. The CREATE OR REPLACE MODEL statement will create a new ML model, or replace a model of the same name, in the data_driven_ml dataset called energy_production. ML models in BigQuery are objects in datasets like tables. Two options are specified for the CREATE OR REPLACE MODEL statement. The first option, model_type, specifies the model type (here linear regression using linear_reg). The second option, input_label_cols, is where you specify the column that serves as your label. In this case, that is the Energy_Production column.

Now run the query to train the model. It should only take a few minutes. Wait for the model to finish training before moving to the next step.

View evaluation metrics of the trained model

You can see the model metrics in the console. After the model table is created, select the Evaluation tab to see the evaluation metrics. An example of these evaluation metrics is shown in Figure 6-23. Note that the metrics that you see may slightly differ from the figure.

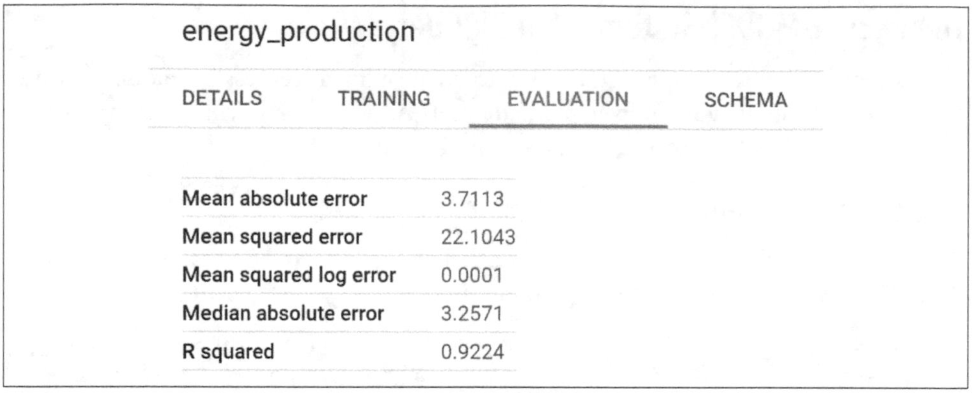

energy_production

DETAILS	TRAINING	EVALUATION	SCHEMA

Mean absolute error	3.7113
Mean squared error	22.1043
Mean squared log error	0.0001
Median absolute error	3.2571
R squared	0.9224

Figure 6-23. Evaluation metrics for the linear regression model predicting energy production.

The ML.EVALUATE function also provides evaluation metrics. Run the following SQL query to return the evaluation metrics for your model:

```
SELECT
  *
FROM
  ML.EVALUATE(MODEL data_driven_ml.energy_production)
```

The output in JSON format is shown in Figure 6-24.

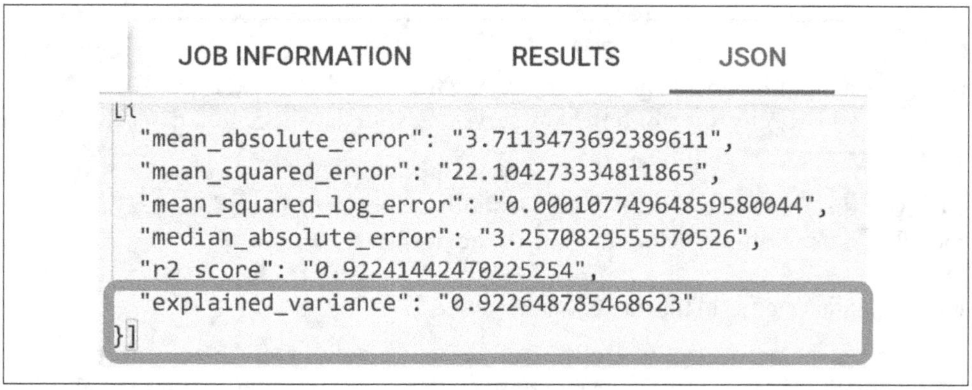

JOB INFORMATION	RESULTS	JSON

```
[{
  "mean_absolute_error": "3.7113473692389611",
  "mean_squared_error": "22.104273334811865",
  "mean_squared_log_error": "0.00010774964859580044",
  "median_absolute_error": "3.2570829555570526",
  "r2_score": "0.92241442470225254",
  "explained_variance": "0.922648785468623"
}]
```

Figure 6-24. Output of the ML.EVALUATE command. The explained_variance output is the only output not included in the console.

As you can see, the output from the console and the ML.EVALUATE function are the same—except for one additional output. The ML.EVALUATE function also provides a metric called "explained variance" via the explained_variance column. Explained variance can be thought of as an answer to the question, "How much of the variance in the label does our model capture in its outputs?" We will not delve into the exact details here, but if the average label value and average predicted value are the same, then we expect explained variance and the R^2 score to be the same. This is called an *unbiased estimator*, and linear regression is such an example.

Why are those scores different here? Because you are not evaluating the model on our training dataset! On the evaluation dataset, as long as the evaluation dataset and training dataset are statistically similar, you only expect that these metrics are close to each other. BigQuery ML automatically splits your dataset into training and evaluation datasets when you train your model, but there are options for having more control on how the data is split that are explored in Chapter 7.

Using the ML.PREDICT function to serve predictions

Now that you have trained your model and explored the evaluation metrics, what is next? The ultimate goal of ML is to serve predictions for your use cases, not to simply train the best model possible. Once you have a model whose performance you are happy with in BigQuery ML, serving predictions with that model is very straightforward using the ML.PREDICT function. Note that ML.PREDICT will only work for predictions on data that is available to BigQuery for processing.

Suppose you want to know the power production during an hour where the temperature is on average 27.45°C, the ambient pressure is 1,001.23 millibar, relative humidity is 84%, and the exhaust vacuum pressure is 65.12 cm Hg. You could run the following query to compute this prediction:

```
SELECT
  *
FROM
  ML.PREDICT(MODEL `your-project-id.data_driven_ml.energy_production`,
    (
    SELECT
      27.45 AS Temp,
      1001.23 AS Ambient_Pressure,
      84 AS Relative_Humidity,
      65.12 AS Exhaust_Vacuum) )
```

Note that the second SELECT statement includes the feature values for the predicted energy production. It is a best practice to alias the columns using the AS keyword to ensure that values are plugged in appropriately to the model. Note that if you include extra columns that do not correspond to features, then they will simply be passed through to the result. This can be useful when you want to include the predicted label as a column in a result table, but also want to include columns that are not used in the model.

Compare your results with the results in Figure 6-25, but note that the predicted label from your model may slightly differ from what is presented here. The column predicted_label contains the predicted energy production.

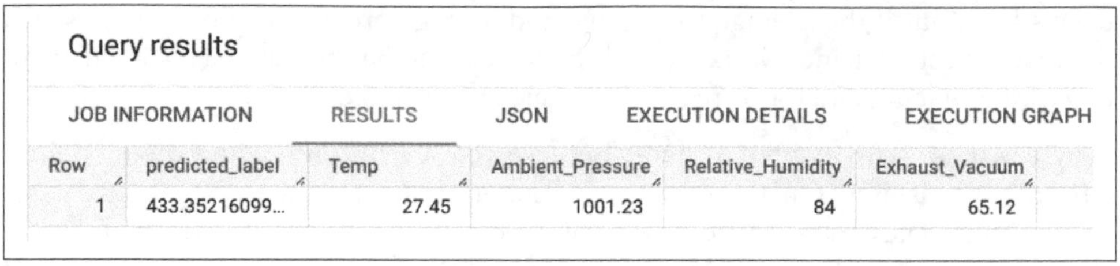

Query results				
JOB INFORMATION	RESULTS	JSON	EXECUTION DETAILS	EXECUTION GRAPH

Row	predicted_label	Temp	Ambient_Pressure	Relative_Humidity	Exhaust_Vacuum
1	433.35216099…	27.45	1001.23	84	65.12

Figure 6-25. The results of the `ML.PREDICT` *function. The predicted energy production for the given feature values was 433.35 MW.*

The method that you did here is great for single predictions, but what if you wanted to predict on a table of feature values instead? You can use the `ML.PREDICT` function to serve predictions on tables just as well. You can replace the second `SELECT` statement in the preceding example to specify a table as a result instead of a single row. For example:

```
SELECT
  *
FROM
  ML.PREDICT(MODEL `your-project-id.data_driven_ml.energy_production`,
    (
    SELECT
      Temp,
      Ambient_Pressure,
      Relative_Humidity,
      Exhaust_Vacuum
    FROM
      `your-project-id.some_dataset.some_table`) )
```

Queries of this form turn BigQuery into a wonderful tool for batch predictions, which is where you need predictions on a large number of instances at once.

Introducing Explainable AI

In the past decade, with the growth of deep learning and more complex models in general, *explainable AI* (or XAI for short) has become a quickly growing field of research. The goal of XAI is to describe a model's behavior in human-understandable terms. This understanding can be used in many different ways: improving the model's performance, understanding issues with the model, ensuring that the model avoids certain biases for compliance or ethical reasons, and many other use cases. This section gives a quick introduction in the context of working in BigQuery ML.

When discussing XAI, often one discusses either local or global explanations. Local explanations focus on a single instance or maybe a small group of instances. You can think of the goal here as being "Why did my model give this prediction for this specific example?" Global predictions look at the model's behavior as a whole over a certain dataset. For example, to answer the question, "Which features tend to contribute the most to this model's predictions?" you could use global explanations.

How do you compute these explanations? Most methods are used *post hoc*, that is, after the model has been trained. These methods can be specific to certain model types or agnostic to the model being used. In general, post hoc methods take a specific dataset (say, your evaluation dataset) and use how the model behaves on this dataset and perturbations to give explanations.

Some models are intrinsically explainable, such as linear regression models. In this case, the explanations can be derived directly from the model itself without the need to use a separate dataset. There is a trade-off, however. In general, the more complex models are less intrinsically explainable. More complex model types, such as deep neural networks used in most image and language models, are impossible to explain from the model definition, and you must rely on post hoc methods.

You will see some of these methods along the way in this chapter and the following chapters, but for a more careful dive into these concepts, *Explainable AI for Practitioners* by Michael Munn and David Pitman (O'Reilly, 2022) is a great resource.

Explainable AI in BigQuery ML

While the `ML.EVALUATE` function provides evaluation metrics, BigQuery also offers a function that provides a way to explain the model and the predictions it produces. Global and local explanations available in BigQuery use Google Cloud's Explainable AI service. Explainable AI in BigQuery provides "feature attributions" that show which input features are most important to your model overall and for specific predictions. To compute global explanations, you will need to modify the `CREATE MODEL` query and add one additional option enabling global explainability:

```
enable_global_explanation = TRUE
```

Global explainability returns the feature's overall influence on the model, often obtained by aggregating the feature attributions over the entire dataset. A higher absolute value indicates the feature had a greater influence on the model's predictions.

Local explanations can be computed without enabling global explanations. You will see examples of both in what follows.

Modifying the CREATE MODEL statement

Copy the original `CREATE OR REPLACE MODEL` query into a new query window. Modify the query by adding the statement `enable_global_explain=TRUE` as shown here:

```
CREATE OR REPLACE MODEL data_driven_ml.energy_production: OPTIONS
    (model_type='linear_reg',
```

```
    input_label_cols=['Energy_Production'],
    enable_global_explain=TRUE) AS
SELECT
  Temp,
  Ambient_Pressure,
  Relative_Humidity,
  Exhaust_Vacuum,
  Energy_Production
FROM
  `your-project-id.data_driven_ml.ccpp_cleaned`
```

Run this altered query to train a new version of the model with global explanations enabled. This should only take a few minutes. Wait until the model has finished training before moving on to the next step.

Using the ML.GLOBAL_EXPLAIN function

To see the explanations, you can create a basic "SELECT * FROM" SQL statement. The difference here is the FROM statement. Rather than the FROM statement referencing the project ID, dataset, and table, the FROM statement is modified as shown in the following code. The ML.GLOBAL_EXPLAIN function calls the model itself (in this case, "energy_production") to retrieve the results. Run the following query in the BigQuery console to explore this for yourself:

```
SELECT
  *
FROM
  ML.GLOBAL_EXPLAIN(MODEL `data_driven_ml.energy_production`)
```

Figure 6-26 contains the query results and shows the features with the largest importance scores for your model overall. Based on the earlier analysis of features using correlation, you would expect that the Temp feature would have the largest attribution score, and this is confirmed here.

Feature Name	Attribution
Temp	12.752
Exhaust_Vacuum	2.721
Relative_Humidity	1.947
Ambient_Pressure	0.297

Figure 6-26. `ML.GLOBAL_EXPLAIN` returns the global feature attributions obtained by taking the mean absolute attribution that each feature receives for all the rows in the evaluation dataset.

Using the ML.EXPLAIN_PREDICT function to compute local explanations

Recall our earlier example: you wanted to know the power production during an hour where the temperature is on average 27.45°C, the ambient pressure is 1,001.23 millibar, relative humidity is 84%, and the exhaust vacuum pressure is 65.12 cm Hg. You used the ML_PREDICT function to predict that the energy production would be 433.35 MW for this hour. You expect that temperature will have the greatest impact based on the global feature attributions for your model. However, global explanations in general aggregate over an entire dataset—what about this example in particular?

You can replace the ML.PREDICT method with the ML.EXPLAIN_PREDICT method to return the prediction with *local* feature attributions instead. Run the following query to get feature attributions for the top three features. Note that your exact output may differ from the output shown in Figure 6-27:

```
SELECT
  *
FROM
  ML.EXPLAIN_PREDICT(
    MODEL `your-project-id.data_driven_ml.energy_production`,
    (
    SELECT
      Temp,
      Ambient_Pressure,
      Relative_Humidity,
      Exhaust_Vacuum
    FROM
      `your-project-id.data_driven_ml.ccpp_cleaned`),
    STRUCT(3 AS top_k_features) )
```

Row	predicted_Energy_Production	top_feature_attributions.feature	top_feature_attributio... attribution
1	450.02603470101332	Relative_Humidity	-2.58330056860657
		TEMP	-1.7340407591690155
		Ambient_Pressure	0.12177258362156519

Figure 6-27. The output of the ML.EXPLAIN_PREDICT function. In this case, the temperature had the largest (in magnitude) contribution to the output for this example.

There is a little syntax and some new columns in the output to explain. The additional argument for ML.EXPLAIN_PREDICT, STRUCT(3 AS top_k_features), restricts the output for feature attributions to the top three features. The top_k_features option is the option for doing so, and ML.EXPLAIN_PREDICT expects this information to be passed in as a STRUCT. You can think of a STRUCT in SQL as a list of values (or columns) with specific names and possibly different types.

Now for the new columns. `top_feature_attributions` is itself a `STRUCT` with two fields, `feature` and `attribution`. The field `feature` gives the corresponding feature name, and `attribution` gives the attribution value for this instance. And there is another new column: `baseline_prediction_value`. This value gives a baseline to compare your instance to for the sake of getting local feature attributions. In the case of linear regression models, this baseline is the average label value (energy production) across the dataset.

How do you interpret the attribution values then? Note that the predicted label is less than the baseline prediction, and the attributions are all negative. The temperature value accounts for about 18.52 MW of decrease on average from the baseline value, relative humidity about on average 2.16 MW, and ambient pressure on average 0.31 MW. Exhaust vacuum pressure is not included here since it was not in the top three, but it had an even smaller contribution than ambient pressure for this example. So, you see that, for this example, most of the deviation from the baseline energy production was because of the temperature, with some minor contributions from the other features.

Another option is to leverage explainability libraries in Jupyter Notebooks, such as Google Colab notebooks. LIME and SHAP are two such popular Python libraries that are commonly used across many different use cases. A full discussion is beyond the scope of this book; we recommend this blog post (*https://oreil.ly/YdZ5x*) and other explainable AI references mentioned already for a deeper discussion and explicit examples.

The phrase "on average" in the previous paragraph may seem a bit odd on first reading. BigQuery ML uses Shapley values to compute attributions for linear models. Shapley values are a tool from coalitional game theory that computes the average contribution of feature values across different coalitions—different combinations of the feature value you are interested in and some baseline feature value. Though there is a more technical definition (see *Interpretable Machine Learning: A Guide For Making Black Box Models Explainable* by Christoph Molnar [self-published, 2022], for example) for linear models, these can be computed simply in terms of the weight corresponding to that feature and the feature value itself for local explanations.

Exercises

In "Feature Selection and Correlation" on page 163, you began gaining a better understanding of the feature selection process and some techniques to use for feature selection. However, you used all of the possible features for training your model in the previous section. Some exercises for the reader:

1. Train new models using a subset of the features. Use what you learned about correlations and collinearity to select your features.

2. Evaluate these new models. Which sets of features performed the best?

3. Use the discussed explainability functions to explore which features contributed most to the models' performance globally and locally. Are there any surprises?

Neural Networks in BigQuery ML

Now that you have trained linear regression models using BigQuery ML, it's time to look at another popular ML model type: neural networks. Neural networks have become incredibly popular in the past decade due to the availability of additional compute resources, new model architectures, and their flexibility to apply knowledge from one problem to another in the form of transfer learning. This section offers a quick introduction to neural networks and then shows how to build such a model in BigQuery ML.

Brief Overview of Neural Networks

As in the case of linear regression models, neural networks are also mathematical functions that take numeric feature values as inputs and output a prediction for the label. Neural networks can be used for both regression and classification problems, but in this section the focus will be on regression models.

To describe neural networks, let us reframe the description of linear regression in visual terms. Recall for the problem of predicting energy production there were four features: temperature, ambient pressure, relative humidity, and exhaust vacuum pressure. For the sake of simplicity, label these as x_1, x_2, x_3, and x_4. A linear regression model using these four features would have the following form:

$$f\left(\overrightarrow{x}\right) = y = w_0 + w_1 x_1 + w_2 x_2 + w_3 x_3 + w_4 x_4.$$

To visualize this as a network, draw a graph like Figure 6-28. Draw a vertex for each of the four features and the output y. Draw arrows from the feature vertices to the output vertex and label those edges with the weights w_1, w_2, w_3, and w_4, respectively. Often, nothing is drawn for the bias w_0 in this representation.

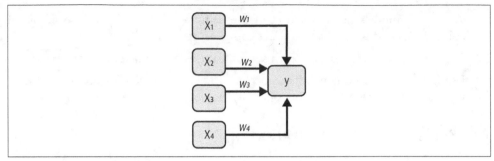

Figure 6-28. A visual representation of a linear regression model.

You have now visualized a linear regression model as a neural network! Before writing any formulas for neural networks in general, we'll start out with a visual representation of one that is not a linear regression model. Now, suppose you want to combine the original features into new hidden features z_1 and z_2, where each of these features is a linear combination of the original features, or what you may consider as a weighted sum of the features. Technically, it is an expression of the form

$$z_1 = c_0 + c_1 x_1 + c_2 x_2 + c_3 x_3 + c_4 x_4$$

where the c_i are some real numbers. The hidden feature z_2 would have a similar definition with different constants (say, d_i instead of c_i). Strictly speaking, the c_0 term makes this something slightly different than a linear combination of the features on their own, but if you include 1 as a constant feature, then the technical definition does align with the usage here.

We call these hidden features together a *hidden layer*. They are *hidden* since you do not see them in the input or the output of the model, but they play a role in computing the output from the inputs. You can draw a visual representation in the same manner as before, but now the feature vertices connect to the new hidden features z_1 and z_2, and the hidden features connect to the output y, as in Figure 6-29.

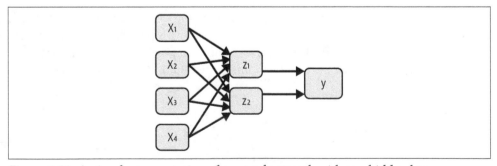

Figure 6-29. A visual representation of a neural network with one hidden layer.

This is an example of a neural network with one hidden layer. How do you determine what these hidden features should be, though? That is, how do you find the best values for the various c_i and d_i? There is no normal equation for neural networks, but you can use gradient descent in the same way as before! Instead of trying different combinations, you can treat the c_i and d_i just like the other weights before for your linear regression model and train the model to find the best weights.

Activation Functions and Nonlinearity

There is still one piece of the neural network puzzle missing, however. To see what this is, consider a simple math problem. Suppose $f(x) = 3 + 2x$ and $g(x) = 1 + 5x$. What is $g(f(x))$? To compute a composition, take the output of the inner function (here $f(x)$) and plug it into the second function:

$$g(f(x)) = g(3 + 2x) = 1 + 5(3 + 2x) = 16 + 10x$$

What was the point of this exercise? Note that $f(x)$ and $g(x)$ are linear functions of the form $mx + b$ for some m and b. The final answer $g(f(x))$ is also a linear function of the same form (just with different m and b). This is not a coincidence! In general, a composition of linear functions is always linear.

How does this relate back to neural networks? The hidden features z_1 and z_2 are linear functions of x_1, x_2, x_3, and x_4; y is a linear function of z_1 and z_2. You can think of your neural network as a composition of two linear functions. The first takes (x_1, x_2, x_3, x_4) to (z_1, z_2), and the second takes (z_1, z_2) to y. Both functions are linear, so the composition is also linear. We just found a more complicated way to write y as a linear function of x_1, x_2, x_3, and x_4!

So, are neural networks with hidden layers pointless? Not at all, but you need to add in one more thing to make them interesting: a nonlinear activation function. *Activation functions* are functions applied to the features in hidden layers before passing along those values to the next layer. This is done so that the functions that go from one layer to the next are no longer linear, and the model can learn more interesting behavior. The most common activation function used for neural networks (and the simplest) is the *rectified linear unit* function, or ReLU for short. ReLU is a very simple function that takes in a single value and returns that value if it's positive, or returns 0 if it's negative (see Figure 6-30).

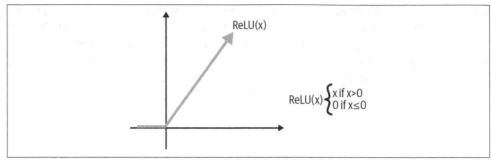

Figure 6-30. Graph of the ReLU activation function.

Activation functions will often be applied to the hidden layers but not the output itself for regression problems. Now you have a definition of neural networks that gives you something more than linear regression models. The resulting functions with ReLU activation are still piecewise linear, but the fact that they are not linear means that you can model more complicated functions. You can see a visual representation of how these activation functions are added in Figure 6-31.

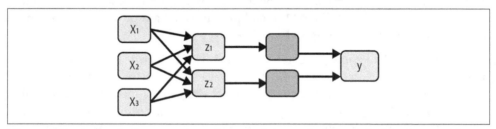

Figure 6-31. A visual representation of a neural network with one hidden layer and activation function ReLU for the hidden layer. The boxes represent ReLU being applied to the value of a hidden feature before being used to compute the final output.

In general, you can build a neural network with as many hidden layers as you like. For example, if you have two hidden layers, you can conceptually think of the neural network doing the following. After training, the model will have learned hidden features for two different hidden layers. You can think of the features for the first hidden layer as being learned from the original input features, and the hidden features for the second hidden layer as being learned from the hidden features from the first hidden layer. You cannot see this directly by looking at the model inputs and outputs, of course, but it does correspond to how neural networks can build up concepts from one layer to another and ultimately apply these to computing the final output. See Figure 6-32 for a visual example of such a neural network.

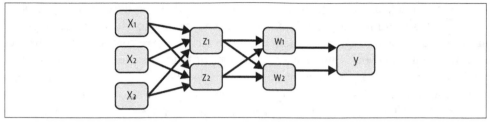

Figure 6-32. A visual representation of a neural network with two hidden layers. The activation function ReLU is not visualized in this example.

 Larger numbers of hidden layers give rise to more powerful models but have more weights to optimize and thus take more data and time to train. Smaller neural networks (fewer hidden layers) are easier to train but may not be able to learn as complex relationships compared with larger neural networks.

Training a Deep Neural Network in BigQuery ML

Now that you know a little bit about neural networks, it is time to train a neural network in BigQuery ML. Training a deep neural network will give you a way to learn critical nonlinear relationships between your input variables and the label, power production. Fortunately, though the concepts are a bit more complicated, the SQL syntax for doing this is just as simple as before, with some small differences. Write and run the following query in the BigQuery console:

```
CREATE OR REPLACE MODEL data_driven_ml.energy_production_nn
  OPTIONS
    (model_type='dnn_regressor',
     hidden_units=[32,16,8],
     input_label_cols=['Energy_Production']) AS
SELECT
  Temp,
  Ambient_Pressure,
  Relative_Humidity,
  Exhaust_Vacuum,
  Energy_Production
FROM
  `your-project-id.data_driven_ml.ccpp_cleaned`
```

This model will take longer to train due to both the model being more complex and the fact that BigQuery is exporting the data to Vertex AI to train a neural network using Vertex AI training.

There are some small changes to the SQL statement that should be addressed while the model is training. First is the model type. dnn_regressor is the model type for deep neural network regression models. The word *deep* here corresponds to the fact that the neural network could have any number of hidden layers, that is, it could be many layers deep. The other new argument is hidden_units. A *hidden unit* or *neuron* is the more technical and commonly used term for what was called *hidden features* earlier. The hidden_units option expects an array of integers, and in this case the array [32,16,8] was given. This means that the neural network has three hidden layers: the first hidden layer has 32 neurons, the second has 16 neurons, and the third has 8 neurons. This would be a bit of a slog to draw out the visual representation of, but hopefully you can understand what this could look like by analogy to earlier diagrams.

Once your model is trained, go to your model and the Evaluation tab as you did for the linear model and look at the evaluation metrics for your model. Your metrics may differ from those that you see in Figure 6-33.

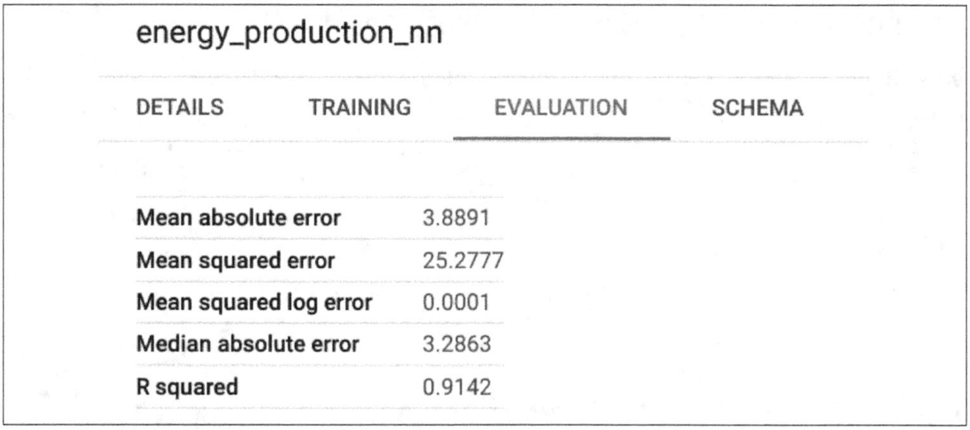

energy_production_nn	
DETAILS TRAINING EVALUATION SCHEMA	
Mean absolute error	3.8891
Mean squared error	25.2777
Mean squared log error	0.0001
Median absolute error	3.2863
R squared	0.9142

Figure 6-33. Trained neural network evaluation metrics.

The new neural network model did slightly worse than the linear regression model based on mean squared error (and RMSE, since RMSE is the square root of mean squared error). This is an example of *overfitting* (as shown in Figure 6-34). The model that is overfitting can more accurately predict the labels for the data in the training set (shown), but this comes at the cost of missing the overall quadratic trend in the data. Models can also underfit. That is, the model is too simple and cannot learn trends in the data. Figure 6-34 shows an example where a linear model was used, so the model is not able to learn the quadratic trend in the data.

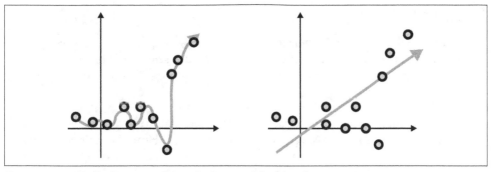

Figure 6-34. Underfitting and overfitting models for a dataset.

When training ML models, you should compare the performance on the training dataset and the evaluation dataset to ensure that the model is not overfitting. You can approach this by altering the model architecture, using early stopping or various other regularization techniques. *Regularization* is a blanket term of techniques that combat overfitting in models. Chapter 8 discusses some of these techniques in more detail for different frameworks, including BigQuery ML.

Naturally, you may have come across a major question along the way. How do you know you have the best number of hidden layers and neurons? You can try some different lists for the `hidden_units` option and see what performs the best, but in theory there are an infinite number of possibilities. The number of hidden layers, neurons per layer, and which activation function is used are all examples of what are called hyperparameters. *Hyperparameters* are different from parameters (such as weights) in that they are set before the model is trained. Hyperparameters define the model architecture, training process, and more, and parameters are what are optimized during the training process to try to find the best model defined by these hyperparameters. Chapter 8 explores different methods for finding the best hyperparameters for your model in BigQuery ML, Vertex AI, and other popular ML frameworks.

Exercises

In "Feature Selection and Correlation" on page 163, you saw the feature selection process and learned some techniques to use for feature selection. However, you used all of the possible features for training your model in the previous section. Here are some exercises to try:

1. Train another model using a larger neural network. You can either add additional neurons for each layer or additional layers. How did this affect mode performance?

2. Train another model using a smaller neural network. You can either remove neurons for each layer or remove layers. How did this affect model performance?

3. Use the discussed explainability functions to explore which features contributed most to the model's performance globally and locally. Are there any surprises?

Deep Dive: Using Cloud Shell to View Your Cloud Storage File

Cloud Shell (*https://cloud.google.com/shell*) is a free service on Google Cloud that gives you terminal access to a small virtual machine with the Google Cloud CLI (command-line interface) preinstalled. This allows you to use the command line to interact with Google Cloud resources. We can't cover all of its capabilities in this book, but you will see a simple example of how you can print off the first few lines of a text file stored in Google Cloud Storage without having to download the file.

To access Cloud Shell, click the Activate Cloud Shell button in the top right corner of the Google Cloud console UI (shown in Figure 6-35). It may take a little time to provision the virtual machine.

Figure 6-35. The Activate Cloud Shell button.

Every time you open Cloud Shell (see Figure 6-36), the underlying virtual machine is different, but the persistent disk is not. What does that mean? It means that your data in Cloud Shell will always be available, but anything that is installed by you will have to be reinstalled whenever you reopen Cloud Shell. Since you will be using the Google Cloud CLI here, this will not be an issue.

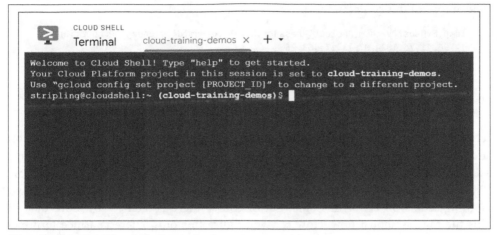

Figure 6-36. The Cloud Shell terminal.

First, ensure that your project is active in Cloud Shell. If it is active, you should see a terminal prompt similar to "`your-login@cloudshell:~ (your-project-id)$`." If you do not see the project ID in the second part of the prompt, you will need to set this. Fortunately, that is very easy to do using the Google Cloud CLI. Type in the following command (replacing your-project-id with your project ID) and hit Enter/Return:

```
gcloud config set project your-project-id
```

You should now see your project ID in the second part of the terminal prompt. You can also check that the project ID is set successfully by running this command:

```
gcloud config list project
```

Now that you have activated the CLI using your project ID, you can look at the first few lines of the CSV file together. Do this by running the following command:

```
gcloud storage cat -r 0-250 gs://low-code-ai-book/ccpp.csv
```

Unlike the previous commands, this one is likely not very obvious in purpose. `gcloud storage` is the family of commands for interacting with Google Cloud Storage, and you are executing the `cat` command. This command is short for *concatenate,* and it's used to read a file from Google Cloud Storage and write it to the standard terminal output. The next part of the command, `-r 0-250`, specifies that you do not want to read the entire file, but rather just the first 250 bytes. For this CSV file, this will allow you to see the first few rows to just get a quick idea of what you are looking at. Finally, you have the file Uniform Resource Identifier (URI) in Google Cloud Storage: `gs://low-code-ai-book/ccpp.csv`

The output of this command is the following:

```
Temp,Exhaust_Vacuum,Ambient_Pressure,Relative_Humidity,Energy_Production
14.96,41.76,1024.07,73.17,463.26
25.18,62.96,1020.04,59.08,444.37
5.11,39.4,1012.16,92.14,488.56
20.86,57.32,1010.24,76.64,446.48
10.82,37.5,1009.23,96.62,473.9
26.27,59.44
```

The last row was not completed, but that is OK! The goal here was to simply get an idea of what you were looking at. Note that this CSV file has five columns: `Temp`, `Exhaust_Vacuum`, `Ambient_Pressure`, `Relative_Humidity`, and `Energy_Production`. These correspond to the columns that were expected. At least in the first few rows, nothing seems off about this data, but of course there is likely a lot more data in this file than is shown now. How can you figure this out? There is a nice terminal command, `wc`, that can count the number of lines in a file:

```
gcloud storage cat gs://low-code-ai-book/ccpp.csv | wc -l
```

The first part of the command is familiar: you are concatenating the CSV file from Google Cloud Storage. You are not specifying how many bytes to read, so the entire file will be read. But the last part of the command is new. This command is really two different commands chained together using the pipe operator `|`. The *pipe* operator takes the output from the first command and "pipes" it to the second command to use as the input. In this case, the second command is the `wc -l` command. This command uses `wc` ("word count") to count the number of lines, words, and characters in the CSV file. The `-l` option is used to only print out the number of lines. In this case, you see that the CSV file has 9,590 lines.

Summary

In this chapter you analyzed power plant production data using SQL and Python. Using what you learned in your analysis, you built both linear regression and deep neural network regressor models to predict power plant production using SQL in BigQuery ML. Along the way, you explored new concepts around topics such as explainability and some of the mathematics behind neural networks.

The focus of this book so far has been on no-code and low-code solutions, but there may be situations where you need something more flexible. In the next chapter, you will be introduced to custom code solutions in Python using scikit-learn and Keras. Both libraries are very approachable and are a great place to start your exploration into using Python for ML.

## CHAPTER 7

Training Custom ML Models in Python

In this chapter, you'll learn how to build classification models to predict customer churn using two popular ML libraries available in Python, scikit-learn and Keras. First, you'll explore and clean your data using Pandas. Then you'll learn how to use scikit-learn to prepare categorical features for training using one-hot encoding, train a logistic regression model, understand model performance using evaluation metrics, and improve model performance. You'll learn how to perform the same steps using Keras to build a neural network classification model using the already prepared data. Along the way, you'll learn more about performance metrics for classification models and how to better understand a confusion matrix to better evaluate your classification models.

The dataset being used for this chapter, the IBM Telco Customer Churn dataset (*https://oreil.ly/Rz3r2*), is a popular dataset for learning how to model customer churn. You should feel encouraged to look at other examples of how to work with this dataset to grow your knowledge after completing the exercises in this chapter.

The Business Use Case: Customer Churn Prediction

Your goal in this project will be to predict customer churn for a telecommunications company. Customer churn is defined as the *attrition* rate for customers, or in other words the rate of customers that choose to stop using services. Telecommunications companies often sell their products at a monthly rate or via annual contracts, so *churn* here will represent when a customer cancels their subscription or contract in the following month.

The data is initially supplied in a CSV file, so you will need to spend some time loading the data into Pandas before you can explore it and ultimately use it to create your ML model using different frameworks. The dataset contains both numeric variables and categorical variables, where the variable takes on a value from a discrete set of possibilities.

There are 21 columns in the dataset. Table 7-1 gives the column names, data types, and some information about the possible values for these columns.

Table 7-1. Schema and field value information for the customer churn dataset

Column name	Column type	Notes about field values
customerID	String	Unique value for every customer
gender	String	"male" or "female"
SeniorCitizen	Integer	1 if customer is a senior citizen, 0 otherwise
Partner	String	Records if the customer has a partner (spouse or domestic partner) in the household
Dependents	String	Records if the customer has dependents in the household or not
tenure	Integer	Number of months the customer has used the telco service
PhoneService	String	Records if the customer pays for phone service
MultipleLines	String	If the customer pays for phone service, do they pay for multiple phone lines?
InternetService	String	What type of internet service does the customer pay for, if any?
OnlineSecurity	String	Does the customer pay for online security?
OnlineBackup	String	Does the customer pay for online backup?
DeviceProtection	String	Does the customer pay for device protection?
TechSupport	String	Does the customer pay for online tech support?
StreamingTV	String	Does the customer pay for streaming television?
StreamingMovies	String	Does the customer pay for streaming movies?
Contract	String	Does the customer have a contract or do they pay month by month?
PaperlessBilling	String	Does the customer use paperless billing?
PaymentMethod	String	What payment method does the customer use?
MonthlyCharges	Float	Monthly charge for customer services
TotalCharges	Float	Total amount customer has paid over lifetime
Churn	String	Did the customer leave the telco service in the following month?

You will discover that many of the features can be consolidated or omitted for training your ML model. However, many of the features will need cleaning and further transformation to prepare for the training process.

Choosing Among No-Code, Low-Code, or Custom Code ML Solutions

Before exploring how to use custom training tools such as scikit-learn, Keras, or other options that were discussed in Chapter 3, it is worth discussing when a custom solution could and should be used over other options discussed in this book so far:

No-code solutions

These are great in two cases in particular. The first is when you need to build an ML model, but do not have any ML expertise. The goal of this book is to give you a bit more insight into how to make the right decisions around your data for ML, but no-code solutions often exist to simplify the decisions and lessen the need for working with more complex solutions. Another place where no-code solutions stand out is in rapid prototyping of models. Because no-code solutions, such as AutoML solutions, manage steps like feature engineering and hyperparameter tuning for the user, this can be an easy way to train a quick benchmark model. Not only that, but as shown in Chapters 4 and 5, it is simple to deploy these models using Vertex AI AutoML. In many cases, these no-code solutions can be robust enough to use in production immediately. In practice, custom solutions can outperform no-code solutions given enough time and effort, but incremental gains in model performance can often be outweighed by the time saved in getting no-code solutions into production.

Low-code solutions

These are great when you do need some customization and are working with data that meets the constraints of the tool you are using. For example, if you are working with structured data and the problem type you wish to solve is supported by BigQuery ML, then BigQuery ML could be a great choice. The advantage of a low-code solution in these cases is that less time needs to be spent on building the model and more time can be spent experimenting with your data and tuning your model. With many low-code solutions, the model can be productionized either directly within the product or via model export and using other tools like Vertex AI.

Custom code solutions

These are by far the most flexible and are often leveraged by data scientists and other AI practitioners who like to build their own custom models. Using ML frameworks like TensorFlow, XGBoost, PyTorch, and scikit-learn, you can build a model using any type of data and the objective of your choice. In some sense, the sky's the limit in terms of flexibility and deployment options. If you need a custom transformation, you can build it. If you need to be able to deploy your model as part of a web application, you can do it. Given the right data, expertise, and enough time, you can achieve the best results using custom code solutions. However, one of the trade-offs is that one needs to spend the time to learn the various different tools and techniques for doing this.

Which should you prefer? There is no single correct answer for every possible use case. Take into account the time you have to train, tune, and deploy the model. Also consider the dataset and the problem objective. Does the no-code or low-code solution support your use case? If not, then a custom code solution may be the only option. Finally, take into account your own expertise. If you know SQL very well but are new to Python, then something like BigQuery ML may be the best choice if it supports the problem you are attempting to solve.

This book does not aim to make you into an expert at using various different custom code ML frameworks. However, the book does take the approach that exposure to these tools and some basic knowledge can go a long way toward solving problems and collaborating with data scientists and ML engineers. If you are not familiar with Python, then Bill Lubanovic's *Introducing Python* (O'Reilly, 2019) is a great resource for getting started. Additionally, if you want to dive deeper into the ML frameworks introduced in this chapter, *Hands-On Machine Learning with Scikit-Learn, Keras, and TensorFlow* (2nd edition) by Aurélien Géron (O'Reilly, 2022) is a wonderful resource that is referenced by data scientists and ML engineers in practice.

Exploring the Dataset Using Pandas, Matplotlib, and Seaborn

Before you begin learning about scikit-learn and Keras, you should follow the workflow discussed in earlier chapters around understanding and preparing data for ML. Though you have used Google Colab briefly in earlier chapters to load the data from BigQuery into a DataFrame and do some basic visualization, you have not gone through the data preparation and model training process completely in the Jupyter Notebook environment.

This section revisits how to load data into a Google Colab notebook using Pandas. Once the data is loaded into a DataFrame, you will explore, clean, and transform the data before creating the datasets that you will use to train your ML model. As you have seen in previous chapters, much of the work goes not into training the model but into understanding and preparing the training data.

All of the code in this section, including some additional examples, is included in a Jupyter notebook in the low-code-ai repo on GitHub (*https://oreil.ly/supp-lcai*).

Loading Data into a Pandas DataFrame in a Google Colab Notebook

First, go to *https://colab.research.google.com* and open a new notebook, following the process discussed in Chapter 2. You may rename this notebook to a more meaningful name by clicking the name as shown in Figure 7-1 and replacing the current name with a new name, say, *Customer_Churn_Model.ipynb*.

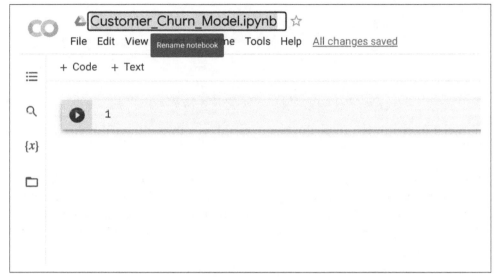

Figure 7-1. Renaming the Google Colab notebook to a more meaningful name.

Now type the following code into the first code block to import the packages needed to analyze and visualize the customer churn dataset:

```
import matplotlib.pyplot as plt
import numpy as np
import pandas as pd
import seaborn as sns
import sklearn
import tensorflow as tf
```

You saw some of these packages before in Chapter 2 when first exploring the use of Colab notebooks, but some of these will be new to you here. The line `import sklearn` imports scikit-learn, a popular ML framework. Scikit-learn was first released in 2007 and was built on top of other Python libraries such as NumPy and SciPy. It is meant to be an easy-to-use framework for building ML models, including linear models, tree-based models, and support vector machines. The next line, `import tensorflow as tf`, imports TensorFlow. TensorFlow is a high-performance numerical computation library that was designed with the training and deployment of deep neural networks in mind. TensorFlow includes Keras, a library meant to ease the development of deep neural networks and the corresponding data transformations. You will be using Keras later in the chapter to train a neural network model.

Now execute the cell containing the `import` statements to import the packages. To do this, click the Run Cell button on the left side of the cell as shown in Figure 7-2, or press Shift + Enter to run the cell.

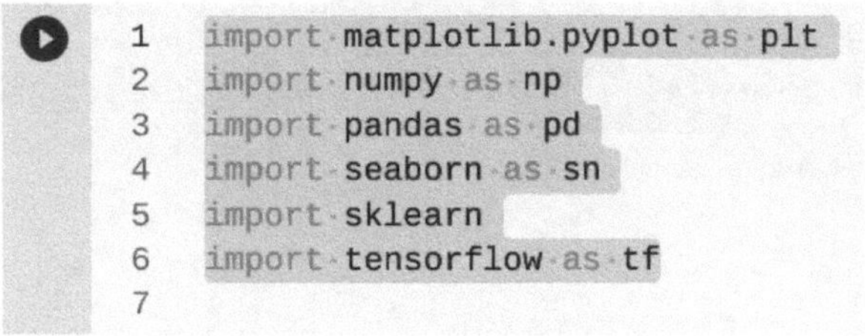

Figure 7-2. The Run Cell button is seen at the top left of the cell as shown here.

You can quickly check that the `import` statements have executed successfully by checking the versions of the packages. Every package includes a special attribute, `__version__`, which returns the version of the package. Type the following code into a new cell, and execute the cell to check your version of the scikit-learn and TensorFlow packages:

```
print("scikit-learn version:", sklearn.__version__)
print("TensorFlow version:", tf.__version__)
```

You should see the versions printed as shown in Figure 7-3. Note that your exact version numbers will depend on when you are walking through this exercise.

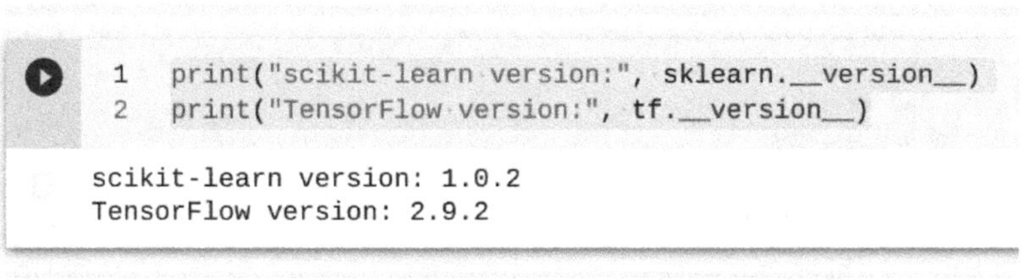

Figure 7-3. Printing the versions of scikit-learn and TensorFlow to ensure they were imported properly.

Now you are ready to import your data. Recall that the dataset is stored in the CSV format, so you will need to download that data, upload it to your notebook, and then import into a Pandas DataFrame, correct? Actually, that is not the case. A very nice feature of Pandas is that you can directly import a CSV file into a DataFrame from a location on the internet without having to download the file first. To do this, type in the following code into a new cell and execute the cell:

```
file_loc = 'https://storage.googleapis.com/low-code-ai-book/churn_dataset.csv'
df_raw = pd.read_csv(file_loc)
```

In general, it is a good idea to look at the first few rows of the DataFrame. Use `df_raw.head()` to explore the first few rows of the DataFrame. You can quickly scroll through the columns of the data and see at a glance that it seems like the types correspond to what was expected. An example of a few of the columns is shown in Table 7-2. Looking at the first few rows is a great quick first step, but of course this dataset is more than just a few rows and there could be some problems lurking where you cannot see them.

Table 7-2. A few columns of the first five rows of the DataFrame df_raw printed using the head() method

Streaming TV	Streaming Movies	Contract	Paperless Billing	Payment Method	Monthly Charges	Total Charges	Churn
No	No	Month-to-month	Yes	Electronic check	29.85	29.85	No
No	No	One Year	No	Mailed check	56.95	1889.5	No
No	No	Month-to-Month	Yes	Mailed check	53.85	108.15	Yes
No	No	One year	No	Bank transfer (automatic)	42.30	1840.75	No
No	No	Month-to-month	Yes	Electronic check	70.70	151.65	Yes

Understanding and Cleaning the Customer Churn Dataset

Now that the data has been loaded into the DataFrame df_raw, you can begin to explore and understand it. The immediate goal is to get an idea of where there could be issues with the data so that you may resolve those issues before moving forward. However, you should also be keeping an eye out for the overall distribution and other properties of the columns of your DataFrame since this will be important when transforming the data later.

Checking and converting data types

First you will check that the data types inferred by Pandas match up with what was expected from Table 7-1. Why is this useful? It can be an easy way to check for mistyped data, which can often come from issues with the data itself. For example, what if there is a string value in a column of integers? Pandas will import this column as a string column because integers can be cast as strings, but not vice versa in most cases. To check the data types for your DataFrame, type **df_raw.dtypes** into a new cell and execute the cell.

Note there are no parentheses after dtypes. This is because dtypes is not a function but rather a property of the Pandas DataFrame df_raw. Anything that was not a floating-point number or an integer was imported as an object in the DataFrame. This is normal behavior for a Pandas DataFrame. If you look through the output more carefully, though, almost every column matches the expected type, except for the TotalCharges column. You can see the output for the last few columns in Table 7-3 and confirm that you see the same thing in your notebook environment.

Table 7-3. The data types for the last six columns of the df_raw DataFrame (note that the TotalCharges column is not a float64 as expected)

Contract	object
PaperlessBilling	object
PaymentMethod	object
MonthlyCharges	float64
TotalCharges	object
Churn	object

This is a good sign that there is something different about the TotalCharges column than expected. Before moving forward, you should explore this column and understand what is happening. Recall that you can work with a single column of a Pandas DataFrame using the syntax df['ColumnName'], where df is the DataFrame name and ColumnName is the column's name.

Begin by getting some high-level statistics about the TotalCharges column using the describe() method. Try to do this without looking at the provided code first, but if you need it, the code is right here:

```
df_raw['TotalCharges'].describe()
```

Your output should be the same as the output in Figure 7-4. Since TotalCharges is being treated as a categorical variable (in this case as a string), you only see the count of elements, the number of unique values, the top value in terms of frequency, and the number of times that value appears.

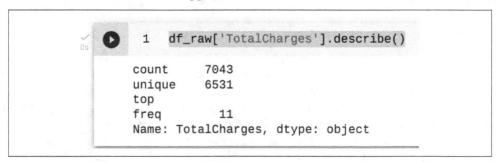

Figure 7-4. Summary statistics of the TotalCharges column. Note that the most frequent value is a string with a single space.

In this case you can see the issue almost immediately. The top value is either a blank or empty string, and it appears 11 times. This is likely why Pandas treated the TotalCharges as an unexpected data type and led you to discover an issue with the data.

When you have missing data, you can ask, "What should be there?" To try to understand this, look at the corresponding rows of data in the DataFrame and see if there is a pattern for which rows are missing. To do that, you will create a *mask* and apply it to the DataFrame. The mask will be a simple statement that returns true or false depending on the input value. In this case, your mask will be of the form mask=(df.raw['TotalCharges']==' '). The == operator checks to see if the value of the TotalCharges column is equal to the string with a single space. If the value is a string with a single space, the operator returns true; otherwise it returns false. Type the following code into a new cell and execute the cell:

```
mask = (df_raw['TotalCharges']==' ')
df_raw[mask].head()
```

The output of the cell is shown in Table 7-4. Now explore the results of this cell. Do you notice anything that may explain why the TotalCharges column is blank for these customers? Look at the tenure column and notice that the value is 0 for each of these customers.

Table 7-4. The first few columns and rows of the DataFrame df_raw whose value for the TotalCharges column is ' '

customerID	gender	SeniorCitizen	Partner	Dependents	tenure	PhoneService
4472-LVYGI	Female	0	Yes	Yes	0	No
3115-CZMZD	Male	0	No	Yes	0	Yes
5709-LVOEQ	Female	0	Yes	Yes	0	Yes
4367-NUYAO	Male	0	Yes	Yes	0	Yes
1371-DWPAZ	Female	0	Yes	Yes	0	No

If the tenure is 0, then this is the first month for these customers with the telco, and they have not been charged yet. This explains why there is no value for TotalCharges for these customers. Now verify this hypothesis by using a different mask to check the rows with tenure equal to 0. Try to write the code for this cell on your own, but the solution follows in case you need any help:

```
mask = (df_raw['tenure']==0)
df_raw[mask][['tenure','TotalCharges']]
```

Note that in the code above, you specify a list of columns ['tenure','Total Charges']. Since you were looking purely at the relationship between tenure and TotalCharges, this will make the results easier to parse. All 11 rows with Total

Charges equal to ' ' have the value 0 for the tenure column. So, indeed, the relationship was as expected. You now know that these odd string values correspond to zero TotalCharges and can replace the string values with the float 0.0. The easiest way to do this is to use the df.replace() method. The syntax for this function can take a little bit to parse, so first type the following code into a new cell and execute that cell to see the results:

```
df_1 = df_raw.replace({'TotalCharges': {' ': 0.0}})
mask = (df_raw['tenure']==0)
df_1[mask][['tenure','TotalCharges']]
```

Your results should be the same as the results in Table 7-5. You can now see that the string values for TotalCharges from before have now been replaced by the float value 0.0.

Table 7-5. The TotalCharges column has been replaced with the value 0.0 for the rows where the value of tenure is 0

	tenure	TotalCharges
488	0	0.0
753	0	0.0
936	0	0.0
1082	0	0.0
1340	0	0.0
3331	0	0.0
3826	0	0.0
4380	0	0.0
5218	0	0.0
6670	0	0.0
6754	0	0.0

With these results in mind, it becomes easier to understand the syntax used in the first line of code, df_raw.replace({'TotalCharges': {' ': 0.0}}). The method takes a Python data structure known as a dictionary. *Dictionaries* are unordered lists of pairs where the first element of each pair is the name of a value, and the second element of each pair is the value itself. In this case, the first element is TotalCharges, the name of the column where you want to replace values. The second element is a dictionary itself, {' ':0.0}. The first element of this pair is the value you want to replace, and the second element of the pair is the new value you'd like to insert.

Before you explore the summary statistics for the TotalCharges column and the other numeric columns, be sure Pandas knows that TotalCharges is a column of float values. To do so, type the following code into a new cell and execute that cell:

```
df_2 = df_1.astype({'TotalCharges':'float64'})
df_2.dtypes
```

Note that the `astype()` method uses similar arguments to the `replace()` method. The input is a dictionary where the first element of each pair is the column whose data type will be changed, and the second argument (here, `float64`) is the new data type for that column. Your output from the cell should be similar to what is shown in Table 7-6.

Table 7-6. The datatypes of the last four columns of the new DataFrame df_2 portrayed in vertical orientation (the rest of the columns are omitted in this figure)

PaymentMethod	object
MonthlyCharges	float64
TotalCharges	float64
Churn	object

Exploring summary statistics

Now that you have solved the datatype issue you encountered, look at the summary statistics of the numeric columns. You saw how to do this back in Chapter 2, so try to do this without looking at the code first, though the code is below in case you need any help, and the results are in Table 7-7:

```
df_2.describe()
```

Table 7-7. Summary statistics for the numeric columns in the customer churn dataset

	SeniorCitizen	tenure	MonthlyCharges	TotalCharges
count	7043	7043	7043	7043
mean	0.162147	32.371149	64.761692	2279.734304
std	0.368612	24.559481	30.090047	2266.79447
min	0	0	18.25	0
25%	0	9	35.5	398.55
50%	0	29	70.35	1394.55
75%	0	55	89.85	3786.6
max	1	72	118.75	8684.8

At a glance, looking at the results in Table 7-7, there are no odd values or anything amiss except for maybe `SeniorCitizen`. Recall that `SeniorCitizen` has the value of either 0 or 1. The average (mean) value for the `SeniorCitizen` column, 0.162..., then represents the percentage of customers that are senior citizens. Though the feature may be better thought of as a categorical variable, the fact that it is a binary 0 or 1 means that summary statistics like the mean can still give useful information.

Speaking of categorical features, how can you explore summary statistics for these features? The describe() method by default only shows numeric features. You can have it include statistics for categorical features by using the optional keyword argument include='object'. This specifies that you want to include only columns of type object, which is the default data type for all non-numeric columns in Pandas. Include this optional argument in the describe() method in a new cell and execute the cell. The code is included here in case you need help:

```
df_2.describe(include='object')
```

You will now see the statistics for the categorical features. These summary statistics are more simplistic since you are working with discrete values instead of numeric values. You can see the number of rows with non-null values or the count, the number of unique values, the most frequent value (or one of the most frequent values in case of a tie), and the frequency of that value.

For example, consider the customerID column. This column has the same number of unique values as it does rows. Another way to interpret this information is that every single value in this column is unique. You can additionally see that by looking at the frequency at which the top value appears.

Explore the summary statistics and see what else you notice. Here is a collection of some observations that will be helpful moving forward but are by no means a complete list of the useful information available from these results:

- The gender and Partner columns are fairly well balanced between two different values.
- A large majority of customers have phone service, but almost half of those customers do not have multiple lines.
- Many of the columns have three different possible values. Though you have information about the top class, you do not know the distribution of different values at this time.
- The label for our dataset, Churn, is somewhat unbalanced with about a 5:2 ratio of No to Yes values.
- All columns, including the numeric columns, have 7,043 elements. There could be other missing values similar to what you discovered for TotalCharges, but there are not any null values.

Exploring combinations of categorical columns

As you saw in Chapter 6, looking at interactions between the different features can often help you understand which features are most important and how they interact. However, for that project, all of your features were numeric. In this project, most of your features are instead categorical. You will explore a method of understanding feature interactions in this case by looking at the distribution of different feature value combinations across multiple columns.

First look at the PhoneService and MultipleLines columns. Common sense dictates that a customer cannot have multiple phone lines if they do not have phone service. You can confirm that this is true in the dataset by using the value_counts() method. The value_counts() method takes a list of columns in your DataFrame as an argument and returns the count of unique value combinations. Type the following code into a new cell and execute that cell to return the unique value combinations across the PhoneService and MultipleLines columns:

```
df_2.value_counts(['PhoneService','MultipleLines'])
```

Your results should be the same as the following results. Note that MultipleLines has three different values, No, Yes, and No phone service. Unsurprisingly, No phone service only occurs when the PhoneService feature has value No. This means that the MultipleLines feature contains all of the information of the PhoneService feature. PhoneService is redundant, and you will remove this feature from your training dataset later.

```
PhoneService MultipleLines
Yes          No                3390
             Yes               2971
No           No phone service  682
```

Are other features in your dataset "correlated" in a similar fashion? Unsurprisingly, this is indeed the case. As an exercise, write code in a new cell to explore the relationship between the InternetService, OnlineSecurity, OnlineBackup, StreamingTV, and StreamingMovies.

Once again you have some redundancy between feature values, but it's not as clear in this case. When the value of InternetService is No, the value of all of the other columns is No internet service. However there are two different internet types, Fiber optic and DSL, and the picture is not as clear in those cases whether there is redundancy or not. Though you did not include the columns here, the DeviceProtection and TechSupport columns have the same relationship with InternetService. You should explore this on your own as well. You will consider how to take this information into consideration in the next section when transforming features.

Beyond looking at counts of specific value combinations, there exist techniques for understanding the correlation between different values of categorical features. Two such examples are the chi-square test and Cramer's V coefficient. The *chi-square test* checks for the independence of a dependent and independent categorical variable, while *Cramer's V coefficient* determines the strength of that relationship, similar to the Pearson correlation coefficient for numeric variables. For more details, you can reference almost any statistics book, such as *Statistics in a Nutshell* by Sarah Boslaugh (O'Reilly, 2012).

You should also explore the relationship between the categorical features and the label Churn. For example, consider the Contract feature. There are three possible values for this feature: Month-to-month, One year, and Two year. What does your intuition say about this feature and how it relates to Churn? You should reasonably expect that longer contract periods lead to churn being less likely, at least if the customer is not at the end of the contract period. You can use the value_counts() method as before to look at this relationship, but often it is easier to visually understand relationships than look at a table of values. To visualize this, write the following code into a new cell and execute that cell:

```
(df_2.groupby('Contract')['Churn'].value_counts(normalize=True)
  .unstack('Churn')
  .plot.bar(stacked=True))
```

This is actually one very long line of code to be parsed. The parentheses at the beginning and end tell Python to treat this as one line of code rather than three separate lines. First the groupby() function is used to group the values by different Contract values. You want to look at how Churn relates, so you select the Churn column and then apply the value_counts function. Note the additional normalize=True argument, which will replace the value counts for each pair with a percentage rather than a number. The advantage of this is that you can see within each value of Contract what percentage of customers churned versus those that did not instead of comparing counts across uneven groups. The unstack() function is used to format the table into a more human-readable format before you use built-in Pandas plotting capabilities to plot the data. In this case, Figure 7-5 uses a stacked bar chart to visually compare the different values for Contract quickly.

You see that there is a higher percentage of customer churn for month-to-month contracts versus one-year or two-year contracts. From the visualization, you see that more than 40% of customers on a month-to-month contract canceled their service versus around 15% on a one-year contract and less than 5% on a two-year contract. This means that the contract type almost certainly will be a useful feature moving forward.

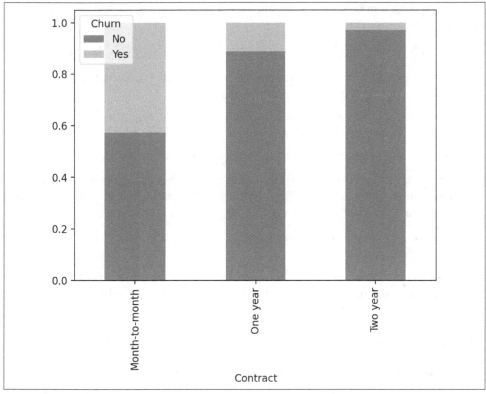

Figure 7-5. Visualization of the proportion of customers that left the telco versus those that did not based on the contract type.

As an exercise, go through this sort of analysis for your other categorical features. Note which features have different percentages of churn across the different values and those that are more or less the same. This will be helpful in choosing features later.

When executing similar blocks of code in Python multiple times, it can be more efficient to create a function to execute instead. For example, you can create a function to create the distribution chart above by using the following code:

```python
def plot_cat_feature_dist(feature_name):
    (df_2.groupby(feature_name)['Churn'].value_counts(normalize=True)
        .unstack('Churn')
        .plot.bar(stacked=True))
```

def is the keyword in Python for defining a function, the function name is plot_cat_feature_dist, and feature_name is the input variable. This way, plot_cat_feature_dist('Contract') will generate the same graph as in Figure 7-5. You can then use this function for all of your categorical variables instead.

Here are some observations you should have made while exploring your categorical features:

- The churn rate was about double for senior citizens versus non-senior citizens.
- The values for the gender, StreamingTV, and StreamingMovies features do not seem to make a difference in the churn rate.
- The larger the household, the lower the churn rate. In other words, having a partner or dependents in the household lowers the churn rate.
- For those with a phone line, having multiple lines increases the churn rate.
- The InternetService feature affects churn rate. Fiber optic internet service has a much higher churn rate than DSL. Those without internet service have the lowest churn rate.
- Internet add-ons (like OnlineSecurity and DeviceProtection) decrease the churn rate.
- PaperlessBilling increases the churn rate. Most values of PaymentMethod are the same except for Electronic Check, which has a much higher churn rate than the others.

Did you notice anything else? Be sure to make a note of these observations for later.

Exploring interactions between numeric and categorical columns

Before moving on to finally thinking through how you will transform your features, you should also explore the relationship between the numeric features and the label. Remember that SeniorCitizen is really a categorical column since the two values represent two discrete classes. The numeric columns that are left are tenure, Monthly Charges, and TotalCharges. The columns would have a simple relationship if a customer had paid the same amount every month. That is, tenure × MonthlyCharges = TotalCharges. You saw this explicitly in the case where tenure was 0 before.

How often is this true? Intuitively, and maybe from experience, the monthly charges tend to change over time. This can be due to promotional pricing ending, but also due to things like changing the services you are paying for. You can check this intuition using Pandas functions. Write the following code into a new cell and execute that cell to see the summary statistics of a new column comparing tenure × MonthlyCharges and TotalCharges:

```
df_2['AvgMonthlyCharge'] = df_2['TotalCharges']/df_2['tenure']
df_2['DiffCharges'] = df_2['MonthlyCharges']-df_2['AvgMonthlyCharge']
df_2['DiffCharges'].describe()
```

Note that you are creating two new columns in your DataFrame df_2. The AvgMonth
lyCharge column captures the average monthly charge over the customer's tenure,
and the DiffCharges column captures the difference between the average monthly
charge and the current monthly charge. The results are shown below:

```
count 7032.000000
mean   -0.001215
std     2.616165
min   -18.900000
25%    -1.160179
50%     0.000000
75%     1.147775
max    19.125000
Name: DiffCharges, dtype: float64
```

A few observations you should make from these summary statistics: first, note that
the count is 11 lower than the total number of rows. Why is this? Recall that you have
11 rows with zero tenure. In Pandas, if you divide by zero, the value is recorded as
NaN instead of throwing an error. Otherwise, note that the distribution seems fairly
symmetric. The mean value is almost zero, the median value is 0, and min and max
values are close to being opposites of one another.

One way to remove the NaN values is to use the replace() method instead for the
undefined values. Use the following code in a new cell to perform this task:

```
df_2['AvgMonthlyCharge'] = (df_2['TotalCharges'].div(df_2['tenure'])
                                        .replace(np.nan,0))
df_2['DiffCharges'] = df_2['MonthlyCharges']-df_2['AvgMonthlyCharge']
df_2['DiffCharges'].describe()
```

The choice of replacing a null value with a zero value is an example of an imputation
strategy. The process of *imputation* is the process of replacing unknown values with
substituted values that are reasonable for the problem at hand. Because you want to
look at the difference between monthly charges and average monthly charges, saying
that "there is no difference" is a reasonable approach to avoid having to throw out
possibly useful data. Without imputation here, you would lose all rows with zero
tenure, so your model would not be able to accurately predict these cases. With large
enough datasets, if the missing data does not focus on a single group, often a strategy
of omitting that data will be taken. This was the approach taken in Chapter 6.

How does the value of the DiffCharges relate to the Churn column? The method
you used to understand the relationship between categorical columns does not quite
work here since DiffCharges is numeric. But you could bucketize the values of
the DiffCharges column and use the approach that was used before. The idea of
bucketization is to break a numeric column into value ranges called *buckets*. The
numeric feature becomes a categorical feature by asking, "Which bucket does this
value belong to?" In Pandas, you use the cut() function to define buckets for a

numeric column. You can either provide the number of buckets to use, or specify a list of cutoff points. To bucketize the DiffCharges column and explore its effect on Churn, type the following code into a new cell and execute that cell:

```
df_2['DiffBuckets'] = pd.cut(df_2['DiffCharges'], bins=5)
plot_cat_feature_dist('DiffBuckets')
```

The resulting graph (in Figure 7-6) shows that the larger the difference (either positive or negative) between MonthlyCharges and AvgMonthlyCharge, the higher the churn rate for the corresponding range of values. As an exercise, explore with different numbers of bins and see what patterns you notice.

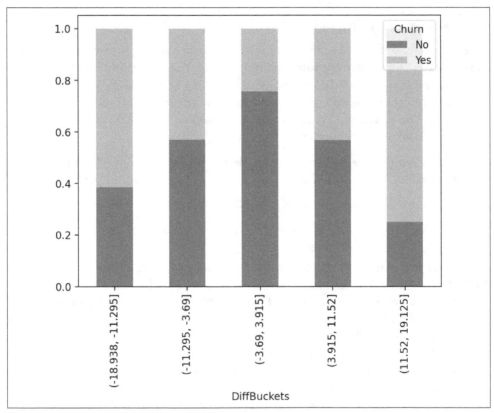

Figure 7-6. The churn rate for each bucket of the DiffCharges column.

Notice that the churn rate for each bucket does not follow a nice linear trend. That is, the churn rate goes down before it goes back up later, depending on how far away the bucket is from the center. In cases such as this, treating bucket membership as a categorical variable can be more advantageous for ML than keeping the feature as a numeric feature.

You can also explore the numeric features without any manipulation. For example, let's explore the relationship between MonthlyCharges and Churn by using the following code. The relationship is visualized in Figure 7-7:

```
df_2['MonthlyBuckets'] = pd.cut(df_2['MonthlyCharges'], bins=3)
plot_cat_feature_dist('MonthlyBuckets')
```

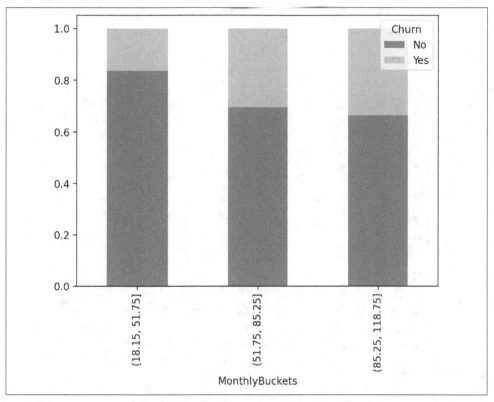

Figure 7-7. Customer churn per bucket for MonthlyCharges. The churn rate increases as the monthly charges increase, with the highest churn rate being for charges between 85.25 and 118.75.

In Figure 7-7, you can see that the churn rate tends to increase as the MonthlyCharges value increases. This implies that the MonthlyCharges column will be useful for predicting churn.

Finding the right number of buckets to use for numeric columns can be tricky. Too few buckets and you may miss important patterns, but too many buckets and the patterns may become very noisy and even misleading. Figure 7-8 shows an example for when too many buckets leads to a noisy pattern where it is hard to gain insights. Also note that the range of values for each bucket is fairly small, so you are capturing a smaller number of customers per bucket.

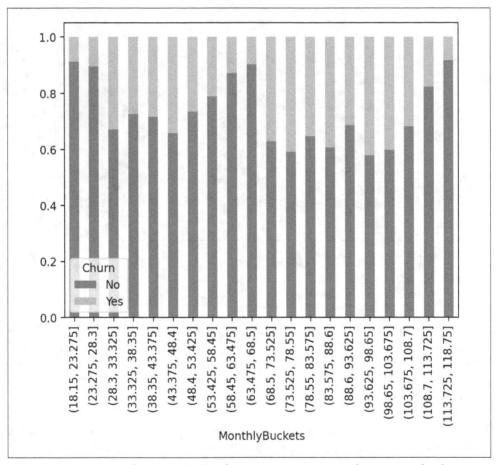

Figure 7-8. Customer churn per bucket for `MonthlyCharges` with too many buckets. The pattern is lost in the noise, and it is hard to understand the relationship from this visualization.

As an exercise, perform this analysis yourself for the `tenure` and `TotalCharges` columns. You should see that as `tenure` and `TotalCharges` increase, the churn rate decreases. It makes sense that both columns have a similar relationship with churn since longer tenures should lead to a larger amount of charges paid over the tenure. Using code from previous chapters, check the correlation between these two features to see that they are indeed highly correlated, with a correlation of about 0.82.

Transforming Features Using Pandas and Scikit-Learn

At this point, you have explored the different columns in your dataset, how they interact with each other, and specifically how they interact with the label. You will now prepare that data for use in custom models. First you will select the columns to use for training your ML model. After that, you will transform those features into forms more amenable to training. Recall that your features must be numeric with meaningful magnitudes. You will take this into account when selecting the features for this project.

Feature selection

The previous section explored the interaction between the different features in the customer churn dataset with the customer churn column Churn. You saw that a few features were either not predictive—that is, the different values did not affect the churn rate—or were redundant with respect to other features. You should make a copy of your DataFrame df_2 and then remove the columns you will not be using for training the model. Why make a copy? If you remove the columns from df_2, then you may have to go back through the code for creating that DataFrame to be able to access that data again. Though not explicitly stated, this is why the DataFrame df_2 was created instead of altering the original DataFrame df_raw. By removing the columns in a copy of the DataFrame, you leave the original data accessible in case you have to access it again.

You discovered that the gender, StreamingTV, and StreamingMovies columns were not predictive of the label Churn in the previous section. Additionally, you found that the PhoneLine feature was redundant and included in the MultipleLines feature, so you will want to remove that as well to avoid problems related to collinearity. In Chapter 6, you learned that collinearity occurs when there are high correlations among predictor variables, leading to unreliable and unstable estimates of regression coefficients. These problems are magnified when using a linear model above more complex model types. One approach to combat this is to only use one column from a set of collinear columns.

The easiest way to drop columns in a Pandas DataFrame is to use the drop() function. Type the following code into a new cell and execute it to make a copy of the Pandas DataFrame and to drop the columns you no longer need:

```
df_3 = df_2.copy()
df_3 = df_3.drop(columns=['gender','StreamingTV',
                          'StreamingMovies','PhoneService'])
df_3.columns
```

The line `df_3.columns` is included to check to see which columns remain. The exact output will differ based on your previous explorations, but as an example you may see an output like the following:

```
Index(['customerID', 'SeniorCitizen', 'Partner', 'Dependents',
       'tenure', 'MultipleLines', 'InternetService', 'OnlineSecurity',
       'OnlineBackup','DeviceProtection', 'TechSupport', 'Contract',
       'PaperlessBilling', 'PaymentMethod', 'MonthlyCharges',
       'TotalCharges', 'Churn', 'AvgMonthlyCharge', 'DiffCharges',
       'DiffBuckets', 'MonthlyBuckets', 'TenureBuckets,
       'TotalBuckets'], dtype='object')
```

For the DataFrame columns shown here, `AvgMonthlyCharge`, `DiffCharges`, `DiffBuck ets`, `MonthlyBuckets`, `TotalBuckets`, and `TenureBuckets` were added. You saw that the `DiffBuckets` feature would be a helpful feature and that the `tenure` feature was highly related to the `TotalCharges` feature. To prevent problems in terms of collinearity, remove the `TotalCharges` feature and all of the additional added features except for `DiffBuckets`. The code needed to do this may differ from the following code, depending on the exploration you performed:

```
df_3 =df_3.drop(columns=['TotalCharges','AvgMonthlyCharge',
                         'DiffCharges','MonthlyBuckets',
                         'TenureBuckets', 'TotalBuckets'])
```

Finally, what about the `customerID` column? This column is too granular to be of any use in a predictive model. Why is this? Remember that the `customerID` column uniquely identifies every row. You risk the model learning to associate the value of this feature to the value of `Churn` in a direct relationship, especially given the transformations that will follow. This is great for your training dataset, but once your model sees a new value for `customerID` for the first time, it will not be able to use that value in a meaningful way. For that reason, it is best to drop this column for training your model. As an exercise, write the code to drop the `customerID` column into a new cell and execute that cell to drop the column. Here's the solution code, but do your best to complete this task without looking at it:

```
df_3 = df_3.drop(columns=['customerID'])
df_3.dtypes
```

In the end, you end up with 15 feature columns and 1 label, `Churn`. The output of the final `df_3.dtypes` line is included here for reference:

```
SeniorCitizen        int64
Partner              object
Dependents           object
tenure               int64
```

```
MultipleLines          object
InternetService        object
OnlineSecurity         object
OnlineBackup           object
DeviceProtection       object
TechSupport            object
Contract               object
PaperlessBilling       object
PaymentMethod          object
MonthlyCharges         float64
Churn                  object
DiffBuckets            category
```

DiffBuckets is a category column, rather than an object. This is because the bucketization process includes additional information, the intervals representing the buckets.

Encoding categorical features using scikit-learn

Before beginning the training process, you need to encode your categorical features as numeric features. SeniorCitizen is a great example of how this could be done. Instead of Yes and No values, the values are encoded as 1 or 0 respectively. In essence, this is what you will be doing for your features moving forward using scikit-learn.

First, note that many of your categorical features are binary features. Partner, Depend ents, OnlineSecurity, OnlineBackup, DeviceProtection, TechSupport, and Paper lessBilling are all binary features. Note that for OnlineSecurity, OnlineBackup, DeviceProtection, and TechSupport, this is not strictly true, but the No internet service value is already captured by InternetService. Before encoding your features, replace all instances of No internet service values in different columns with the value No. You can do this by using the following code:

```
df_prep = df_3.replace('No internet service', 'No')
df_prep[['OnlineSecurity', 'OnlineBackup',
        'DeviceProtection', 'TechSupport']].nunique()
```

The nunique() method computes the number of unique values per column. You should see in the output for this cell there are two unique values for the OnlineSecur ity, OnlineBackup, DeviceProtection, and TechSupport corresponding to No and Yes. You will keep this DataFrame, df_prep, as one that you can come back to later for any additional feature engineering.

Now you are ready to perform one-hot encoding. *One-hot encoding* is a process of transforming a categorical feature with independent values to a numeric representation. This representation is a list of integers, with one integer for each possible feature value. For example, the InternetService feature has three possible values: No, DSL, and Fiber Optic. The one-hot encoding of these values would be [1,0,0], [0,1,0], and [0,0,1] respectively. Another way to think of this is that we have created a new feature column for every feature value. That is, the first column asks, "Is the value of `InternetService` equal to `No`?" If so, the value is 1, and if not, the value is 0. The other two columns correspond to the same question, but for values of `DSL` and `Fiber Optic` respectively. With this way of thinking of one-hot encoding, often a feature like `Partner` with only two values `No` and `Yes` will be encoded as 0 and 1 respectively instead of `[1,0]` and `[0,1]`.

Scikit-learn includes a preprocessing library with transformers specifically for this purpose for your features and labels. For transforming categorical features into one-hot encoded features, you will use the `OneHotEncoder` class in scikit-learn. The following code is an example of how to one-hot encode the categorical columns you are working with in this example:

```
from sklearn.preprocessing import OneHotEncoder

numeric_columns = ['SeniorCitizen', 'tenure', 'MonthlyCharges']
categorical_columns = ['Partner', 'Dependents', 'MultipleLines',
                       'InternetService','OnlineSecurity',
                       'OnlineBackup','DeviceProtection',
                       'TechSupport','Contract','PaperlessBilling',
                       'PaymentMethod','DiffBuckets']

X_num = df_prep[numeric_columns]
X_cat = df_prep[categorical_columns]

ohe = OneHotEncoder(drop='if_binary')
X_cat_trans = ohe.fit_transform(X_cat)
```

It is worth understanding this code line-by-line before moving forward. First you import the `OneHotEncoder` class from scikit-learn via `from sklearn.preprocessing import OneHotEncoder`. Next you separate the columns into numeric and categorical columns. Since `SeniorCitizen` has already been encoded, you can simply include it in the numeric columns. After that, the next two lines of code split the DataFrame into two separate DataFrames: `X_num` for the numeric features and `X_cat` for the categorial features.

Finally, you are ready to use scikit-learn's `OneHotEncoder`. First you create the one-hot encoder via the line `ohe = OneHotEncoder(drop='if_binary')`. The argument `drop='if_binary'` will replace a binary feature value with either 0 or 1 rather than returning the full one-hot encoding.

The final line is where the actual transformation occurs. The `fit_transform` function does two different things. The *fit* part of `fit_transform` refers to the `OneHotEncoder` learning the different values for the different features and the assignment of the one-hot encoded values. This will be important since you may want to reverse the process at times and go back to the original values. For example, after making a prediction, you want to see what payment method the customer was using. You can use the `inverse_transform()` method of `OneHotEncoder` to transform the numeric input after encoding back to the original input. For example, consider the following two lines of code run in separate cells:

```
X_cat_trans.toarray()[0]
ohe.inverse_transform(X_cat_trans.toarray())[0]
```

The first line returns this output:

```
[1., 0., 0., 1., 0., 1., 0., 0., 0., 1., 0., 0., 1., 0., 0., 1., 0., 0., 1.,
0., 0., 0., 1., 0., 0., 0.]
```

The second line returns this output:

```
Partner                              Yes
Dependents                            No
MultipleLines           No phone service
InternetService                      DSL
OnlineSecurity                        No
OnlineBackup                         Yes
DeviceProtection                      No
TechSupport                           No
Contract                  Month-to-month
PaperlessBilling                     Yes
PaymentMethod           Electronic check
DiffBuckets                (-3.69, 3.915]
```

Once the `OneHotEncoder` has been fit to the data, you can move back and forth between the original values and the encoded values using `transform()` and `inverse_transform()`.

Finally, you need to combine the numeric features and the encoded categorical features back into a single object. The one-hot encoded categorical features are returned as a NumPy array, so you will need to convert the Pandas DataFrame to a NumPy array and concatenate the arrays into a single array. Additionally, you will need to create a NumPy array for the label `Churn`. To do this, execute the following code in a new cell:

```
X = np.concatenate((X_num.values,X_cat_trans.toarray()), axis=1)
y = df_prep['Churn'].values
```

The `concatenate()` function in NumPy takes two arrays and returns a single array. `X_num` is a Pandas DataFrame, but the actual values of the Pandas DataFrame are stored as a NumPy array. You can access this array by looking at the `values` property of the DataFrame. `X_cat_trans` is a special type of NumPy array called a sparse array. *Sparse* arrays, arrays where most of the entries are 0, can be nice since there are a lot of clever optimizations that can be used to store them more efficiently. However, you need the actual corresponding array. You can use the `toarray()` method to access that. Finally, you want to concatenate the DataFrames "horizontally," where you are combining the columns side by side, so you need to specify the additional argument axis=1. Similarly, axis=0 would correspond to stacking the arrays "vertically," that is, appending one list of rows to the other.

Generalization and data splitting

After all the work preparing your dataset, you are finally ready to start training your model, correct? Not quite. You need to perform the training-test data split to ensure that you can properly evaluate your model.

Scikit-learn has a nice helper function for doing this, called train_test_split, in the model_selection module. Though splitting your dataset for training and evaluation is something that you have to manage yourself in scikit-learn and other custom training frameworks, most (if not all) frameworks have tools in place to make the process easier.

To split your dataset into training and test datasets, execute the following code in a new cell:

```
from sklearn.model_selection import train_test_split

X_train, X_test, y_train, y_test = train_test_split(X,y,test_size=0.20,
                                                    random_state=113)

X_train.shape
```

The first line imports the train_test_split function from the model_selection library in scikit-learn. The second line is where the splitting occurs. train_test_split takes in a list of arrays that you are splitting (here, your X and y) and the test_size to specify the size of the training dataset as a percentage. You can optionally also provide a random_state so anyone else who executes this code will get the same rows in the training and test datasets. Finally, you can see the final size of the training dataset with X_train.shape. This is an array of shape (5634, 29). That is, there are 5,634 examples in the training dataset with 29 features after one-hot encoding. This means that the test dataset has 1,409 examples.

Building a Logistic Regression Model Using Scikit-Learn

With prepared training and test datasets in hand, you are ready to begin training your ML model. This section covers the basics of the model type you will be training, logistic regression, and how to begin training models in scikit-learn. After that, you will learn about different ways to evaluate and improve your classification model. Finally, you will be introduced to *pipelines* in scikit-learn, a way to consolidate the different transformations you are performing on your dataset and the training algorithm you want to use.

Logistic Regression

The goal of a logistic regression model is to predict membership in one of two discrete classes. For the sake of simplicity, denote these two classes as $y = 1$ and $y = 0$. You will often think of one of the classes as the "positive" class and the other as the "negative" class. Like linear regression, the inputs are a list of numeric values, but the output is the predicted probability of the positive class given the list of features $\overrightarrow{x}$. You may see this probability denoted as $P\left(y = 1 \mid \overrightarrow{x}\right)$. In the case that $y = 1$, you want this probability to be as close to 1 as possible, whereas for $y = 0$, you want this probability to be as close to 0 as possible.

How is this probability calculated? Recall that for linear regression you used the model $f(x) = w_0 + w_1 x_1 + \ldots + w_n x_n$ for some weights $w_0, \ldots, w_n$. For logistic regression, the equation is similar:

$$g\left(\overrightarrow{x}\right) = \frac{1}{1 + \exp\left(-f\left(\overrightarrow{x}\right)\right)}$$

At first glance, this formula may seem scary, but it is worth parsing. $g(x)$ is the composition of two functions: the so-called *logit* $f(x)$ and the *sigmoid (or logistic) function*:

$$\sigma(t) = \frac{1}{1 + \exp\left(-t\right)}$$

The sigmoid function (and its variations) shows up in many different fields, including ecology, chemistry, economics, statistics, and of course ML. The sigmoid function has some nice properties that make it appealing for classification models. First, its values range between 0 and 1, allowing for the outputs to be interpreted as a probability. In technical terms, this is an example of a cumulative distribution function since the values are always increasing as the independent variable increases. Second, the *derivative* (rate of change at any given instant) of the function is easy to compute. This is important for the sake of gradient descent, making training such a model a very reasonable process. A graph of the logistic function can be seen in Figure 7-9.

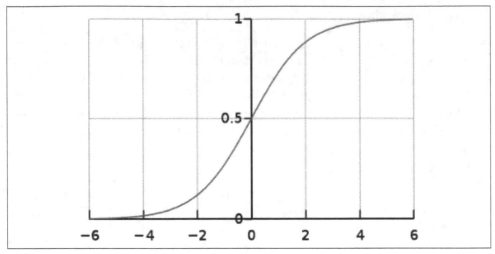

Figure 7-9. A graph of the logistic function. Note the range of values is between 0 and 1.

Recall, when training a linear regression model, that the goal you used was to minimize the mean squared error. For logistic regression, you use a different loss function known as the cross-entropy. The *cross-entropy* loss function is defined as follows:

$$L(g, D) = -\frac{1}{N}\Sigma\left(\log\left(g(\vec{x})\right)y + \log\left(1 - g(\vec{x})\right)(1 - y)\right)$$

Here, the sum is over all examples in the dataset D. The argument D is included here as a reminder that the cross-entropy depends on the dataset that is being used to compute it, just as much as the model that you are evaluating. Either y or $1 - y$ will be zero, so only one of the terms in the sum for each example will be nonzero. The corresponding term $\log\left(g(\vec{x})\right)$ or $\log\left(1 - g(\vec{x})\right)$ will be what contributes to the loss function. If the model is 100% confident about what ends up being the correct answer, then this term will be zero. If not, then the value contributed to the loss function increases exponentially as the confidence decreases.

Here's a concrete example: suppose that $g(\vec{x}) = 0.6$ and $y = 1$. In other words, the model gives a 60% chance of the label being 1. How does this contribute to the loss function? Well, for this single term, the only contribution is from $\log\left(g(\vec{x})\right)$. log(0.6) is about equal to –0.222. In the computation of the loss function itself, the sign is ultimately swapped due to the minus sign out in front. However, if $g(\vec{x}) = 0.4$ instead, then log(0.4) is about equal to –0.398. The further the predicted probability $g(\vec{x})$ is away from 1 in this case, the larger the contribution to the loss function.

Cross-entropy first arose as a concept in an area of study known as *information theory*. Roughly speaking, cross-entropy measures the amount of information needed to represent an event when you assume one probability distribution, but the actual probability distribution is different. In the case of logistic regression, the assumed probability distribution is from the output of the model, and the actual distribution is given by our labels.

Training and Evaluating a Model in Scikit-Learn

You have prepared your data and have identified a model type, logistic regression, that you want to train to predict customer churn. Now you are ready to train your first model using scikit-learn. The process for creating and training a model is very straightforward in scikit-learn. First, you create the model of the type you want to train, and then you train the model. To build and train a logistic regression model, type the following code into a new cell and execute that cell:

```
from sklearn.linear_model import LogisticRegression

cls = LogisticRegression()

cls.fit(X_train, y_train)
```

After executing the cell, you will likely see the following, or a similar, message:

```
/usr/local/lib/python3.10/dist-packages/sklearn/linear_model/_logistic.py:814:
ConvergenceWarning: lbfgs failed to converge (status=1):
STOP: TOTAL NO. of ITERATIONS REACHED LIMIT.

Increase the number of iterations (max_iter) or scale the data as shown in:
    https://scikit-learn.org/stable/modules/preprocessing.html
Please also refer to the documentation for alternative solver options:
    https://scikit-learn.org/stable/modules/linear_model.html#logistic-regression
  n_iter_i = _check_optimize_result(
LogisticRegression()
```

What went wrong? By default, scikit-learn will perform gradient descent to try to find the best weights for the model for a certain number of iterations. An *iteration* in this context means computing gradient descent over the entire dataset. The training process will terminate once the improvement in our loss function, cross-entropy, becomes very small (by default, 10^{-4}) between iterations. In your case, your model never hit that threshold. In practice, this means that there is still room for the model to improve by training for longer.

What would cause such an issue, though? There are a few different reasons, but one of the most basic issues has to do with feature ranges. If the ranges of values for feature ranges differ greatly, gradient descent tends to take more iterations to converge to the best solution.

One way to think about this is to consider an analogy of rolling a ball down from the edge of a bowl. First, suppose that you have a bowl that is perfectly round, meaning the top is a perfect circle. If you place a ball on the edge of the bowl and give it a little nudge, it immediately rolls down to the bottom point of the bowl. What about if the bowl has more of an oval or oblong shape? If you give the ball a nudge, it may not roll straight toward the center, but oscillate back and forth along the way. In essence, this is exactly what is happening with gradient descent. The *curvature*, how far away the "bowl" is from being perfectly flat, affects the behavior of gradient descent. When the curvature is a constant—for example, when the bowl is perfectly round—then we have the nice behavior discussed previously. However, when the curvature is not constant, as in the situation where the feature values have different scales, we risk the wobbling behavior discussed before.

How do you address this issue? One approach is to simply train the model for more iterations. You can easily do this in scikit-learn by providing your own value for the optional `max_iter` argument. This is a fine approach for smaller datasets, but once you start working with larger and larger ones, this is no longer feasible. A better way of approaching this problem is to rescale the features to a standard range, say between 0 and 1. In scikit-learn, you can use the `MinMaxScaler()` transformer to do just that. Type the following code into a new cell and execute it to rescale your training dataset and then train a new logistic regression model:

```
from sklearn.preprocessing import MinMaxScaler

scaler = MinMaxScaler()
X_train_scaled = scaler.fit_transform(X_train)

cls = LogisticRegression()

cls.fit(X_train_scaled, y_train)
```

This time your model should have converged successfully. Instead of having to spend more computing time for the model to converge, you were able to simply rescale the data to make the training process more efficient. This is a best practice in general for training ML models, and not just when using scikit-learn or when training a logistic regression model.

Now that your model has been trained, the next step is to evaluate it. In scikit-learn, you can use the `score` method of the trained model to do this with your testing dataset. The output of the `score` method is the mean accuracy of the model on the test dataset expressed as a decimal. Execute a new cell with the code `cls.score(X_test, y_test)` to compute the accuracy of your trained model on the test dataset.

The accuracy of your model is likely around 48%, though it may slightly vary depending on random states. This does not seem like a good model, as likely you could get slightly better results from a random coin flip. However, you may have noticed an issue with the approach here. Before training the model, you scaled the training features to be between 0 and 1. But you did not perform the same transformations on the testing dataset. Since the model was trained expecting a different range of values than was presented for evaluation, the model performed poorly. This is a textbook example of *training-serving skew*.

You want to perform the same scaling on the test dataset as you did on the training dataset. You used the `fit_transform()` method so the `MinMaxScaler()` could learn the minimum and maximum value for each feature and scale the values to a range of 0 to 1 based on that. You do not want to refit the transformer, but you can use the same transformer to transform the testing dataset to prepare for evaluation. Do this by using the following code and then compare the difference in performance:

```
X_test_scaled = scaler.transform(X_test)
```

```
cls.score(X_test_scaled, y_test)
```

The accuracy of your model should now be around 80%. This is much better than the accuracy you received before when not scaling the evaluation dataset. The important takeaway from this example is that you must perform the same transformations at training and evaluation time to be sure you are receiving accurate results. This is true at prediction time as well. It is important to document the transformations you are performing on your data and leverage tools like pipelines in scikit-learn to ensure that these transformations are being applied consistently.

Classification Evaluation Metrics

Accuracy is a simple and easy-to-understand metric that is commonly used for classification models. However, there are some possible issues with solely using accuracy as a metric. Your model has an accuracy of around 80%, but a model that just predicts that there is no customer churn has an accuracy of about 73.5%. Eighty percent is better than 73.5%, but the model that predicts no churn would have a significantly lower business value compared to a different model that may have higher business value. If your goal was to predict customer churn and try to prevent customers from leaving, then the "no churn" model will never give any actionable insights and effectively has no value.

As you learned in Chapter 5, you can use metrics like recall and precision together with accuracy to get a clearer picture of your model's performance. To review, *recall* can be thought of as the true positive rate. In this example of customer churn, the recall represents the percentage of customers who canceled their account that the model correctly predicts. *Precision* can be thought of as the positive predictive power of the model. In the case of the customer churn problem, precision represents the percentage of the predicted customers canceling their account that indeed do cancel their account. If your goal is to proactively contact customers who may cancel their accounts, then recall would be a very important metric to consider. You would likely be willing to sacrifice a little bit of accuracy or precision to improve recall. Of course, this is still something you want to balance as there is a resource cost to contacting customers who were not planning to cancel.

Take the example of a model that predicts no customer churn. The recall in this model is 0 because none of the customers that canceled their accounts are correctly identified. However, you would expect that the recall is higher for the model that you trained.

Remember that the confusion matrix breaks down the predictions into a table based on the predicted class and the actual class. A reminder of this is shown in Table 7-8.

Table 7-8. Confusion matrix for a general problem

	Predicted positives	Predicted negatives
Actual positives	True positives (TP)	False negatives (FN)
Actual negatives	False positives (FP)	True negatives (TN)

The confusion matrix for the model you trained is easy to compute using scikit-learn. To do so, you can use the `confusion_matrix` function from the `sklearn.metrics` library. Type the following code into a new cell and execute it to compute the confusion matrix for your model:

```
from sklearn.metrics import confusion_matrix

y_pred = cls.predict(X_test_scaled)

confusion_matrix(y_test, y_pred, labels=['Yes','No'])
```

`confusion_matrix` takes three arguments as used here. The first argument is the actual labels from your testing dataset, `y_test`. The second is the predicted labels from your model. To compute these predictions, you use the `predict` method for your model, passing in the transformed test inputs `X_test_scaled`. The last argument is optional, but useful. The `labels` argument expects a list of label values, here `'Yes'` and `'No'`. This determines the order of the labels in the confusion matrix. Your confusion matrix should look similar to the following:

```
array([[187, 185],
       [ 98, 939]])
```

What does this mean? Of the examples in your test dataset, 187 + 185 = 372 customers canceled their service, and 98 + 939 = 1,037 customers kept their service. Your model correctly predicted that 187 customers would cancel (true positives) and missed 185 customers who canceled (false negatives). Your model also correctly predicted that 939 customers would keep their service (true negatives) but predicted that 98 customers who kept their service would cancel instead (false positives).

From this, you can compute precision and recall in two different ways. You can compute them by definition, using the information from the confusion matrix, or you can leverage the `precision_score` and `recall_score` functions in scikit-learn. Use the following code to follow the second approach to compute the precision and recall for your model:

```
from sklearn.metrics import precision_score, recall_score

print("Precision:", precision_score(y_test, y_pred,
                                    labels=['Yes','No'], pos_label='Yes'))

print("Recall:", recall_score(y_test, y_pred,
                              labels=['Yes','No'], pos_label='Yes'))
```

A few notes about that code before exploring the results. The first three arguments are the same as for the `confusion_matrix` function before. Note that the `labels` argument is required for `precision_score` and `recall_score` if you are not using indexed labels (such as 0 and 1). You also included an additional argument, `pos_label`, which defines the "positive class." Since recall and precision are metrics pertaining to a "positive class," you need to define which class should be treated as such. Your results should be similar to the following:

```
Precision:0.656140350877193
Recall:0.5026881720430108
```

In other words, of the customers your model predicted would cancel their account, 65.6% of those customers actually did cancel. On the other hand, your model only captured 50.3% of those customers who actually did cancel. There is still room for improvement in your model, but you can clearly see that this model brings more business value than a model that cannot detect any churn.

Serving Predictions with a Trained Model in Scikit-Learn

In the previous section, you saw how to serve predictions using the `predict` method so you could evaluate your model using various different metrics. One issue you encountered naturally in this process was training-serving skew, where in your case the data at prediction time was not transformed yet and you received inaccurate results. Training-serving skew can arise in different fashions.

Another common problem is that the format of the incoming data for predictions may be different than the data used for training. In this case, your training data was in the CSV format, but maybe the incoming data for predictions is in the JSON format, a common data interchange format used in web applications.

When thinking about how to serve predictions in your models, it is important to think back through all of the transformations you have done. It can be convenient to include these into a single function and include that function with your model at prediction time.

Here are the steps you took to transform your data:

1. Cleaned the data to ensure that `TotalCharges` was a float.

2. Created a new `DiffBuckets` feature.

3. Dropped the `CustomerID`, `gender`, `StreamingTV`, `StreamingMovies`, `PhoneService`, and other intermediate columns.

4. One-hot encoded your categorical features.

5. Scaled your numeric features to a range of 0 to 1.

You would need to perform the same steps when serving predictions. Now you will gather all of the preprocessing code into a single function so you can easily apply it to new data coming in. Suppose you want to predict whether a specific customer will cancel their account at the end of the month. The data has been given to you in the JSON format:

```
{"customerID": "7520-HQWJU", "gender": "Female", "SeniorCitizen": 0,
"Partner": "Yes", "Dependents": "Yes", "tenure": 66, "PhoneService": "Yes",
"MultipleLines": "Yes", "InternetService": "DSL", "OnlineSecurity": "Yes",
"OnlineBackup": "Yes", "DeviceProtection": "Yes", "TechSupport": "No",
"StreamingTV": "No", "StreamingMovies": "No", "Contract": "Month-to-month",
"PaperlessBilling": "Yes", "PaymentMethod": "Bank transfer (automatic)",
"MonthlyCharges": 67.45, "TotalCharges": "4508.65"}
```

You will need to parse this data, perform the transformations listed previously, and serve a prediction with your trained model. To parse the data, you can use the built-in *json* package in Python. This package has a useful function, `json.loads()`, that loads JSON data into a Python dictionary. From there you will be able to easily transform the data. Type in the following code, or copy and paste the code from the solution notebook (*https://oreil.ly/_XAAH*), and execute the cell:

```
import json

example = json.loads("""{"customerID": "7090-HPOJU", "gender": "Female",
"SeniorCitizen": 0, "Partner": "Yes", "Dependents": "Yes", "tenure": 66,
"PhoneService": "Yes", "MultipleLines": "Yes", "InternetService": "DSL",
"OnlineSecurity": "Yes", "OnlineBackup": "Yes", "DeviceProtection": "Yes",
"TechSupport": "No", "StreamingTV": "No", "StreamingMovies": "No",
"Contract": "Month-to-month", "PaperlessBilling": "Yes",
"PaymentMethod": "Bank transfer (automatic)", "MonthlyCharges": 67.45,
"TotalCharges": "4508.65"}""")

ex_df = pd.DataFrame([example])
```

```
ex_df['TotalCharges'] = ex_df['TotalCharges'].astype('float64')
ex_df = ex_df.drop(columns=['customerID','gender',
                            'StreamingTV','StreamingMovies',
                            'PhoneService'])

ex_df['AvgMonthlyCharge'] = ex_df['TotalCharges']/ex_df['tenure']
ex_df['DiffCharges'] = ex_df['MonthlyCharges']-ex_df['AvgMonthlyCharge']
ex_df['DiffBuckets'] = pd.cut(ex_df['DiffCharges'],
                              bins=[-18.938,-11.295,-3.69,3.915,11.52,19.125])
ex_df.pop('DiffCharges')

numeric_columns = ['SeniorCitizen', 'tenure', 'MonthlyCharges']
categorical_columns = ['Partner', 'Dependents', 'MultipleLines',
                       'InternetService','OnlineSecurity','OnlineBackup',
                       'DeviceProtection','TechSupport','Contract',
                       'PaperlessBilling','PaymentMethod','DiffBuckets']

X_num = df_prep[numeric_columns]
X_cat = df_prep[categorical_columns]

X_cat_trans = ohe.transform(X_cat)

X = np.concatenate((X_num.values,X_cat_trans.toarray()), axis=1)
X_scaled = scaler.transform(X)

cls.predict(X)
```

At first glance, this may seem like a lot of code, but almost everything here is something you have worked through before. The first part may be the part that is the most different from before. There you are loading the JSON data using `json.loads()` as a dictionary. Since many of your transformations were performed in a Pandas DataFrame, it is convenient to load the incoming data into a Pandas DataFrame as well. After that, you ensure `TotalCharges` is of type `float64`, and you drop the columns you do not need for your model. Next you create the `DiffBuckets` feature. Note that for the `pd.cut()` function, you specify the endpoints for the bins rather than the number of bins. The cut points are data-dependent, and you want to ensure you're using the same buckets as you did at training time. Finally, you will separate out the categorical columns to perform one-hot encoding and min-max scaling before serving the prediction.

In this case, you will see that this customer is not expected to cancel her account. If you wanted to make this code easier to run, you could create a function to execute this code. Here is an example of what that would look like:

```
def custom_predict_routine(example):
    # Insert the code from above, indented once
    return cls.predict(X)
```

You should only use the `fit_transform` method for transformers like `OneHotEncoder` and `MinMaxScaler` at training time. At prediction time, use the `transform` method instead to ensure that you are transforming your features in a consistent manner to how they were transformed at training time.

Often you will be serving predictions from a different environment than where you trained the model. You will need to not just transport the model files, but any of the preprocessing code and transformers. You can store objects, like your trained model `cls`, using packages like *joblib*. The `dump` method in *joblib* serializes the Python object and saves the object to disk, where it can be reloaded using the `load` method. For example:

```
import joblib

joblib.dump(cls, 'filename.joblib')

cls = joblib.load('filename.joblib')
```

This can be used not just for the model, but for the transformers and other objects being used.

Pipelines in Scikit-Learn: An Introduction

This section dives into a more advanced topic known as pipelines in scikit-learn. Feel free to treat this section as optional on a first reading and return later or as needed to learn how to manage transformers in scikit-learn.

When combining the various different transformations into a single function, you likely found the process to be a bit tedious. However, this is a very important step to ensure that you are able to avoid training-serving skew. Scikit-learn includes a construction known as a `Pipeline` to ease this process. A `Pipeline` in scikit-learn contains a sequence of objects where all of the objects are transformers (like `OneHot Encoder`) except for the final object, which is a model (like `LinearRegression`).

However, some of your processing code involved Pandas operations that did not directly involve scikit-learn transformers. How do you include these into a scikit-learn pipeline? You can use the `FunctionTransformer()` from scikit-learn in these situations. The `FunctionTransformer()` takes a Python function as an argument when defining the transformer. When you call `fit_transform()` or `transform()` on that transformer, it simply applies the included function to the input and returns the output of that function. This is a great way to include NumPy or Pandas processing logic into your scikit-learn pipeline.

What would the pipeline look like in your case? In essence, you did the following steps:

1. Loaded the data into a Pandas DataFrame
2. Cleaned and prepared the data using Pandas functions
3. Split the categorical and numeric columns to be transformed separately
4. One-hot encoded the categorical features and recombined the features
5. Performed min-max scaling on the dataset before training the model

The steps here are purposely reorganized slightly compared to the previous section to make the transition to a scikit-learn Pipeline a little more seamless. The first step (loading the DataFrame) would not change here. For the second and third steps, you will use a FunctionTransformer(). For the fourth step, you will need two transformers: the OneHotEncoder() you are familiar with from before and a new transformer, the ColumnTransformer(). The ColumnTransformer() allows you to apply different transformations on different columns. This is exactly what you need for your use case. The OneHotEncoder() will be applied to the categorical columns, and the MinMaxScaler() will be applied to the numeric columns.

First, combine the Pandas preprocessing logic into a single function:

```
def transform_fn(df):

    df = df.replace({'TotalCharges': {' ': 0.0}})
    df = df.astype({'TotalCharges':'float64'})

    df['AvgMonthlyCharge']= df['TotalCharges'].div(df['tenure'],
                                                fill_values=0.0)

    df['DiffCharges'] = df['MonthlyCharges']-df['AvgMonthlyCharge']

    df['DiffBuckets'] = pd.cut(df['DiffCharges'], bins=5)

    df = df.drop(columns=['AvgMonthlyCharge', 'gender','StreamingTV',
                        'StreamingMovies','PhoneService',
                        'customerID', 'DiffCharges'])
    return df
```

Next, include code to specify the numeric and categorical columns:

```
numeric_columns = ['SeniorCitizen', 'tenure', 'MonthlyCharges']
categorical_columns = ['Partner', 'Dependents', 'MultipleLines',
                    'InternetService','OnlineSecurity',
                    'OnlineBackup', 'DeviceProtection',
                    'TechSupport','Contract',
                    'PaperlessBilling','PaymentMethod',
                    'DiffBuckets']
```

Now define the transformers and the model you plan to use in your pipeline:

```
from sklearn.compose import ColumnTransformer
from sklearn.preprocessing import FunctionTransformer


fn_transformer = FunctionTransformer(transform_fn)
col_transformer = ColumnTransformer(
  [('ohe', OneHotEncoder(drop='if_binary'), categorical_columns),
   ('sca', MinMaxScaler(), numeric_columns)])
model = LogisticRegression()
```

A few notes about the preceding code. The `import` statements for the `Function Transformer` and `ColumnTransformer` are shown in the first two lines. The `FunctionTransformer` takes in a single argument: the Python function containing the transformation logic. Since you want to *include* the function and not *call* the function, you pass in `transform_fn`, not `transform_fn(df)`. In Python, functions are objects, so we can use them as inputs to other functions, as seen here. For the `ColumnTransformer`, you pass in a list of ordered triples. The first element of each triple is a name that you assign to the transformer, the second element is the transformer itself, and the third element is the columns to be transformed.

Now, to define the `Pipeline`, use the following code:

```
from sklearn.pipeline import Pipeline

pipe = Pipeline([('preproc', fn_transformer),
                 ('col_trans', col_transformer),
                 ('model', model)])
```

The `Pipeline` takes a list of ordered pairs. The first element of each pair is the name of that object (transformer or model), and the second element is the transformer or model itself. The final `Pipeline` is a nice way to package up all of the code, but is there an advantage to doing so other than cleaner code?

The `fit` method of a `Pipeline` will call `fit_transform` on all of the transformers and then the `fit` method on the model. The `predict` method will apply each transformer's `transform` methods in order before calling `predict` on the model. In essence, you can think of a `Pipeline` as a model with all of the transformations built in.

A final advantage of working with a `Pipeline` is portability. A `Pipeline` can be exported using the *pickle* or *joblib* libraries after running the `fit` method. This exported pipeline will not only contain the information of the trained model, it will contain the fit transformers as well. This is a nice way to transfer both transformations and model to a different location to keep consistency for serving predictions.

As an exercise, finish rewriting your model code to use a `Pipeline`, train the model using the `fit` method, then evaluate your model to compute its accuracy, precision, and recall.

Building a Neural Network Using Keras

You were able to build a logistic regression model using scikit-learn and train your first ML model using custom code. In this section you will build another type of model using Keras, a framework for easily building custom neural networks as part of the larger TensorFlow software development kit (SDK).

Recall that a neural network consists of multiple layers, with each layer having some number of neurons, and each neuron having a corresponding activation function. In regression models, often the ReLU function is used as the activation function for the hidden layers, and no activation function is used for the final output. For classification models, the idea is very similar, but you need to convert the final output into a probability for the positive class. In logistic regression you used the sigmoid function to do this, and it will play the same role in neural networks for classification.

Introduction to Keras

TensorFlow was introduced in late 2015 as a free and open source SDK for developing ML models. The name *TensorFlow* refers to both tensors and the notion of a flow or computation graph. A *tensor* is simply an array with some number of dimensions, where the number of dimensions is called the *rank* of the tensor. For example, you can think of a line of text as a rank 1 tensor of words or strings. A page of text would be a rank 2 tensor since it is an array of lines. A book could be a rank 3 tensor, and the analogy goes on. Tensors are a common data structure when working with scientific computing and are used in many different contexts. The *computation graph* is the set of directions that TensorFlow builds for the CPU (or GPU/TPU) to perform the needed computations. Advantages of graph-based approaches to computation include optimization techniques that can be applied behind the scenes and the ability to easily split up that computation over multiple devices.

Though TensorFlow has all of these advantages, the original version of TensorFlow was known to be difficult to learn due to the approach it took. Over time, new libraries and functionalities were added to TensorFlow to make it easier to use and more approachable for those new to the framework. In 2019, TensorFlow 2.0 was released and introduced Keras as the high-level interface of choice for building, training, and serving predictions with artificial neural networks. Keras was first developed as a Python interface to create neural networks for Theano, a Python library defining, optimizing, and efficiently evaluating mathematical expressions involving multidimensional arrays. Keras was extended to include support for TensorFlow, and with TensorFlow 2.0, Keras is now officially part of the TensorFlow framework. Keras is easy to use, and you will be able to use it to create a neural network with just a few lines of code.

Training a Neural Network Classifier Using Keras

Since the data has already been prepared using scikit-learn and Pandas, you will be able to quickly jump into training a new ML model. You will create TensorFlow datasets using the Dataset API for your training and test datasets, then you will define your neural network model, and finally you will train and evaluate your neural network. You will be able to rework the custom function you wrote previously for your scikit-learn model to serve predictions for your Keras model as well.

Before starting this process, a little additional preprocessing is needed. Using the LogisticRegression model in scikit-learn, you can build a binary classification model to predict two classes, Yes and No. In Keras, you must use numeric labels 1 and 0 instead of string labels as you used before. Luckily, scikit-learn includes a LabelEncoder transformer for performing this task. Use the following code to encode your labels Yes and No as 1 and 0 respectively:

```
from sklearn.preprocessing import LabelEncoder

le = LabelEncoder()
y_train_enc = le.fit_transform(y_train)
y_test_enc = le.transform(y_test)

le.inverse_transform([1])
```

In the output, you will see that Yes is being treated as the positive class, or 1. Note that you can also ensure the order of the labels by fitting the transformer on the set ["No","Yes"] instead and simply transforming y_train and y_test.

With the labels properly encoded, now create the TensorFlow datasets. The tf.data.Dataset API allows you to create data ingestion pipelines to stream data in while training your model. Since data is streaming in one batch at a time, the data can be distributed across multiple machines. This allows you to train large models on possibly massive datasets across multiple different machines. In your case, the dataset does fit into memory, but using this API makes it easier to change scale without having to change your training code. The Dataset API is easy to use and is considered a best practice when using TensorFlow and Keras.

The common pattern that is used with the tf.data.Dataset API is to first create a source dataset from your input data. Here the source will be your NumPy arrays that you created from your Pandas DataFrames. After that, you will perform any transformations you want, using features like the map() or filter() functions. In this case, those transformations have already been completed. The tf.data.Dataset

API will handle sending batches of your data to the training loop and keep the training process running seamlessly.

Since you are already working with NumPy arrays, you will be creating your Dataset using the from_tensor_slices method. This method takes a NumPy array and treats each "slice" as an example in your training dataset. For example, X_train is a rank 2 array or a matrix. from_tensor_slices will treat each row of that matrix as a separate example. Additionally, you can pass in a pair of arrays, and Keras will treat the first as examples and the second as labels, which is precisely what you want in this scenario. To create your Dataset objects, use the following code:

```
import tensorflow as tf
import tensorflow.keras as keras

train_dataset=(tf.data.Dataset.from_tensor_slices((X_train_scaled, y_train_enc))
                    .batch(128))

test_dataset=(tf.data.Dataset.from_tensor_slices((X_test_scaled, y_test_enc))
                    .batch(1))
```

The only portion of the code that may need some explanation is the batch() method. Recall that Dataset objects send batches of data from your dataset to the training loop. The batch() method defines the size of those batches. The exact right batch size will depend on the dataset and the model type you are working with and often takes a bit of tuning to get perfect. As a general rule of thumb, the larger your model or example size, the smaller your batch size should be. However, the smaller the batch size, the *noisier* the training process may be. In other words, gradient descent will take a less direct path toward the optimal set of weights, so it could take more compute time to converge to an optimal model. Batch size is a perfect example of a hyperparameter that defines the model and model training process.

Now that the data is ready for training, you should create your model. Recall in BigQuery ML you specified a list of integers. The number of elements in the list was the number of hidden units, and the value of each integer is the number of neurons in that hidden layer. You will use the same information in Keras, but in a slightly different format. The keras.Sequential API allows you to give a list of the layers you want in your model and then builds a model from that information. The layers discussed in the previous chapter are what Keras calls Dense layers. Dense layers are layers where all of the neurons from the previous layer connect to every neuron in the next layer, forming the weighted sums you saw in Chapter 6. An example of a Dense layer is shown here:

```
keras.layers.Dense(
        units=64, input_shape=(28,), activation="relu",
        name="input_layer"
    )
```

There are four arguments shown in this example. First is the number of `units`. This is simply the number of neurons in this layer. The second argument is the `input_shape`. If you are defining the first layer in the model, you need to specify the shape of the incoming examples. If this is not the first layer of the model, then you can omit this argument, as Keras will receive this information from the previous layer. Recall that after one-hot encoding, there were 28 distinct features. You can double-check this by looking at the output of `X_train.shape`. The shape of `X_train` is (5634, 28). There are 5,634 examples, and each has 28 feature values. The notation `(28,)` may seem odd, but it is how Python represents a list of one element. In the case that the incoming examples are higher dimensional (for example, with image data), then the `input_shape` will be a list of many elements. The third argument is `activation`, for defining the activation function. For a binary classification model, the final layer will need 1 output and `sigmoid` as the activation function. For the hidden layers, the most commonly used activation function is the ReLU (or rectified linear unit) function, as discussed in Chapter 6. Finally, you can assign your own custom name to the layer with the `name` argument.

Use the following code to define your neural network in Keras. This code will create a neural network with three hidden layers of 64, 32, and 16 neurons respectively:

```python
model = keras.Sequential(
    [
        keras.layers.Dense(
            units=64, input_shape=(28,), activation="relu",
            name="input_layer"
        ),
        keras.layers.Dense(units=32, activation="relu",
                            name="hidden_1"),
        keras.layers.Dense(units=16, activation="relu",
                            name="hidden_2"),
        keras.layers.Dense(units=1, activation="sigmoid",
                            name="output"),
    ]
)
```

Now that the model has been defined, it needs to be compiled. This is the process that translates the model into TensorFlow operations and configures the model for training. Luckily, Keras handles all this with only a few inputs from you.

Use the following code to compile your model:

```python
loss_fn = keras.losses.BinaryCrossentropy()
metrics = [tf.keras.metrics.BinaryAccuracy(),
           tf.keras.metrics.Precision(),
           tf.keras.metrics.Recall()]

model.compile(optimizer="adam", loss=loss_fn, metrics=metrics)
```

`keras.losses.BinaryCrossentropy()` is Keras's implementation of the cross-entropy loss function discussed earlier in this chapter. You also included three metrics to be included for evaluating the performance of the model. `BinaryAccuracy()`, `Precision()`, and `Recall()` are Keras's implementation of the accuracy, precision, and recall metrics, respectively, that you used for your model created in scikit-learn. When compiling the model using the `compile()` method, you include the loss function, any metrics you want to use, and the optimizer. A deep discussion of optimizers is beyond the scope of this book, but the Adam optimizer is considered a good default choice for training neural network models. In short, Adam takes the original gradient descent algorithm and makes some changes to address some possible pitfalls of using gradient descent. For a deeper discussion on optimizers, please see *Hands-On Machine Learning with Scikit-Learn, Keras, and TensorFlow* by Aurélien Géron (O'Reilly, 2022).

With the model now defined and compiled, the next step is to train it. In Keras, you use the `fit()` method to train a compiled model. You need to specify the dataset you want to use for training and evaluation, and you need to specify how long you wish to train the model. The following code shows an example of this:

```
history = model.fit(
    x=train_dataset,
    epochs=20,
    validation_data=test_dataset
)
```

The argument x corresponds to the training dataset. If you are not using a `tf.data.Dataset`, then you will have to specify the labels separately in the argument y, but your `train_dataset` contains both the features and the labels. `validation_data` is similar to the first argument x except it is specifically for the evaluation dataset. This argument is optional, but it tends to be a good idea to monitor how the metrics for training and evaluation evolve side by side. Finally, the middle argument, `epochs`, is a measurement of how long the training process will last. In ML terms, an *epoch* is an entire pass through your dataset for the sake of training. Recall that your dataset is sending the data to the training loop in batches of 128, and your training dataset has 5,634 examples. After 44 batches (or what are often called *steps*), you will have gone through the entire dataset, and thus an epoch. The next epoch will then begin as Keras goes back through the dataset once again.

How long should the model train for? There is no nice rule of thumb to rely on in practice. However, there are a couple of signs you can look out for. First, if the model is no longer improving from one epoch to another, that's a sign that the training process has converged. A second sign is that the model is starting to perform worse on the evaluation dataset. This is a sign that the model has begun overfitting and that you want to stop training it, even if the performance continues to improve on the training dataset.

The `fit()` method also has an optional argument for callbacks. A *callback* is a function that can perform actions at various stages of training—for example, saving checkpoints of the model every epoch, or stopping training if model performance has stalled or is getting worse on the evaluation dataset. The latter example is called *early stopping*. Use the following code to train your model, using the `keras.callbacks.EarlyStopping()` callback function to impose early stopping if needed:

```
early_stopping = keras.callbacks.EarlyStopping(patience=5,
                                                restore_best_weights=True)


history = model.fit(
    x=train_dataset,
    epochs=100,
    validation_data=test_dataset,
    callbacks = [early_stopping]
)
```

The argument `patience` for `keras.callbacks.EarlyStopping()` specifies that you want to wait for five epochs of stalled or worsening performance before stopping the training process. The training process, due to various places where randomness comes into play, can be noisy. You do not want to terminate training early due to noisiness, so the `patience` argument is useful in preventing that. However, just in case the model performance is getting worse during that waiting period, the `restore_best_weights` argument being set to `True` will return the model back to its best performance before terminating the training process. If you have not already, run the code above to train your model. This will take a couple of minutes in Colab to complete training.

While training the model, you will see metrics for every epoch of training. The first few metrics are specific to the training dataset, and the second half is related to the test datasets. You can also use the `model.evaluate(x=test_dataset)` method to evaluate the model. This can be used for the test dataset or for other datasets, depending on how you split your dataset for training and evaluation. Your output from `model.evaluate()` should look similar to the following:

```
12/12 [==============================] - 0s 6ms/step - loss: 0.4390
- binary_accuracy: 0.7928 - precision: 0.6418 - recall: 0.4866
```

Good news, you have trained a successful ML model using Keras. Unfortunately, in this case the neural network model had slightly lower accuracy, precision, and recall. What does this mean? It doesn't mean that a neural network model is automatically worse, but it does mean that likely some further tuning and feature engineering will be needed to improve the performance of this model.

Building Custom ML Models on Vertex AI

You have successfully built, trained, and evaluated multiple ML models. You used scikit-learn to train a logistic regression model and used Keras to train a neural network classifier. In this case, the dataset you were using was fairly small, but in practice you may want to train custom code models on large datasets. You saw in Chapter 5 how to train a classification model using Vertex AI AutoML. In this section, you will get a brief introduction to training custom code models using Vertex AI Training. This section introduces you to more complex topics in Python, such as creating packages. You will not dive into the fine details here, but you'll see enough to get you started.

Vertex AI allows you to train your model in a containerized environment on a cluster of machines of your choice. Roughly speaking, you can think of a *container* as a computer where the hardware and operating system are abstracted away so that a developer can focus purely on the software they want to run. When using standard ML frameworks, you can use prebuilt containers. Prebuilt containers are available for scikit-learn, TensorFlow, XGBoost, and PyTorch. To use the Vertex AI Training service in the Cloud Console, do the following steps:

1. Ensure that your dataset is available in Google Cloud Storage, BigQuery, or Vertex AI managed datasets.

2. Gather the Python code into a single script.

3. Update your code to save results in a Google Cloud Storage bucket.

4. Create a source code distribution.

Fortunately, the first step has already been completed. The dataset is available already in a public Google Cloud Storage bucket. The next step is to gather the Python code into a single script. This code includes all of the code that has been used to load the data into a Pandas DataFrame, prepare the data for training, and build and train an ML model, and you will need to also add code to be sure that the model is saved somewhere off of the Vertex AI resources being used to train the model.

Vertex AI provisions resources for a training job for just the duration of the job, and then those resources are torn down. This means you need to be sure to save anything locally that you do not want to lose, but it also means that you only use the resources that you need.

Before moving forward, you will need to create a directory to hold the files you will be creating for your Python package. To do this in Colab, run the following code in a new cell:

```
!mkdir trainer
```

The exclamation point at the front of the code tells Colab to run this as a Linux terminal command. The `mkdir` command creates a new directory, and you are calling this new directory *trainer*.

The Python code from this chapter has been combined into a single file and is available in the low-code-ai GitHub repo (*https://oreil.ly/supp-lcai*). You should try to build this file yourself as well. You can do this in a notebook by using a special cell magic, `%%writefile`. The `%%writefile` cell magic tells Colab to write the contents of the cell to a specified file rather than execute the code in the cell. The format for the cell will be the following:

```
%%writefile trainer/trainer.py

<Your Python code to be written to trainer.py>
```

Before reading further, you should go ahead and either combine the code from your notebook into a single cell to write out to `trainer/trainer.py` using the `%%writefile` cell magic, or you should copy the solution at the link above. Note that you do not need to include code for visualizations or where you were checking the output. You should use the solution to check your work if you are combining the Python code yourself into a single file.

When looking at the solution, the first thing you will notice is that all the `import` statements have been moved to the top of the script. This is considered a Python best practice, though if the import is done before the module being imported is used, it will not be an issue. Toward the end of the file, `print` statements have been added for printing out the various different metrics from the model. If you do not print the results, they will be lost. Using `print` statements will allow you to find these metrics later in the training logs.

Finally, in the last line of the Python script you will see the use of `joblib.dump()` to write the model out to Google Cloud Storage. Note that the reference for Cloud Storage is different here: `'gcs/<YOUR-BUCKET-NAME>/sklearn_model/'`. Google Cloud Storage buckets are mounted in Vertex AI Training using Cloud Storage FUSE and are effectively treated like a file system. You will need to include your Cloud Storage bucket name for the bucket you created in Chapter 4 or create a new bucket.

Now that the script has been written to `trainer\trainer.py`, the next step is to create the other files in the package. An easy way to do this is using the `%%writefile` cell magic. To have Python recognize a folder as a package, it needs an *__init__.py* in the *trainer* directory. This file contains any initialization code for the package, but this can be an empty file as well if no such code is needed. The other file you will need is a *setup.py* file. The objective of the *setup.py* file is to ensure that the package is installed correctly on the machine(s) executing the training job and is a standard part of a Python package. That all being said, when using the standard prebuilt container for scikit-learn training on Vertex AI, most of this process is straightforward and involves mostly boilerplate code. To create the *__init__.py* file in the *trainer* directory, run the following code in a new cell:

```
%%writefile trainer/__init__.py
#No initialization needed
```

The line #No initialization needed is an example of a comment in Python. The # symbol denotes that Python should not parse the line, but is there for human readability. Since there will be no initialization needed for your package, Python will simply treat this *__init__.py* file as a blank file. To create your *setup.py* file, run the following code in a new cell:

```
%%writefile setup.py
"""Using `setuptools` to create a source distribution."""

from setuptools import find_packages, setup

setup(
    name="churn_sklearn",
    version="0.1",
    packages=find_packages(),
    include_package_data=True,
    install_requires=['gcsfs'],
    description="Training package for customer churn.",
)
```

The code here is mostly boilerplate code. Within the setup function you define the package name, the version number, what packages should be installed as part of the distribution, and the description of the package. The find_packages() function automatically detects the packages in your directory for you. The install_requires=['gcsfs'] argument ensures that the *gcsfs* package is installed for using Cloud Storage FUSE.

All of the files are in place, so now you can create your package by executing the following code in a new cell:

```
!python ./setup.py sdist --formats=gztar
```

The command is to execute the Python script ./setup.py with the sdist option. This creates a Python source distribution with the compression format tar.gz. Your files, with relevant folders expanded, should look like what is shown in Figure 7-10.

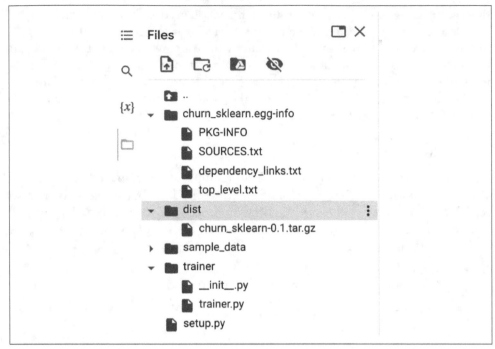

Figure 7-10. File structure after creating the source code distribution for your trainer package.

The difficult part of the process has now been completed. Now you should move the package to a location on Google Cloud Storage for use on Vertex AI. The easiest way to do this is to authorize Colab to access your Google Cloud account and then use the gcloud storage tool. To authorize Colab to access your Google Cloud resources, run the following code in a new cell and follow the prompts:

```
import sys
if "google.colab" in sys.modules:
    from google.colab import auth
    auth.authenticate_user()
```

After following the prompts, you can then move the file to the Cloud Storage bucket of your choice. Run the following code in a new cell, replacing your-project-id with your project ID and your-bucket-name with your bucket name:

```
!gcloud config set project your-project-name
!gcloud storage cp ./dist/churn_sklearn-0.1.tar.gz gs://your-bucket-name/
```

Now everything is in place and you're ready to train your model. You will submit your training job through the Cloud Console. Open a new browser window or tab and go to *console.cloud.google.com*. After that, select Vertex AI on the left-hand side menu, and then select Training. If you are having problems finding the Training option, see Figure 7-11.

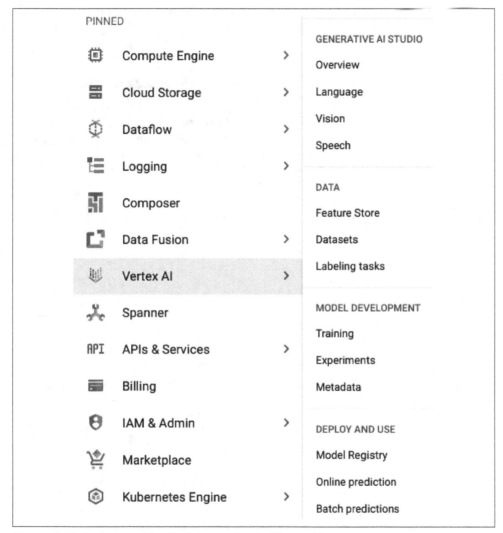

Figure 7-11. Location of the Training option in Vertex AI.

After selecting the Training option, click Create to start creating your new training job (see Figure 7-12). You have a few options to set before you can start the training process. The inputs on the different pages are shown in Figure 7-13 through Figure 7-16, and the inputs are shown in Table 7-9. Any options not mentioned here should be left as the default value. Once you have input all of the options on each page, click Continue until the Start Training button is available to press.

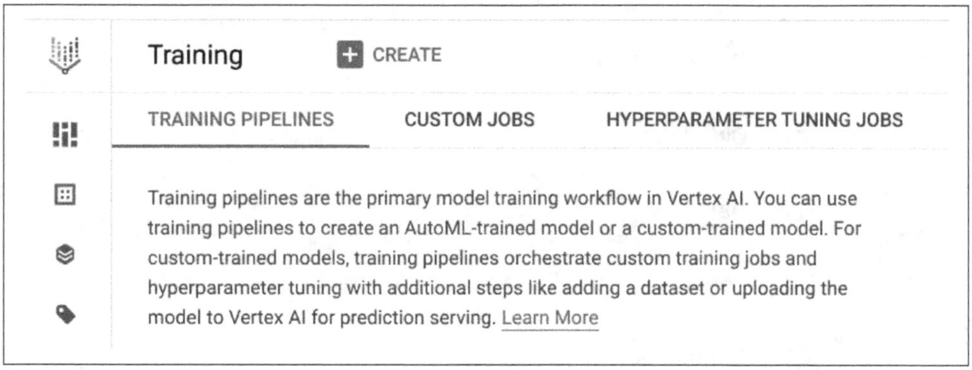

Figure 7-12. Location of the Create button in the Vertex AI Training console.

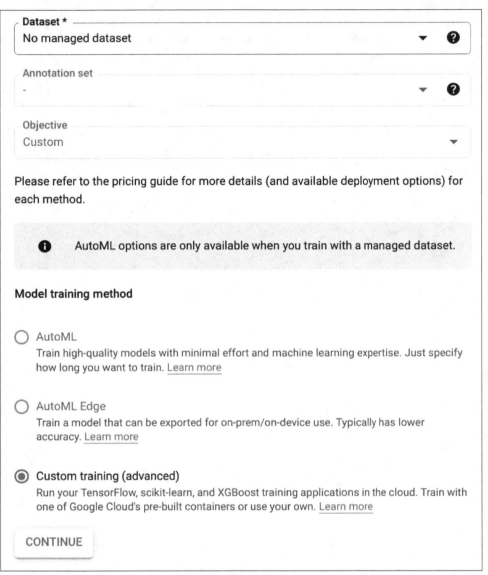

Figure 7-13. Input on the Training Details page for your training job.

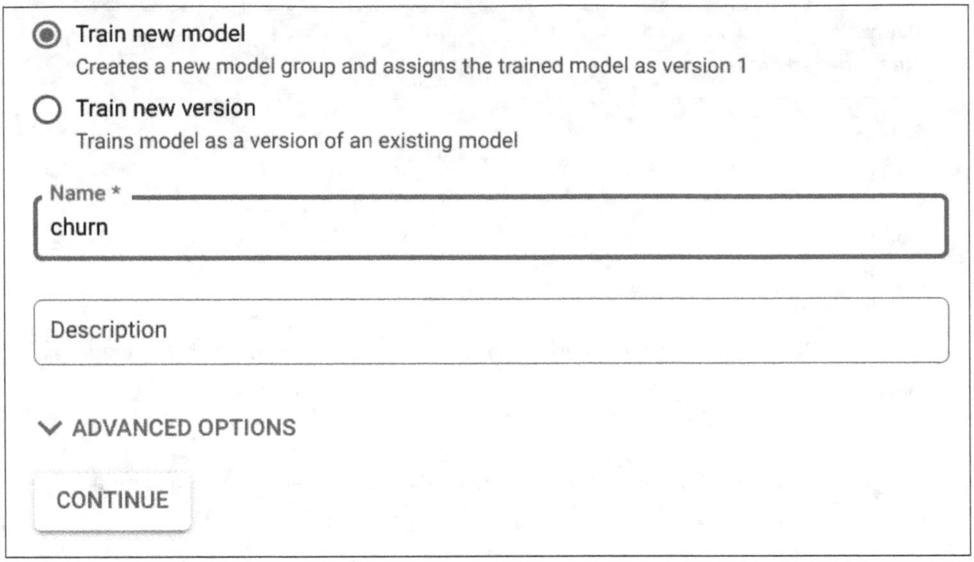

Figure 7-14. Input on the Model Details page for your training job.

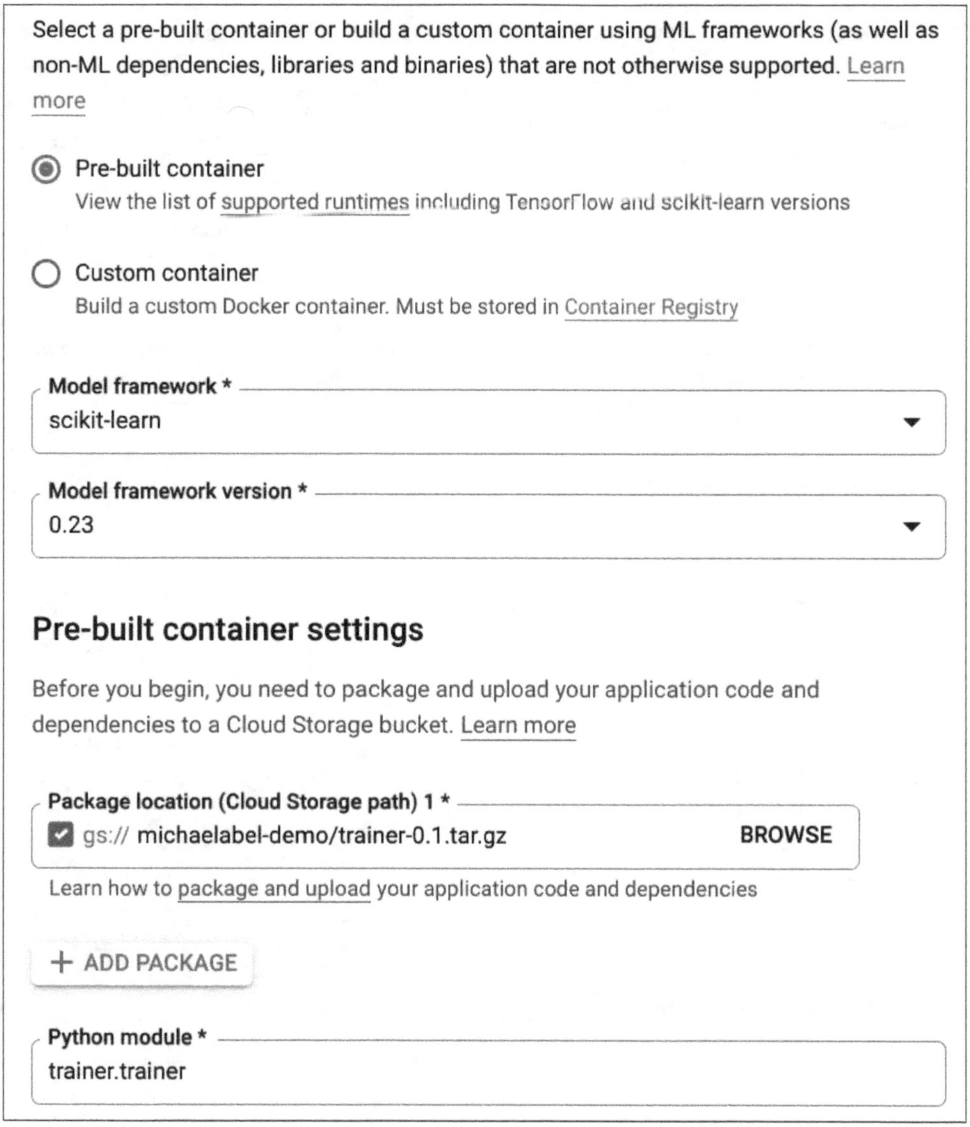

Select a pre-built container or build a custom container using ML frameworks (as well as non-ML dependencies, libraries and binaries) that are not otherwise supported. Learn more

◉ Pre-built container
   View the list of supported runtimes including TensorFlow and scikit-learn versions

○ Custom container
   Build a custom Docker container. Must be stored in Container Registry

Model framework *
scikit-learn ▼

Model framework version *
0.23 ▼

Pre-built container settings

Before you begin, you need to package and upload your application code and dependencies to a Cloud Storage bucket. Learn more

Package location (Cloud Storage path) 1 *
☑ gs:// michaelabel-demo/trainer-0.1.tar.gz   BROWSE

Learn how to package and upload your application code and dependencies

＋ ADD PACKAGE

Python module *
trainer.trainer

Figure 7-15. Input on the "Training container" page for your training job. Be sure to replace the bucket with the bucket you are using.

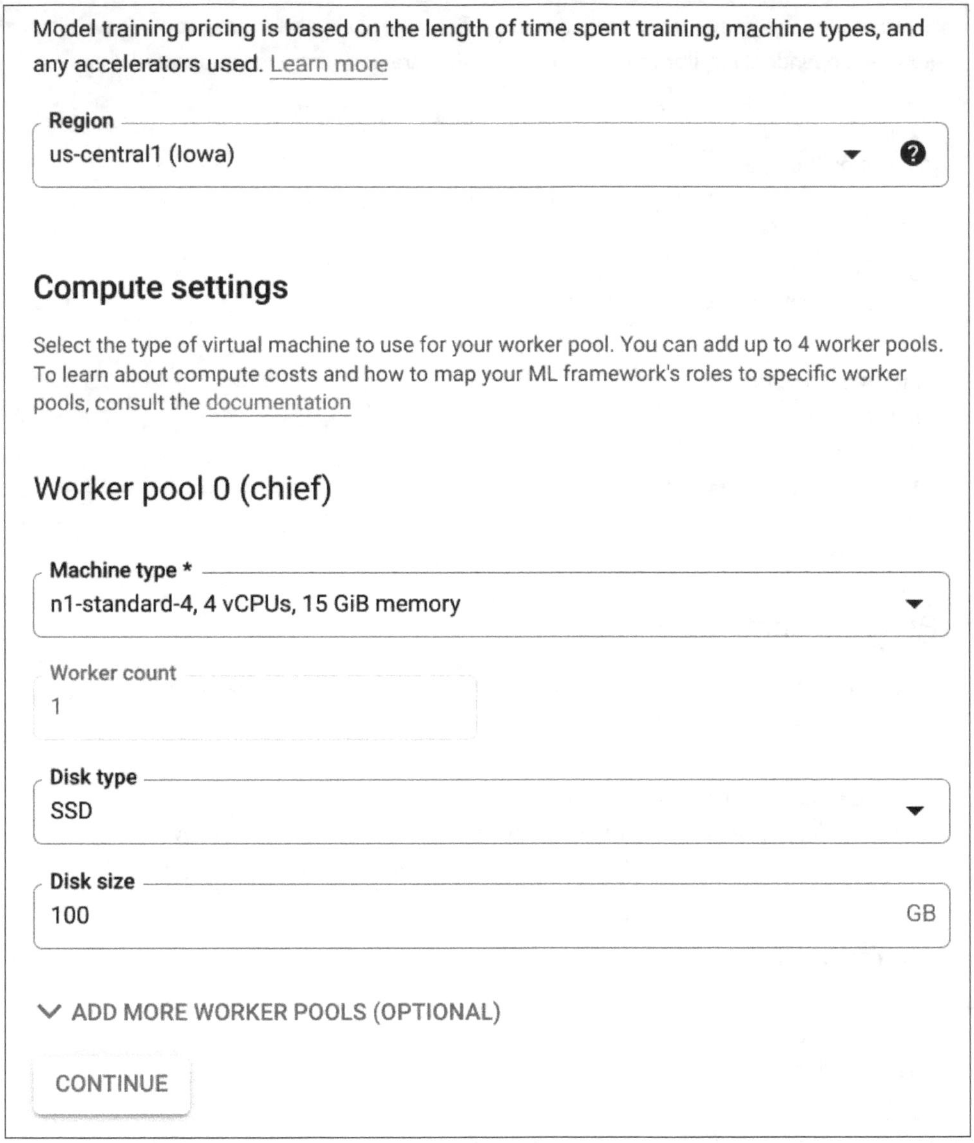

Model training pricing is based on the length of time spent training, machine types, and any accelerators used. Learn more

Region
us-central1 (Iowa) ▾ ❓

Compute settings

Select the type of virtual machine to use for your worker pool. You can add up to 4 worker pools. To learn about compute costs and how to map your ML framework's roles to specific worker pools, consult the documentation

Worker pool 0 (chief)

Machine type *
n1-standard-4, 4 vCPUs, 15 GiB memory ▾

Worker count
1

Disk type
SSD ▾

Disk size
100   GB

⌄ ADD MORE WORKER POOLS (OPTIONAL)

CONTINUE

Figure 7-16. Input on the Compute and Pricing page. Be sure to choose a location close to your bucket.

Table 7-9. Inputs for your training job in Vertex AI Training

Training Method page	
Dataset	No managed dataset
Model training method	Custom training (advanced)

Model Details page	
Radio buttons	Train new model
Model name	churn
"Training container" page	
Radio buttons	Pre-built container
Model framework	scikit-learn
Model framework version	0.23
Package location	gs://your-bucket-name/trainer-0.1.tar.gz
Python module	trainer.trainer
Compute and Pricing page	
Region	Choose a region close to your bucket location
Machine type	n1-standard-4

The training pipeline that Vertex AI will create takes around three minutes to run. Once it has finished, you can see the logs by going back to the Vertex AI link and then Training. Once on that page, click Custom Jobs and then click "churn-custom-job" (see Figure 7-17). Once on the page for the custom job, you will see a table of information. At the bottom of that table, click the link for "View logs." If you scroll down, you will then see the printout of the metrics from the training job. An example of the metrics shown in logs is displayed in Figure 7-18.

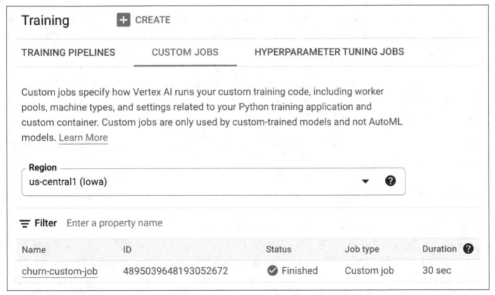

Figure 7-17. The Custom Jobs page with the finished custom job `churn-custom-job`.

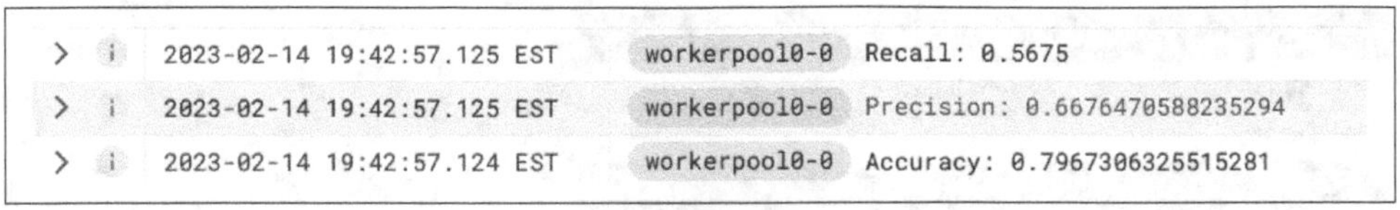

```
>  i    2023-02-14 19:42:57.125 EST      workerpool0-0  Recall: 0.5675

>  i    2023-02-14 19:42:57.125 EST      workerpool0-0  Precision: 0.6676470588235294

>  i    2023-02-14 19:42:57.124 EST      workerpool0-0  Accuracy: 0.7967306325515281
```

Figure 7-18. Metrics from the custom training job.

You have successfully trained a model using scikit-learn on Vertex AI. Of course, this process likely feels like overkill given the amount of time it took to set up and the amount of data you were working with. For working with smaller datasets, working locally or in a Colab notebook is a reasonable approach. But, as datasets become larger and larger, eventually it becomes more advantageous to take advantage of larger pools of resources. In Vertex AI, the same basic process will work when working with ever-growing datasets. Now your model is stored as a *.joblib* file and ready to load wherever needed for serving predictions.

As an exercise, go through this same process with the Keras model. A few hints:

- Be sure to use a prebuilt container for TensorFlow. You can check the version being used in your Colab notebook by running the command `tf.__version__`.

- The TensorFlow prebuilt images include the *sklearn* package, so you can easily reuse your preprocessing code.

- Instead of using `joblib.dump()` to save the model, TensorFlow models include a built-in method, `save()`. Use `model.save()` to store your model in Google Cloud Storage.

Finally, for those who went through the optional section on pipelines in scikit-learn, package up the code for the `Pipeline` version of the model code and submit that for training to Vertex AI Training.

For further resources, see the official Vertex AI Custom Training (*https://oreil.ly/A127h*) documentation.

Summary

In this chapter you learned how to build a custom code model to predict customer churn for a telco company. You explored two of the most popular ML frameworks in scikit-learn and TensorFlow and built simple classification models in each. You then learned how to train your model using the Vertex AI Training service on Google Cloud. All the topics you covered in this chapter are simply the tip of the iceberg and hopefully serve as a stepping stone into deeper knowledge about ML. In the next chapter, you will see how to improve your models using techniques such as hyperparameter tuning in BigQuery ML and using custom code in Vertex AI.

## CHAPTER 8

Improving Custom Model Performance

In Chapters 6 and 7, you learned how to prepare data and build custom models using SQL, BigQuery ML, and Python using scikit-learn and Keras. You will revisit those tools in this chapter with an eye toward additional feature engineering and hyperparameter tuning. In contrast to previous chapters, you will start with prepared data and an already trained model and work to improve from there. If you are confused when exploring the code for the previously built models or the user interface for BigQuery, please revisit the discussions in Chapters 6 and 7.

The Business Use Case: Used Car Auction Prices

Your goal in this project will be to improve the performance of an ML model trained to predict the auction price of used cars. The initial model is a linear regression model built in scikit-learn and does not quite meet your business goals. You will ultimately explore using tools in scikit-learn, Keras, and BigQuery ML to improve your model performance via feature engineering and hyperparameter tuning.

The dataset used for training the linear regression model has been supplied to you as CSV files. These datasets have been cleaned (missing and incorrect values have been remedied appropriately), and the code that was used to build the scikit-learn linear regression model has also been provided. Your teammate who trained the linear regression model has shared some notes with you on model performance and their initial explorations into using Keras for training the ML model. Your colleague has also shared the data split that they used to train and evaluate their model. They created a separate test dataset that has not been used yet that you will be able to use to validate your final model performance. Your task will be to explore the use of feature engineering to improve the feature set for the model and to leverage hyperparameter tuning to ensure that the best model architecture is being used. You will see how to perform these tasks in scikit-learn, Keras, and BigQuery ML.

In the wholesale car sales industry, one of the leading indicators of wholesale prices is the Manheim Market Report (MMR) (*https://www.manheim.com*). MMR pricing calculations are based on over 10 million sales transactions for the previous 13 months. In your dataset, you have access to pricing calculations for the car sales that have been shared when the data was initially pulled. However, you are not certain if you will have access to this information in the future. For that reason, you have been asked to avoid using this feature in your explorations. The business goal that has been shared with you is to have an RMSE in the sales price of $2,000 or less without using the MMR feature. You will start by using the notebook provided by your colleague to load the data and replicate the model training they performed.

There are 13 columns in the dataset. Table 8-1 gives the column names, data types, and some information about the possible values for these columns.

Table 8-1. Schema and field value information for the car sales dataset

Column name	Column type	Notes about field values
year	Integer	Year vehicle was manufactured
make	String	Brand of the vehicle
model	String	Specific version or variation of a vehicle make
trim	String	Specific version or variation of a vehicle model
body	String	Body style of vehicle (e.g., sedan)
transmission	String	Automatic or manual transmission
state	String	State in which the car will be sold
condition	Float	Condition of the car as rated from 0 to 5
odometer	Integer	Odometer reading at time of sale
color	String	Vehicle color
interior	String	Interior color
mmr	Float	Manheim Market Report pricing
sellingprice	Float	Actual selling price for vehicle (label)

Model Improvement in Scikit-Learn

In this section you will work to improve the linear regression model in scikit-learn that was shared with you by your teammate. You will first quickly explore the data, the preprocessing pipeline, and the model itself in scikit-learn. Then you will explore the features more carefully and see how you can improve the model performance using both new and familiar feature engineering techniques. Finally, you will leverage hyperparameter tuning to ensure that you are optimally creating the new features for your specific problem.

Loading the Notebook with the Preexisting Model

First, go to *https://colab.research.google.com*. You will load a notebook from the low-code-ai repository (*https://oreil.ly/supp-lcai*) directly rather than create a new notebook. Click the GitHub button and type in the URL for the low-code-ai GitHub repo, *https://github.com/maabel0712/low-code-ai*, under the prompt "Enter a GitHub URL or search by organization or user." Figure 8-1 shows what it should look like.

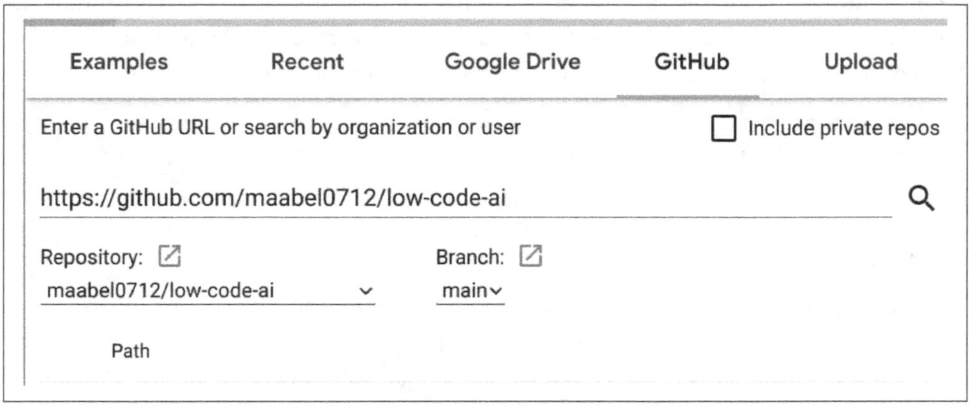

Examples	Recent	Google Drive	GitHub	Upload

Enter a GitHub URL or search by organization or user ☐ Include private repos

https://github.com/maabel0712/low-code-ai 🔍

Repository: ⤢
maabel0712/low-code-ai ⌄

Branch: ⤢
main⌄

Path

Figure 8-1. Connecting to GitHub in Google Colab to open a notebook directly.

Hit Enter (or click the magnifying glass) to search the repo for notebooks. Scroll down until you see `chapter_8/sklearn_model.ipynb` and click the "Open notebook in new tab" button on the far right. This will open up the `sklearn_model.ipynb` notebook in a new browser tab.

The code for loading the vehicle auction sales data, preparing the data for training, training the ML model, and evaluating the ML model is already included in the notebook. In this chapter, you will not go through this code in the level of detail that you did in Chapter 7, but you will spend some time reviewing the code before beginning the process of model improvement.

Loading the Datasets and the Training-Validation-Test Data Split

First, execute the cell to load the training, validation, and test datasets into corresponding DataFrames:

```
!wget -q https://storage.googleapis.com/low-code-ai-book/car_prices_train.csv
!wget -q https://storage.googleapis.com/low-code-ai-book/car_prices_valid.csv
!wget -q https://storage.googleapis.com/low-code-ai-book/car_prices_test.csv

import pandas as pd
train_df = pd.read_csv('./car_prices_train.csv')
valid_df = pd.read_csv('./car_prices_valid.csv')
test_df = pd.read_csv('./car_prices_test.csv')
```

This code should be mostly familiar from previous chapters, but the wget bash command may be new to you. wget simply downloads the file at the given URL into the local file directory. The -q flag suppresses the logs from the wget command. When loading the data into DataFrames, note that the file location starts with ./. The . is a shorthand for "the current working directory," which is where the wget command will download the three files you specified.

After loading the datasets into their respective DataFrames, quickly ensure that the data is what you expect by using the head() method on each DataFrame. The first few columns of output from the train_df.head() method are shown below:

```
   Unnamed: 0  year        make       model        trim       body
0           0  2012     Infiniti     G Sedan  G37 Journey    g sedan
1           1  2012    Chevrolet       Cruze           LS      Sedan
2           2  2005         Jeep    Wrangler            X        SUV
3           3  2011          Kia     Sorento           SX        SUV
4           4  2002   Volkswagen  New Beetle          GLS  Hatchback
```

The very first column is the index in your DataFrame train_df, but where is the second column, Unnamed:0, coming from? This column is an unnamed column in the CSV files that you are loading to create your DataFrames, and it was not mentioned in Table 8-1. Most likely this was the index from a previous DataFrame that got carried over by mistake and not an important feature. You will see in the next section that your colleague dropped this column as part of preprocessing the data.

Note that you could also use Pandas to read directly from the file location in Google Cloud Storage as you did in Chapter 7. The advantage of using the wget command is that you will now have your own local copy of the data. Which approach is the most advantageous depends on your workflow and how you are manipulating the data.

Before moving forward, recall that in the previous chapters you used two datasets, a training dataset and a test dataset, for evaluating the model after training. Now there are three datasets: a training dataset, a validation (or evaluation) dataset, and a test dataset. Why are there three datasets? The training dataset is of course used for training the model, and the validation dataset is used for evaluating the model. In this project, you are going to be comparing many different models to each other. You will use the training dataset to train each model and then evaluate the models using the validation dataset. The "final model" will be the model whose performance was the best on the validation dataset. However, the final model you choose may be biased toward the validation dataset since you specifically choose the model that performed the best on the validation dataset.

The role of the test dataset is to have a final independent dataset to verify the final model's performance. If the final model has similar performance on the test dataset as it does to the validation data, then that model is ready to use. In the case that the model has significantly worse performance on the test dataset, then you know you have a problem before you take the model and use it in your workloads.

One way to help avoid this scenario is to ensure that your training, validation, and test datasets have similar data distributions. As an exercise, explore the datasets using the describe(include='all') method and see that the three datasets have similar distributions up to a few outliers.

Exploring the Scikit-Learn Linear Regression Model

Now go to the next cell in the notebook. This cell contains the code to prepare the data, train the ML model, and evaluate the model all using scikit-learn. There will not be a careful walkthrough of all the code in this section, as the concept of a scikit-learn pipeline was covered in Chapter 7. However, a quick overview with some additional notes will be discussed along the way. First consider the data processing portion of code after the import statements:

```
y_train = train_df['sellingprice']
X_train = train_df.drop('sellingprice', axis=1)

def drop_columns(df, columns):
    return df.drop(columns, axis=1)

preproc_cols = FunctionTransformer(drop_columns,
    kw_args={"columns":['Unnamed: 0', 'mmr']})

numeric_columns = ['year', 'condition', 'odometer']
categorical_columns = ['make', 'model', 'trim', 'body',
                       'transmission', 'state', 'color', 'interior']

col_transformer = ColumnTransformer(
  [
    ('ohe', OneHotEncoder(drop='if_binary',
                          handle_unknown='infrequent_if_exist'),
                          categorical_columns),
    ('minmax', MinMaxScaler(), numeric_columns)
  ]
)
```

First, you are splitting the DataFrame into a separate column of labels (selling price) and the rest of the feature columns as a single DataFrame. Then, you are dropping the Unnamed: 0 and mmr columns of your training, validation, and test datasets. This is being done by defining a function drop_columns and applying that function using a FunctionTransformer. Note that there's a new parameter in defining the FunctionTransformer. The kw_args parameter takes in values for arguments in the chosen function beyond the first. For `preproc_cols`, the first argument is the DataFrame we wish to drop columns from, and that will be provided in the pipeline. The second parameter is the list of columns we wish to drop, and that will be passed in as the corresponding value of a dictionary for the key `columns`.

The `Unnamed: 0` column may seem odd, but as discussed before this is likely an artifact of how the data was shuffled using the Pandas DataFrame method `sample()`, which kept the original index as a new column. Within the context of your problem, this column has no relation to the target and has been discarded. The `mmr` column is unsurprisingly highly correlated with the target `sellingprice`, but given that you have been instructed to avoid using that feature, it is being dropped as well.

Otherwise, the rest of the preceding code will seem familiar "Pipelines in Scikit-Learn: An Introduction" on page 228 in Chapter 7. You are splitting the columns into numeric columns and categorical columns (`numeric_columns` and `categorical_columns`, respectively) and then using a `ColumnTransformer()` to apply different transformations to the different sets of columns. The `OneHotEncoder()` will be used for the categorical columns, and a `MinMaxScaler()` will be used for the numeric columns.

Now consider the rest of the code in the cell where you define the model and the pipeline:

```
model = LinearRegression()

pipeline = Pipeline(steps=[('preproc_cols' , preproc_cols),
                           ('col_transformer', col_transformer),
                           ('model', model)])

pipeline.fit(X_train, y_train)
```

The model that is being used here is a linear regression model. You are also using a `Pipeline` object to define the preprocessing and the model together as a sequence of steps. First the `preproc_cols` `FunctionTransformer()` will be applied to the DataFrame, then `col_transformer` `ColumnTransformer()` will be used to apply the appropriate transformation to columns depending on their type. Finally, the linear regression model will be trained as the last part of the pipeline when `pipeline.fit` is called. The last line fits the transformers and trains the model together. The fit transformers are stored as part of the pipeline at prediction time. After training the model, you will see a graphical representation of the pipeline, as shown in Figure 8-2. If you wish, you can expand this to see more details and confirm that they align with your expectations from the code.

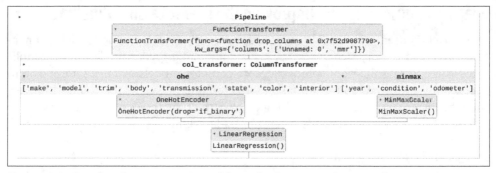

Figure 8-2. Graphical representation of the scikit-learn `Pipeline` used to train your model.

Now that the model has been trained in your notebook environment, you can evaluate the model. Recall that when using scikit-learn pipelines, you can use the `score()` method in the same way you would for any model object. You can also import other metrics such as RMSE and MAE. Run the following code in the following cell to look at evaluation metrics for your model:

```
import math
from sklearn.metrics import mean_squared_error, mean_absolute_error

y_valid = valid_df['sellingprice']
X_valid = valid_df.drop('sellingprice', axis=1)

print('R2:', pipeline.score(X_valid, y_valid))
print('RMSE:',math.sqrt(mean_squared_error(y_valid, pipeline.predict(X_valid))))
print('MAE:', mean_absolute_error(y_valid, pipeline.predict(X_valid)))
```

You will see that the R^2 score is about 0.876. This means that, roughly speaking, your features describe 87.6% of the variability in the label. You will also see that the RMSE is about 3,384.60 and the MAE is about 2,044.26. Recall that your business goal was to have an RMSE of less than $2,000. As expected, based on the communication from your colleague, the model does not meet those needs, but now you have everything ready to work on improving the model.

In general, when collaborating across a team, you want to avoid any randomness from splitting and the training process when comparing results. Otherwise, you may be misled by comparing different model results being trained in different environments. In this case, the actual data split was shared with you rather than the code. This is often preferable since a random shuffle and split will often be used. You can set a random seed to make that split deterministic or save the corresponding training, validation, and test datasets, as was done here. Additionally, this is something to consider when initializing and training models as well.

Feature Engineering and Improving the Preprocessing Pipeline

Often, well-chosen and carefully created features, even with simple model architectures, can lead to very strong results. Just simply making your model more complicated is not always the right approach. More complex models will need more data to successfully train the model and take more compute power to train and ultimately tune the hyperparameters. Even looking for easy fixes, such as looking out for strange values and removing unrelated features, can lead to significant model improvement.

Looking for easy improvements

Your colleague did a careful analysis of the original dataset and communicated to you that they removed all null values and columns (such as the VIN) that were in a one-to-one relationship with the label. Now it is a good idea to explore the dataset to see if anything else could be improved. To do this, run the command `train_df.describe()` in your notebook environment in a new cell if you have not already done so. A sample of the expected output is shown in Table 8-2.

Table 8-2. Partial output of `train_df.describe()`

	year	condition	odometer	mmr	sellingprice
count	385000.000000	385000.000000	385000.000000	385000.000000	385000.000000
mean	2010.120177	3.339402	67732.957974	13695.356558	13544.324018
std	3.879672	1.117698	52521.619238	9525.243974	9599.953488
min	1990.000000	-1.000000	1.000000	25.000000	1.000000
25%	2008.000000	2.700000	28494.000000	7200.000000	7000.000000
50%	2012.000000	3.600000	52122.000000	12200.000000	12100.000000
75%	2013.000000	4.200000	98188.000000	18150.000000	18000.000000
max	2015.000000	5.000000	999999.000000	182000.000000	183000.000000

Recall that you are dropping the `Unnamed: 0` and the `mmr` columns in the preprocessing pipeline, so you do not need to worry about those columns in your analysis. Nothing seems out of place in the `year` column at a glance; the model year of the cars range between 1990 and 2015, with the data distribution skewed toward newer cars. You should notice something odd about the `condition` column. You have a minimum value of `-1.0` in the `condition` column. This likely means that a magic number slipped by your colleague. When analyzing many columns across a dataset, it is easy to sometimes miss something simple like this. This is a good reason an extra pair of eyes is always valuable.

Since `condition` is a floating-point number, we cannot easily just treat `-1.0` as a separate value without doing some transformation. You have a few options. If you expect that the selling price has a linear relationship with the `condition` value, then you could create a new feature `condition_recorded` as a binary 0 or 1 value and replace instances of -1.0 with 0.0 so that those values are treated differently than normal condition values. However, as you may have experienced with other rating systems, often the effect of ratings is not linear. An easy way to address this is to bucketize the values and then one-hot encode the corresponding bucket membership. This way, the case of no rating will be treated entirely differently than cases of other ratings (say, between 2 and 3), and you can tune the number of buckets to see which gives your model the best performance.

To take the second approach, create a new cell in the notebook and add the following code, but do not run the code yet:

```
import pandas as pd

from sklearn.preprocessing import (OneHotEncoder, MinMaxScaler,
                                    FunctionTransformer,
                                    KBinsDiscretizer)
from sklearn.compose import ColumnTransformer
from sklearn.linear_model import LinearRegression
from sklearn.pipeline import Pipeline

y_train = train_df['sellingprice']
X_train = train_df.drop('sellingprice', axis=1)

def preproc_cols(df, drop_cols):
    return df.drop(drop_cols, axis=1)

drop_cols = FunctionTransformer(preproc_cols,
                               kw_args={"drop_cols":['Unnamed: 0', 'mmr']})
ohe = OneHotEncoder(drop='if_binary', handle_unknown='infrequent_if_exist')
minmax = MinMaxScaler()
bucket_cond = KBinsDiscretizer(n_bins=10, encode='onehot', strategy='uniform')
```

This code is mostly the same as what was shared with you before, but take the time to spot a few changes. The KBinsDiscretizer transformer has been added; this transformer is the tool in scikit-learn that can be used to bucketize data. Note that the transformers are now defined on separate lines rather than in the ColumnTransformer as before. This is done for increased readability, but also for *modularity*, the ability to split up code more easily as you continue to improve your model.

In the last of these lines is where the KBinsDiscretizer is defined. The n_bins argument is set to 10 for 10 different buckets, the encode argument tells the transformer to perform one-hot encoding, and the strategy, uniform, tells the transformer to split the buckets evenly. This way, -1.0 will be in its own bucket separate from the other ranges. Finish defining the pipeline using the following code, and run the cell to train your new model:

```
numeric_columns = ['year', 'odometer']
categorical_columns = ['make', 'model', 'trim', 'body',
                       'transmission', 'state', 'color', 'interior']
```

```
col_transformer = ColumnTransformer(
  [('ohe', ohe, categorical_columns),
   ('minmax', minmax, numeric_columns),
   ('bucket_cond', bucket_cond, ['condition'])])

pipeline = Pipeline(steps=[('drop_cols' , drop_cols),
                           ('col_transformer', col_transformer),
                           ('model', model)])

pipeline.fit(X_train, y_train)
```

You can evaluate the new model by executing the code you used before in a new cell:

```
print('R2:', pipeline.score(X_valid, y_valid))
print('RMSE:',math.sqrt(mean_squared_error(y_valid, pipeline.predict(X_valid))))
print('MAE:', mean_absolute_error(y_valid, pipeline.predict(X_valid)))
```

The change did lead to a small increase in the performance of the model. The RMSE dropped from about 3,384.60 to 3,313.63. Though it is a small improvement in this case, in many cases catching issues like this can lead to a large improvement in the model performance.

As you were evaluating the model, you likely noticed a warning message in the results:

```
UserWarning: Found unknown categories in columns [2, 3] during transform.
These unknown categories will be encoded as all zeros
```

What does this warning actually mean? Here columns 2 and 3 correspond to `trim` and `body`. This warning means that there are values for these columns in the validation dataset that are not in the training dataset. Checking for skew between the datasets, such as different values appearing in the training and validation datasets, is an important step of understanding your data in preparation for training. However, it is very possible that an issue you were not expecting could appear while training and evaluating models, so it is useful to know what to look out for.

You can quickly check, using the following code, how many values for the `trim` column appear exactly once:

```
(train_df.trim.value_counts()==1).sum()
```

You will see that there are 124 values that are unique in the training dataset for the `trim` column. Likewise, in the validation dataset you can see there are 273 values that are unique. It seems as if your colleague may have caught on to this and addressed it in their `OneHotEncoder` definition. They included the `handle_unknown='infrequent_if_exist'` parameter and value. `handle_unknown` defines the behavior that is followed when an unknown value appears at prediction time, and the `'infrequent_if_exist'` value will assign unknown features to an infrequent category if it exists. To create an "infrequent" category, you can set the `min_frequency` argument. This again is something that can be tuned.

Setting the `min_frequency` too high will mean that many categories will have the same contribution to output of the model, lowering the usefulness of the feature. On the other hand, if the `min_frequency` is set too low, then you can run across the issue of having a large number of features that only appear once or the issue you have already seen where it is difficult to get a proper distribution of feature values between datasets.

Set the `min_frequency` to 1 and then rerun the training code to see if there is any difference in performance. You will see that the performance only changed very slightly this time. In essence, you said that you treat all categories that appear less than 1 time (or 0 times) in the training set as the same. It may make sense to increase the `min_frequency` so that you treat all infrequent variables as the same category, the `infrequent` category. You will explore this later when performing hyperparameter tuning.

Feature crosses

Consider the `model` and `trim` features for a moment. Often you think of these features together rather than separately, correct? When you say "I bought a Honda CR-V," that does not completely describe the car. There can be many different *trims* or packages for the car. For a 2023 Honda CR-V, for example, three of the trims are "LX," "EX," and "EX-L." It is entirely possible that the same names can be used across different vehicles as well. For example, the 2023 Honda Pilot also has the "LX" and "EX-L" trims. Therefore, the value of the `trim` variable also does not tell the entire story either. You need the value of both features to be able to identify the vehicle.

However, in your model, you treat `model` and `trim` as completely separate variables. Recall, when using one-hot encoding you create a binary feature for each feature value, and a linear regression model will assign a weight to each of these binary features. The `trim` value of LX will have its own weight associated with it, independent of the value of the `model` variable since you are using one-hot encoding. That is, the `trim` feature value of "LX" will be treated the same regardless if the `model` is "Pilot" or "CR-V." It makes sense to still consider the `make` feature separately since certain makes tend to be more expensive than others.

How do you capture both feature values as a pair? One way of approaching this is by using something known as a *feature cross*. A feature cross is a synthetic feature formed by concatenating two or more features. One way to intuitively think about this is that you are considering the value of both variables at the same time, rather than separately.

How does this work for categorical features? Recall that the feature value corresponding to one-hot encoding is a binary 0 or 1. The idea of a feature cross in this case would be that the crossed feature value would be 1 if the *pair* of features have the corresponding values, but 0 otherwise. For example, take "CR-V LX" as the `model` and `trim`. The value for the "CR-V" feature (under one-hot encoding) would be 1, and the value for the "LX" feature would be 1. So the value for the "CR-V LX" feature for the feature cross of `model` and `trim` would be 1. However, the value for the "Pilot LX" feature would be 0 since the "Pilot" feature has a value of 0 in this example.

This seems like a simple feature to create and use, and when you used AutoML in Chapters 4 and 5 it created these sorts of features (and more) for you in its process of finding the best model for your dataset. However, feature crosses can be extremely powerful features even in simple linear regression models. Can you think of other pairs of features that may benefit from using a feature cross?

To see this in action, first replace the code for the `preproc_cols` function with the following:

```
def preproc_cols(df, drop_cols):

    df['model_trim'] = df['model'] + df['trim']
    df['model_trim'] = df['model_trim'].str.lower()

    df['color_interior'] = df['color'] + df['interior']
    df['color_interior'] = df['color_interior'].str.lower()

    return df.drop(drop_cols, axis=1)
```

Consider the first two lines of this function. You are creating a new column, `model_trim`, in your DataFrame. This new column is formed by concatenating the value of the `model` and the `trim` column. So, the value of the `model_trim` column will depend on both the model and the trim of the car. The second line converts the corresponding string into all lowercase. This is a good practice to ensure that random differences in capitalization do not lead to different feature values. `color` and `interior` are another good example of features that have a relationship that can be represented well by a feature cross, so the third and fourth line implement the same ideas.

Finally, you need to be sure that the new feature cross columns are being one-hot encoded just as the other categorical variables; to do this, update the list `categorical_columns` with the new feature names. Your final list should look like this:

```
categorical_columns = ['make', 'model', 'trim', 'model_trim', 'body',
                       'transmission', 'state', 'color', 'interior',
                       'color_interior']
```

Now execute the model code with the preceding changes and reevaluate the performance of the model. The complete code is available in the solution notebook if you get stuck. You should see that the RMSE is now about 3,122.14. By adding feature crosses, you were able to decrease the RMSE by about 2% and get even closer to your ultimate goal.

As an exercise, before moving on to the next section, explore other features that could be bucketized and crossed with other features. As a goal, see if you can get the RMSE for your model under 3,000 before moving on to the next section.

Hyperparameter Tuning

In the previous section you included new and useful features to lower the RMSE for your model. You may not have quite reached your goal of $2,000 RMSE yet, but you have made good progress. The next process that you will explore is known as *hyperparameter tuning*. Recall that a *hyperparameter* is a variable that is not updated during training but defines things such as the model architecture (such as number of hidden layers or neurons per hidden layer for neural networks), how features are engineered (such as how many buckets), and how the training process is executed (such as the learning rate or batch size). When you bucketized the condition feature, you selected a number of buckets. But how do you know what the optimal number of buckets would be? The process of hyperparameter tuning aims to answer these sorts of questions for you.

Hyperparameter tuning strategies

There are three main strategies that are commonly used for hyperparameter tuning: grid search, random search, and Bayesian search. For all three, the first step is the same. First you select a range of candidate values for the hyperparameters you wish to tune. You can choose a range of values or a discrete set of values depending on the hyperparameter you want to tune. For example, if you want to tune the optimizer learning rate, you could set a range such as [0, 1] for the candidate range. In your case, you bucketized the condition feature and set 6 as the number of buckets. This was really an arbitrary choice, and there may be a better choice. For example, you could set the candidate range between 5 and 15.

If you choose too low a number of buckets, you are treating large ranges of condition values the same in the model. For example, with two buckets, all condition values between 3.0 and 5.0 could be in the same bucket. On the other hand, if you have too many buckets, then you risk overfitting, as you will have a small number of examples per bucket that could be memorized by the model. With all of this in mind, 5 to 15 seems like a reasonable candidate range.

Once you have set the candidate ranges for the hyperparameters you wish to tune, the next step is to choose a tuning method. The *grid search* method is very simply a "try everything and see what works the best" approach. For example, suppose you are tuning for two hyperparameters. The first has 4 candidate values and the second has 3 candidate values, so there are 12 combinations of hyperparameters to check. A visual representation of this is shown in Figure 8-3.

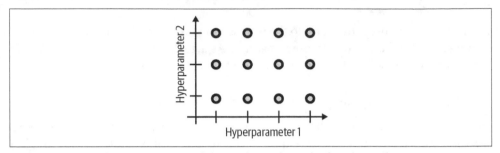

Figure 8-3. Visual representation of the grid search method with two hyperparameters tuned.

To select the best set of hyperparameters, you train a model for each set of hyperparameters using the training dataset and evaluate the models using the validation dataset. In this case, you know for sure that you have the best hyperparameters (in the candidate ranges) since you tried every possible value.

The downside of the grid search method should be apparent at this point. If you want to work with a couple of hyperparameters each with a small range of candidate values, then there are a reasonable number of models to train. However, if you want to tune a large number of hyperparameters with a large number of candidate values each, then this can quickly become infeasible. For example, if you have four hyperparameters to tune with 10 candidate values each, then there are 10,000 candidate models to train.

There are two alternate approaches that are often used. The *random search* approach is a partial search strategy that randomly selects some preset number of the candidate models. Those models are trained and compared. The advantage of this approach is that you can control how much time and effort is taken in searching through the set of candidate models, but the downside is that you may miss the best model in the search space because you got unlucky in the random selection process.

The third approach is *Bayesian search* or *optimization*, which is a more intelligent approach to a partial search. The full details of the approach are beyond the scope of this book, but the core idea is fairly simple. You randomly train a small number of the candidate models as a starting point. Based on the evaluation metrics of those initial models, the Bayesian optimization algorithm chooses the next set of candidate models in the search space. These are the candidates, based on the earlier models, that are expected to have the best evaluation metrics. This process continues for some number of steps that are set up front. The next set of candidate models are chosen based on the previous candidates' performance. Though this has the same downside as random search in terms of not exhausting the search space, the upside is that the search is a "more intelligent" search than random search.

Hyperparameter tuning in scikit-learn

In scikit-learn, both the grid search and random search strategies are easy to implement. In the remainder of this section, you will implement a variant of the grid search strategy to find a better set of hyperparameters for your model. First, add a couple of new transformers to bucketize the odometer and year columns, and remove the list of numeric columns since those will now be bucketized as categorical columns. Also, include the new KBinsDiscretizer transforms in the ColumnTransformer. For convenience, the corresponding code is included here:

```
bucket_cond = KBinsDiscretizer(n_bins=10, encode='onehot',
    strategy='uniform')
bucket_odo = KBinsDiscretizer(n_bins=10, encode='onehot',
    strategy='quantile')
bucket_year = KBinsDiscretizer(n_bins=10, encode='onehot',
    strategy='uniform')

categorical_columns = ['make', 'model', 'trim', 'model_trim', 'body',
                       'transmission', 'state', 'color', 'interior',
                       'color_interior']

col_transformer = ColumnTransformer(
  [('ohe', ohe, categorical_columns),
   ('minmax', minmax, numeric_columns),
   ('bucket_cond', bucket_cond, ['condition']),
   ('bucket_odo', bucket_odo, ['odometer']),
   ('bucket_year', bucket_year, ['year'])]
  )
```

You will tune the following four hyperparameters: the number of buckets for the odometer, condition, and the year columns, and the minimum frequency for the OneHotEncoder transformer for a feature to not be encoded as infrequent. In scikit-learn, you need to define the candidate ranges as a dictionary of values. Since you are using a pipeline for your model and transformations, the syntax may look a little odd at first glance. The code for this case is the following:

```
grid_params = {'col_transformer__bucket_cond__n_bins': range(8,13),
               'col_transformer__bucket_odo__n_bins': range(8,13),
               'col_transformer__bucket_year__n_bins': range(8,13),
               'col_transformer__ohe__min_frequency': range(1,6)
              }
```

The dictionary has pairs of the form 'hyperparameter_name' : candidate_range. The hyperparameter range may look odd here at first glance, but it is not too bad to parse. For example, the first hyperparameter has the name col_trans former__bucket_cond__n_bins. This corresponds to the n_bins value for the bucket_cond transformer, which is part of the col_transformer. The corresponding candidate range is a list of possible values for the n_bins parameter of bucket_cond. range(8,13) is a convenient syntax for the list [8,9,10,11,12]. Note that the second endpoint 13 is not included in the list. For the min_frequency hyperparameter, the candidate range is range(1,6).

Now that the candidate ranges have been defined, you need to define the strategy and then train the corresponding models—in this case, 625 candidate models with the different choices of hyperparameters that you have defined. This is not an excessively large number of models to train, but it will likely take at least an hour or so to fully train them all. Scikit-learn offers a variant of the grid search strategy known as a *halving grid search*.

To perform a halving grid search, first train all candidate models, but only for a small portion of the training data. Based on the evaluation of those models, you keep some portion of the candidate model pool. The name implies that you keep half, but you can reduce the number of models more aggressively if you wish. After you remove models from the candidate pool, you then train the remaining candidate models using more of the training data. You repeat the overall process until you have chosen the best candidate model.

It is entirely possible that models that perform well on a subset of the data will not perform as well on the entire dataset and be eliminated in later rounds of the process. Additionally, it's possible that a model that performed poorly on a small subset of the dataset would have actually performed very well on the entire training dataset. That candidate model could be discarded before you see the improvement in the model using more data. In general, any method you use other than grid search has some risk along these lines, but halving grid search tends to be more effective than random search in finding the best candidate model.

To implement halving grid search in scikit-learn takes just a few lines of code:

```
from sklearn.experimental import enable_halving_search_cv
from sklearn.model_selection import HalvingGridSearchCV

grid_search = HalvingGridSearchCV(pipeline, grid_params,
                                  cv=3, verbose=1,
                                  scoring='neg_root_mean_squared_error')
```

At the time of writing, the halving grid search strategy is experimental in scikit-learn, so it has to be enabled with the first line. The second line imports the HalvingGrid SearchCV class for performing halving grid search. The third line is where we create the object that will be performing the halving grid search. The first argument is the model or pipeline that you wish to use and the second argument is the grid_params dictionary you defined earlier. The keyword argument cv refers to a resampling method known as cross-validation. Briefly, cv corresponds to the number of trials per candidate model using different splits of the training dataset into a smaller training set and evaluation dataset. Higher cv values will lead to more precise evaluation metrics but take more time to process. The verbose argument takes an integer from 0 to 3. The higher the number, the more information will be output during the tuning process. Finally, you have to set the metric that you are trying to optimize in the tuning process. Since we are trying to optimize RMSE, we use the neg_root_mean_squared_error score.

 You may wonder why we use the negative root mean squared error for the scoring argument. In statistical modeling, a score function should increase when a model improves. On the other hand, a loss function should decrease when the model improves. Hyperparameter tuning methods in scikit-learn are set to use score functions. Fortunately, we can get a score function by taking the negative RMSE instead.

Now you are ready to perform hyperparameter tuning. Add the following code after the definition of the grid_search object, and execute the code cell to perform hyperparameter tuning to find the best candidate model:

```
grid_search.fit(X_train, y_train)
print(grid_search.best_params_)
```

The second line that was added will print the hyperparameters for the best candidate model. The hyperparameter tuning process will take 35–40 minutes in Google Colab. You should see a similar result to the following, though the exact output may differ based on randomness in the sampling process:

```
{'col_transformer__bucket_cond__n_bins': 11,
 'col_transformer__bucket_odo__n_bins': 12,
 'col_transformer__bucket_year__n_bins': 11,
 'col_transformer__ohe__min_frequency': 1}
```

You can check the best model's performance on our validation dataset so you can compare performance with the earlier models. Execute the following code in a new cell to output the evaluation metrics (RMSE) for the best model from the grid search:

```
# Load validation dataset in case it is not currently loaded
y_valid = valid_df['sellingprice']
X_valid = valid_df.drop('sellingprice', axis=1)

print('RMSE:', math.sqrt(mean_squared_error(y_valid,
                                    grid_search.predict(X_valid))))
```

Note that when you call the predict() method on the grid_search method, it calls the predict() method on the best model from the grid search. The RMSE on the best model was 2,915.02. Compared with where you started, with an RMSE over 3,300, this is a significant improvement using both feature engineering and hyperparameter tuning. As an exercise, continue experimenting to see if you can find new features and tune any new hyperparameters that come up to see if you can improve the model further.

Finally, once you believe you have the best model that you can get, you should evaluate the model on the testing dataset. However, in this chapter, you will still explore new model architectures using Keras, so you should hold off for now on performing this step.

Model Improvement in Keras

This section explores different neural network model architectures for your car auction selling price problem using Keras. You will not go back through the feature selection and engineering conversation from before, but you will be introduced to Keras preprocessing layers as an analogue to the transformers you used in scikit-learn. After re-creating the feature engineering part of the scikit-learn pipeline, you will learn how to perform hyperparameter tuning using the Keras Tuner package and the Bayesian optimization method discussed in the previous section.

Introduction to Preprocessing Layers in Keras

Keras preprocessing layers allow for you to easily build your data preprocessing functions into the model function in the same way that you created a pipeline in scikit-learn. You saw in Chapter 7 and the previous section how convenient it was to include the preprocessing logic into the model itself. Though you did not export the model in the previous section, you can easily export the entire trained pipeline using the *joblib* library as you did in Chapter 7.

Think back through the transformations you performed on the dataset in the previous section. You one-hot encoded the categorical features, bucketized the numeric features, and created feature crosses. Before starting to build the model in Keras, it is good to understand the preprocessing layers that you will be using.

The `Discretization` layer is used in Keras to bucketize numerical features just as the `KBinsDiscretizer` transformer was used in scikit-learn. You can provide the endpoints of the buckets or use the `adapt()` method to have Keras choose the endpoints based on the data and a specified number of bins. When using the `adapt()` method, you must specify the dataset that you wish to use. The range of values in this dataset is what will be used to choose the bucket boundaries. Typically, you should use your training dataset or a representative sample of your training dataset for the `adapt()` method.

The result of the adapt() method is a list of boundary points corresponding to the number of bins you chose. The left-most boundary point is actually the right endpoint for a bin and the right-most boundary point is actually the left endpoint for another bin.

For example, if you set the number of bins to be four and receive the boundary points [0.0, 1.0, 2.0] then the actual bins are (-inf, 0.0), [0.0, 1.0), [1.0, 2.0), and [2.0, +inf). In other words, all values less than 0 will belong to the first bin and all values greater than 2.0 will belong to the last bin.

Another preprocessing layer that corresponds to the transformations being done in scikit-learn is the StringLookup layer. The StringLookup layer is used to encode categorical columns with string values. You can encode the values in different manners, but you will use one-hot encoding for your model. Another option is to encode the columns as integers and then perform one-hot encoding, or other possible transformations, in later layers.

Finally, you also performed feature crossing when preprocessing your features in scikit-learn. In scikit-learn, this was a somewhat manual process: you concatenated the strings corresponding to the values for each feature, then one-hot encoded the concatenated values. In Keras, there is a preprocessing layer that handles feature crosses, known as the HashedCrossing layer. The HashedCrossing layer takes two categorical features and creates the feature cross for you.

There are many more useful preprocessing layers to explore. For details about additional layers, see the "Working with Preprocessing Layers" (https://oreil.ly/K6TLx) guide in the TensorFlow documentation.

Creating the Dataset and Preprocessing Layers for Your Model

Now you will re-create the preprocessing pipeline that you created in scikit-learn so you can explore new model architectures in Keras.

Return to https://colab.research.google.com. Open a new notebook and name the notebook keras_model.ipynb. You will be adding code to this notebook throughout the next few sections, but if you are stuck, there is a solution notebook in the chapter8 directory also called keras_model.ipynb (https://oreil.ly/AVf5n).

First, import the training and validation datasets into DataFrames as you did before with scikit-learn. Also split the datasets into a DataFrame of features and series of labels. If you need help doing so, here is the solution code:

```
import pandas as pd

!wget -q https://storage.googleapis.com/low-code-ai-book/car_prices_train.csv
!wget -q https://storage.googleapis.com/low-code-ai-book/car_prices_valid.csv
!wget -q https://storage.googleapis.com/low-code-ai-book/car_prices_test.csv

train_df = pd.read_csv('./car_prices_train.csv')
y_train = train_df['sellingprice']
X_train = train_df.drop('sellingprice', axis=1)

valid_df = pd.read_csv('./car_prices_valid.csv')
y_valid = valid_df['sellingprice']
X_valid = valid_df.drop('sellingprice', axis=1)
```

You will need to prepare the input features in Keras. When using different preprocessing layers on different features, you cannot use the Sequential API that you
leveraged in Chapter 7 to build a neural network in Keras. The alternative API, the
Functional API, is very similar to use with a slightly different syntax. To use the
Functional API, you need to start by creating an Input for each input feature. First,
copy the following code to a new cell in your notebook and execute the cell:

```
import tensorflow as tf
from tensorflow.keras.layers import (StringLookup, HashedCrossing,
                                      Discretization, Concatenate)

cat_cols = ['make', 'model', 'trim', 'body', 'transmission', 'state',
            'color', 'interior']
num_cols = ['odometer', 'year', 'condition']

inputs = {}

for col in cat_cols:
  inputs[col] = tf.keras.Input(shape=(1,), name=col,
                               dtype = tf.string)

for col in num_cols:
  inputs[col] = tf.keras.Input(shape=(1,), name=col, dtype = tf.int64)
```

Before moving forward, take a moment to parse this code. First you import the
preprocessing layers you will be leveraging in later steps. Then you split the list of
columns into numeric and categorical columns (num_cols and cat_cols respectively)
as you did in scikit-learn. Then you create an empty dictionary for the Input layers.
You then create an Input for each feature. The for col in cat_cols statement
means that the following code will be executed for every column in the cat_cols list.
tf.keras.Input is the full name for Input layers. The first argument, shape, states
that for each example, each feature will be just a single value. You set the name of
each Input to the corresponding column name in cat_cols. Finally, you set the data
type (dtype) to tf.string, which is the implementation of the string data type in

TensorFlow. The concepts are the same for the num_cols column except that the data type is set to tf.int64, TensorFlow's implementation of 64-bit integers.

Now that the Input layers have been created, you are ready to create the preprocessing layers. First, one-hot encode each categorical column using the following code:

```
preproc_layers = {}
for col in cat_cols:
    layer = StringLookup(output_mode='one_hot')
    layer.adapt(X_train[col])
    preproc_layers[col] = layer(inputs[col])
```

First you create an empty dictionary to hold the layers you will use for preprocessing. Then you create a StringLookup layer for every categorical column, and then you set the output_mode to 'one_hot' so that the output is one-hot encoded. You then use the adapt() method on the corresponding column in the training dataset to learn the vocabulary for one-hot encoding. Note that if an unknown value appears when transforming data in the model, it will be assigned an unknown value '[UNK]'. The behavior of how unknown values are treated can be set. Finally, you specify the input for the column at training and prediction time and store that in the dictionary preproc_layers. You should reference the documentation for StringLookup (https://oreil.ly/cGDlm) for more details.

Next up are the Discretization layers for bucketizing your numeric columns. Use the following code to create the Discretization preprocessing layers:

```
for col in num_cols:
    layer = Discretization(num_bins=10,
                           output_mode='one_hot')
    layer.adapt(X_train[col])
    preproc_layers[col] = layer(inputs[col])
```

The idea here is similar to before, where for each numeric column you create a Discretization layer. Each layer (for now) will split the data into 10 buckets and then one-hot encode the bucket membership. Finally, you use the adapt() method to fit the bucketization to the individual columns.

The last type of feature engineering you performed with your scikit-learn model was feature crossed. Now, re-create these features using HashedCrossing layers using the following code:

```
model_trim=tf.keras.layers.HashedCrossing(num_bins=1000, output_mode='one_hot')(
        (inputs['model'], inputs['trim']))
color_int=tf.keras.layers.HashedCrossing(num_bins=400, output_mode='one_hot')(
        (inputs['color'], inputs['interior']))

preproc_layers['model_trim'] = model_trim
preproc_layers['color_int'] = color_int
```

Note that the HashedCrossing column is slightly different from performing a feature cross as we did in scikit-learn. A *hashing* function is a special type of function that takes a string input and returns an integer in return. The output is deterministic—that is, you always get the same output integer when inputting the same string, but the outputs are distributed in such a way it is nearly impossible to predict. The HashedCrossing column takes the output of the hashing function and uses that to choose a bin to place the corresponding element into. For the model_trim layer, there are 1,000 bins, and for the color_interior layer, there are 400 bins.

Where do these numbers come from? Well, there are over one million different model and trim combinations possible from the values that come up in our dataset. Likewise, there are about 300 combinations of color and interior values that are possible. Since the distribution of values is effectively random, possibly multiple values could end up in the same bin. Overestimating the number of bins helps to lower the likelihood of that scenario. There is a trade-off, though: each bin corresponds to a feature in your model, and this corresponds to multiple weights depending on how many neurons there are in the first hidden layer. This trade-off is the reason that we chose 1,000 bins for the model_trim feature rather than including over one million bins. This trade-off also makes the number of bins a great candidate for hyperparameter tuning.

Building a Neural Network Model

Now that you have created the preprocessing layers, it is time to put everything together. The first thing you should do is concatenate all of the preprocessing layers into a single layer for input into the neural network. Use the following code to perform this task:

```
prepared_layer = Concatenate()(preproc_layers.values())
prepared_layer = tf.reshape(prepared_layer, [-1,3903])
```

This code is fairly straightforward: you create a Concatenate layer and then give it a list of input layers. Since you have been creating all of your preprocessing layers in a dictionary, you simply need to extract the values of the dictionary. prepared_layer is a length 3903 tensor, taking into account all of the possible feature values for the one-hot encoded and bucketized features. The second line reshapes prepared_layer into a rank 2 tensor, which is expected in the Functional API for the next layer.

With all of your inputs as a single layer, the rest of the process of building a model is more or less the same as in Chapter 7. There is a minor difference with the Functional API in Keras, but this is easier to explain after seeing the code:

```
hid_1 = tf.keras.layers.Dense(16, activation='relu')(prepared_layer)
hid_2 = tf.keras.layers.Dense(16, activation='relu')(hid_1)
output = tf.keras.layers.Dense(1)(hid_2)

model = tf.keras.Model(inputs=inputs, outputs=output)
```

The first line creates a new layer, hid_1, which is a dense layer with 16 neurons and ReLU activation. In the Functional API, you have to specify an input for each layer just as you would for a function. In this case, this will be the prepared_layer from before. Next, you define a second layer, hid_2, with the same parameters as the first hidden layer, but with hid_1 as the input layer. Finally, you define the output layer, output, as a dense layer with a single output neuron and no activation function. Recall that for regression models, your output should be a single number, the predicted value.

You need to now create the Model object. You do this by using tf.keras.Model and specifying the inputs for the model (inputs that you defined earlier) and the output for the model (the output layer). From here, the process is the same as it was in Chapter 7, with a few minor differences. Use the following code to compile and train the model:

```
model.compile(optimizer='adam', loss='mse')

train_ds = tf.data.Dataset.from_tensor_slices(
    (dict(X_train), y_train)).batch(100)
valid_ds = tf.data.Dataset.from_tensor_slices(
    (dict(X_valid), y_valid)).batch(1000)

history = model.fit(
    x=train_ds,
    epochs=25,
    verbose=1,
    validation_data=valid_ds
)
```

First you compile the model, setting the optimizer to be the Adam optimizer and the loss function to be the mean squared error, or MSE. Next you create the tf.Datasets for training and validation from the corresponding DataFrames. You set the batch size to 100 for training and 1000 for validation. To train the model, you use the fit() method as before.

Your model performance may vary slightly depending on the randomness involved with initializing and training a neural network, but you should see an MSE of around $10,719,103 after training completes, which translates to an RMSE of $3,274. The performance is similar to your model's performance in scikit-learn before hyperparameter tuning. Note that your MSE may differ due to randomness in how the neural network was initialized. The choice of neural network architecture was arbitrary, though, so there is likely still further room for improvement.

Hyperparameter Tuning in Keras

Now that you have a working model in Keras, it is time to work on improving it. When building Keras models, you can use the Keras Tuner package to easily perform hyperparameter tuning.

Google Colab does not include the Keras Tuner package by default, but it is easy to install. `pip` (a recursive acronym for Pip Installs Packages) is a package-management tool for Python to install and manage packages. The `pip install` command will allow you to download and install packages from the Python Package Index or PyPI. Run the following command in a new cell to install the Keras Tuner package:

```
!pip install -q keras-tuner
```

`pip` is a command-line tool, so as before you use the ! line magic to run the line as a bash command. The `-q` flag suppresses most of the output from the install to avoid cluttering up the notebook environment. Now that Keras Tuner is installed, you can start to alter your model code to prepare it for hyperparameter tuning.

When using Keras Tuner you need to create a function (which you will call `build_model`) that takes hyperparameters as inputs and returns your compiled model. For every candidate model, this function will be executed with different hyperparameters to create the model for training. As you noticed earlier, it takes a few minutes to perform the `adapt()` method for all of your preprocessing layers, so ideally you will have this code outside of the `build_model` function. Use the following code to create the `build_model` function for Keras Tuner:

```
import keras_tuner as kt
from functools import partial

def _build_model_fn(hp, prepared_layer):

    units_1 = hp.Int('units_1', min_value=8, max_value=64, step=4)
    units_2 = hp.Int('units_2', min_value=4, max_value=64, step=4)
    units_3 = hp.Int('units_3', min_value=4, max_value=32, step=2)

    hid_1 = tf.keras.layers.Dense(units_1,
                                    activation='relu')(prepared_layer)
    hid_2 = tf.keras.layers.Dense(units_2, activation='relu')(hid_1)
    hid_3 = tf.keras.layers.Dense(units_3, activation='relu')(hid_2)
    output = tf.keras.layers.Dense(1, activation='linear')(hid_3)

    model = tf.keras.Model(inputs=inputs, outputs=output)

    model.compile(optimizer='adam', loss='mse')

    return model

build_model = partial(_build_model_fn, prepared_layer=prepared_layer)
```

First you import the keras_tuner package and the partial function, both of which will be used later. Next you define an "intermediate" function: _build_model_fn. The underscore at the front of the function name is a Python convention that this is a function that is not meant to be used directly. Note that this function has two arguments, hp and prepared_layer. The hp argument will be provided by Keras Tuner, and the prepared_layer argument will correspond to the layer of the same name you created earlier.

The line units_1 = hp.Int('units_1', min_value=8, max_value=64, step=4) is an example of how to define a hyperparameter using Keras Tuner. hp.Int defines an integer-valued hyperparameter. You can also define floating-point hyperparameters (hp.Float), Boolean hyperparameters (hp.Boolean), or choose from a list of possible values (hp.Choice). For more details, see the Keras Tuner documentation (*https://oreil.ly/ZnCKe*).

In the case of integer hyperparameters, you set a minimum value, a maximum value, and a step size. So in this case, the possible values would be 8, 12, 16, 20, ..., 64. In the preceding code, you create three hyperparameters: units_1, units_2, and units_3. Next you define the three hidden layers for your model. Note that for each hidden layer, the number of neurons is replaced with the hp.Int objects that were defined. Otherwise, the process is similar to the code you used for building and compiling a model. The _build_model_fn function returns the compiled model as the output.

The build_model function needs to take only hp as an argument for use with Keras Tuner. This is where the partial function comes into play. The partial function allows you to create a new function from an old function, but with certain fixed arguments already plugged into the original function. partial(_build_model_fn, prepared_layer=prepared_layer) takes the function _build_model_fn and creates a new function where your prepared_layer layer is always plugged in for the corresponding argument.

Now that the build_model function has been created, next create the tuner that will manage the hyperparameter tuning process. Use the following code to create the tuner object and perform the hyperparameter search:

```
tuner = kt.BayesianOptimization(
    build_model,
    objective=kt.Objective("val_loss", direction="min"),
    max_trials=20)

tuner.search(
    x=train_ds,
    epochs=5,
    verbose=1,
    validation_data=valid_ds)
```

The `tuner` is an example of a `Tuner` in Keras Tuner using Bayesian optimization to optimize hyperparameters. You create an `Objective` to define the goal of the tuning process. In this case, you want to minimize the loss (MSE) of the validation dataset, so you set `val_loss` as the goal and `direction` as `min` to specify that you wish to minimize the `val_loss`. You also set a maximum number of trials or candidate models to be trained.

To perform the tuning process, you use the `search()` method on `tuner`. You specify the training dataset, the number of epochs to train the candidate models for, the verbosity (how much detail you want from 0 to 3), and the validation dataset. Note that the number of epochs is fairly small here since you are training many models. Often, but not always, you can understand which models will perform better after only a few epochs of training, without having to train them until convergence. Your output and results should look similar to those in Figure 8-4.

```
[12]  1   tuner = kt.BayesianOptimization(
      2       build_model,
      3       objective=kt.Objective("val_loss", direction="min"),
      4       max_trials=20)
      5
      6   tuner.search(
      7       x=train_ds,
      8       epochs=5,
      9       verbose=1,
     10       validation_data=valid_ds)

     Trial 20 Complete [00h 03m 04s]
     val_loss: 6105608.5
```

Figure 8-4. An example of the output from the hyperparameter tuning process using Keras Tuner.

Your exact results will vary depending on some randomness in the process, but likely your results will have the best model's `val_loss` around $6,000,000, which corresponds to an RMSE of $2,470. This is an improvement over the previous model's results, even after only five epochs. You should now train this best candidate model for longer to see if you can get even better results. To do this, you need to be able to retrieve the best hyperparameters. Execute the following code in a new cell to find the hyperparameters from the best candidate model:

```
best_hps=tuner.get_best_hyperparameters(num_trials=1)[0]
print('units_1:', best_hps.get('units_1'))
print('units_2:', best_hps.get('units_2'))
print('units_3:', best_hps.get('units_3'))
```

The best hyperparameters found once again can vary from run to run due to randomness in the process. For the run being discussed in this chapter, the best values for `units_1`, `units_2`, and `units_3` were 52, 64, and 32 respectively.

To make things easier, Keras Tuner includes the `tuner.hypermodel.build()` method where we can provide the best hyperparameters, and it will pass those values to the `build_model` method to re-create our best candidate model. Use the following code to do just that, create an early stopping callback, and train the best model until the `val_loss` stops improving:

```
best_model = tuner.hypermodel.build(best_hps)

early_stopping = tf.keras.callbacks.EarlyStopping(monitor='val_loss',
                                                  patience=5)

history = best_model.fit(
    x=train_ds,
    epochs=1000,
    verbose=1,
    callbacks = [early_stopping],
    validation_data=valid_ds
)
```

After training the model, the validation RMSE has decreased even further, to under 2,000. You finally have a model that meets your initial goals! As an exercise, implement hyperparameter tuning for other hyperparameters such as the number of bins for the `HashedCrossing` layers.

However, we chose the model based on performance on the validation dataset, so we could have happened to choose a model that was just simply biased toward that dataset. This is where the test dataset comes in. The test dataset has not been used at any point during the model training process, so it is the closest thing that we have to data "in the wild" or that your model would see in production.

Since we have chosen our final model, we can use the test dataset as a final verification of performance. To do so, use the following code:

```
test_df = pd.read_csv('./car_prices_test.csv')
y_test = test_df['sellingprice']
X_test = test_df.drop('sellingprice', axis=1)
test_ds = tf.data.Dataset.from_tensor_slices(
                    (dict(X_test), y_test)).batch(1000)

best_model.evaluate(test_ds)
```

How did your model perform on the test dataset? If the performance was similar, then you are in great shape and ready to pass the model along to be deployed. Otherwise, you may need to recombine the datasets, do a new training-validation-test data split, and start the process over from the beginning. In the process of doing so, be sure to ensure that your training, validation, and test datasets have similar distributions of examples. In practice, different distributions in the different datasets is a very common reason to see a large drop in performance when evaluating on the test dataset.

Having to start over can be frustrating, but once the independence of the test dataset is compromised by using it to make a decision, this is the best approach if you need to continue to improve your model performance.

Hyperparameter Tuning in BigQuery ML

In this section you will revisit the model you created in scikit-learn and Keras in BigQuery ML. You will load the car auction price datasets you were using before into BigQuery, explore feature engineering in BigQuery ML, and train a neural network model. Finally, you will learn how to perform hyperparameter tuning in BigQuery ML.

You will not be doing a full review of the concepts of BigQuery and BigQuery ML again in this chapter, so please reference Chapter 6 for additional details on certain tasks being performed in this chapter.

Loading and Transforming Car Auction Data

First go to the Google Cloud Console (*http://console.cloud.google.com*) and navigate to BigQuery (either using the side menu or the search bar). In the Explorer to the right of your project ID, click the View Actions button, which is represented by three vertical dots to the right of your project ID. Then click "Create dataset." A reminder of the location of these items in the UI is shown in Figure 8-5.

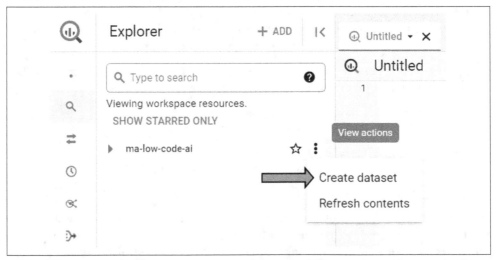

Figure 8-5. The location of the View Actions button and "Create dataset" action in the BigQuery UI.

Create a new dataset, `car_sales_prices`, in the US region. Once the dataset is created, you can use the View Actions button beside your dataset to create a BigQuery table. Select the dataset, click "View actions," then select "Create table." Create three tables, with one for each of the three datasets, using the information in Table 8-3. Note that you will need to replace the *<dataset>* part of the "Select file from GCS bucket or use a URI pattern" and "Table" fields with `train` , `valid` , and `test` for the three different datasets.

Table 8-3. Options for the three tables to be created

Field	Value
Create table from	Google Cloud Storage
Select file from GCS bucket or use a URI pattern	low-code-ai-book/car_prices_*<dataset>*.csv
File format	CSV
Table	car_prices_*<dataset>*
Schema	Auto detect

Before beginning to build the model, you need to replicate the transformations that you performed in scikit-learn and Keras. First, recall that you performed one-hot encoding on the categorical columns. Remember that in BigQuery ML, all string-valued columns are automatically one-hot encoded, so there will be nothing you need to do for those columns.

What about the numeric columns that you bucketized? BigQuery ML provides two functions for bucketizing numeric features. First is the `ML.BUCKETIZE` function, which takes in two arguments. The first argument is the column you wish to bucketize, and the second is a list of bucket endpoints which you provide. Note that you need to know what buckets you wish to use up front.

There is also the `ML.QUANTILE_BUCKETIZE` function. This function also takes two arguments. The first argument is again the column you wish to bucketize, but the second column will now be the number of buckets you wish to split the data into. `ML.QUANTILE_BUCKETIZE` will split the data into quantile-based buckets based on the number of buckets you specify. For example, if you specify four buckets, the first quartile (25% of data) will be placed into the first bucket, the second quartile into the second bucket, and so on. The actual output of these functions will be of the form `bin_n` for data placed into bucket n, and then BigQuery ML will one-hot encode this column just like any other string column.

The final transformation you performed was a feature cross. The function that implements feature crosses in BigQuery ML is the `ML.FEATURE_CROSS` function. This function takes in a `STRUCT` of feature columns and returns feature crosses of those columns. If you provide just a pair of columns, then it will return the feature cross of those two columns. If you provide three columns, then you will receive three feature crosses, one for each possible pair.

The syntax for `ML.FEATURE_CROSS` may seem a little odd at first:

```
ML.FEATURE_CROSS(STRUCT(column1,column2))
```

The `STRUCT` keyword is needed to create a `STRUCT`, which is an ordered list of columns possibly of different types. Without this keyword, you will receive an error from this line of code.

Now you are ready to preprocess your data. Write and execute the following SQL query in the BigQuery console to perform the desired transformations:

```
SELECT
  * EXCEPT (int64_field_0, mmr, odometer, year, condition),
  ML.QUANTILE_BUCKETIZE(odometer, 10) OVER() AS odo_bucket,
  ML.QUANTILE_BUCKETIZE(year, 10) OVER() AS year_bucket,
  ML.QUANTILE_BUCKETIZE(condition, 10) OVER() AS cond_bucket,
  ML.FEATURE_CROSS(STRUCT(make,model)) AS make_model,
  ML.FEATURE_CROSS(STRUCT(color,interior)) AS color_interior
FROM
  `car_sales_prices.car_prices_train`
LIMIT 10
```

The `SELECT * EXCEPT(...)` statement returns all columns in the table except for the ones listed. Here `int64_field_0` is the name for the `Unnamed: 0` column from before. You want to also remove the `mmr` column since you were not going to be able to use it for training. Finally, you did not use the numeric values for `odometer`, `year`, and `condition` before, as you had bucketized those features, so you will not return those features in the results.

Next, you bucketize the `odometer`, `year`, and `condition` columns using `ML.QUAN TILE_BUCKETIZE` and 10 buckets. The `OVER()` clause at the end allows you to split up the data into different sets (based on the inside of the `OVER` statement) and then bucketize into quantiles. Here, you simply bucketize into quantiles without any additional splitting.

Finally, you implement the feature crosses with `ML.FEATURE_CROSS`. For this example, you have the `LIMIT 10` statement, so you can look at just the first few rows of data. An example of what the results could look like is shown in Table 8-4.

Table 8-4. *The output from the preprocessing queries for the* ML.QUANTILE_BUCKETIZE *and* ML.FEATURE_CROSS *transformations*

odo_bucket	year_bucket	cond_bucket	make_model	color_interior
bin_10	bin_1	bin_1	Nissan_300ZX	red_red
bin_7	bin_1	bin_1	Chevrolet_Corvette	red_–
bin_10	bin_1	bin_?	Lexus_LS 400	silver_silver
bin_10	bin_1	bin_4	Jeep_Cherokee	white_gray
bin_9	bin_1	bin_2	Mazda_MX-5 Miata	red_blue
bin_10	bin_1	bin_2	Honda_Accord	blue_–

Note that for the bucketized columns, the output is bin_n as expected. Also, the output for the feature cross columns has the form value1_value2. These concatenated values will be one-hot encoded by BigQuery ML, taking a very similar approach to what you did in scikit-learn earlier in the chapter.

Training a Linear Regression Model and Using the TRANSFORM Clause

Now you are ready to train a linear regression model using the preceding query you wrote for preprocessing the data. Note that if you transform the data using that query, save the results, and then train the model using the new table, everything works just fine. However, you must perform the same transformations at prediction time. This becomes very tricky when you do not know exactly how the one-hot encoding was done nor do you have the bucket endpoints for the bucketization.

BigQuery ML provides the TRANSFORM clause to enable you to build these transformations into the model. The overall structure of the CREATE MODEL statement is as follows:

```
CREATE OR REPLACE MODEL `dataset.model_name`
TRANSFORM (<transformation_sql>)
OPTIONS (<model_options>)
AS SELECT …
```

The <transformation_sql> is the SELECT part of the preceding query where you specified the columns you wanted to use and the transformations on those columns. Write and execute the following SQL statement to train a linear regression model using your transformations in a TRANSFORM clause:

```
CREATE OR REPLACE MODEL
  `car_sales_prices.linear_car_model`
  TRANSFORM (
    * EXCEPT (int64_field_0, mmr, odometer, year, condition),
    ML.QUANTILE_BUCKETIZE(odometer, 10) OVER() AS odo_bucket,
    ML.QUANTILE_BUCKETIZE(year, 10) OVER() AS year_bucket,
    ML.QUANTILE_BUCKETIZE(condition, 10) OVER() AS cond_bucket,
    ML.FEATURE_CROSS(STRUCT(make,model)) AS make_model,
```

```
    ML.FEATURE_CROSS(STRUCT(color,interior)) AS color_interior)
  OPTIONS (
    model_type='linear_reg',
    input_label_cols=['sellingprice'],
    data_split_method='NO_SPLIT') AS
SELECT
  *
FROM
  `car_sales_prices.car_prices_train`;
```

This query should seem mostly familiar from what you did before in Chapter 6 up to a few changes. First, the TRANSFORM clause is included to build the transformation logic into the model so that it can be referenced at inference time. When you call ML.PREDICT to serve predictions, the TRANSFORM clause will be executed on the input table before being passed to the model for predictions. This means that things like the bucket endpoints will be included in the model itself now. In scikit-learn and Keras, you used pipelines and preprocessing layers, respectively, to manage this process.

The other thing that you may have noticed is that there is a new option. The data_split_method option dictates how the data will be split for training and validation. Since you already have a separate validation dataset, the NO_SPLIT option is employed to use the entire training dataset for training. You can evaluate your trained model using your validation dataset using the following SQL statement:

```
SELECT SQRT(mean_squared_error)
FROM ML.EVALUATE(MODEL `car_sales_prices.linear_car_model`,
    (SELECT * FROM `car_sales_prices.car_prices_valid`))
```

Since you used the RMSE for evaluation before, you will use it again here for consistency. Your RMSE here could be fairly high, and possibly over $8,000. You can check the RMSE for the training set as well by running the following query:

```
SELECT SQRT(mean_squared_error)
FROM ML.EVALUATE(MODEL `car_sales_prices.linear_car_model`,
    (SELECT * FROM `car_sales_prices.car_prices_train`))
```

The RMSE on the training dataset will be closer to $3,000 and what you expected from your scikit-learn model before. This is a classic example of overfitting, but where is this coming from? The feature crosses involve a very large number of possible values, thus leading to a very large number of features for the model. You can compute the number of features coming from the feature crosses by running the following query:

```
SELECT
    COUNT(ML.FEATURE_CROSS(STRUCT(color,interior))) +
    COUNT(ML.FEATURE_CROSS(STRUCT(make,model)))
FROM
    `car_sales_prices.car_prices_train`
```

You will see that there are 770,000 different feature values from the feature crosses. Such a large number of features compared to the number of examples can lead to overfitting very easily. In the next section, you will learn how regularization techniques can address overfitting with large numbers of features.

Finally, you can predict using your model in the same way as before in Chapter 6:

```
SELECT *
FROM ML.PREDICT(MODEL `car_sales_prices.linear_car_model`,
    (SELECT * FROM `car_sales_prices.car_prices_valid`))
```

You can train a deep neural network regression model in a very similar manner by simply changing the options, as you can see in the following SQL statement:

```
CREATE OR REPLACE MODEL
  `car_sales_prices.dnn_car_model`
  TRANSFORM (
    * EXCEPT (int64_field_0, mmr, odometer, year, condition),
    ML.QUANTILE_BUCKETIZE(odometer, 10) OVER() AS odo_bucket,
    ML.QUANTILE_BUCKETIZE(year, 10) OVER() AS year_bucket,
    ML.QUANTILE_BUCKETIZE(condition, 10) OVER() AS cond_bucket,
    ML.FEATURE_CROSS(STRUCT(make,model)) AS make_model,
    ML.FEATURE_CROSS(STRUCT(color,interior)) AS color_interior)
  OPTIONS (
    model_type='dnn_regressor',
    hidden_units=[64, 32, 16],
    input_label_cols=['sellingprice'],
    data_split_method='NO_SPLIT') AS
SELECT
  *
FROM
  `car_sales_prices.car_prices_train`;
```

Configure a Hyperparameter Tuning Job in BigQuery ML

Once you have written the code to train a model, then you only need to make a few small alterations to begin hyperparameter tuning. First you will need to include a new option, num_trials. This option sets the number of different models that will be trained during the hyperparameter tuning process. You can optionally also set a value for the num_parallel_trials option. This will allow you to run multiple trials in parallel at the same time. The total number of resources used to train all the models will be the same, but being able to run multiple models in parallel will make it take less time overall. However, there is a trade-off when using Bayesian optimization as implemented in BigQuery ML and Vertex AI in general. The more parallel trials you run, the fewer iterations you go through until you get to the maximum number of trials, and in general Bayesian optimization learns from each iteration.

After setting the `num_trials` option, the next step is to set up your hyperparameters. In BigQuery ML, only certain hyperparameters can be tuned. For deep neural network (DNN) models, you can tune the `batch_size`, `dropout`, `hidden_units`, `learn_rate`, `optimizer`, `l1_reg`, `l2_reg`, and `activation_fn`. You will focus on drop out, `l1_reg`, and `hidden_units` here, but you should explore other hyperparameters as an exercise.

Regularization

You are familiar with `hidden_units` from earlier examples. But what about `dropout` and `l1_reg`? *Dropout* is a type of regularization technique. In general, regularization techniques are used to reduce the risk of overfitting for a model. *Overfitting* occurs when the model performs much better on the training dataset than evaluation datasets. This often happens because the model "memorizes" the dataset and starts to miss the general patterns that are needed to perform well on other datasets. One main way of reducing this risk of overfitting is to lower the model's complexity.

L1 and L2 regularization are commonly the first regularization techniques that ML practitioners learn about. Suppose you have a loss function $L(x, D)$. Recall that the goal of the training process is to minimize this loss function. The idea of L1/L2 regularization is to add an additional term to the loss function to force the learning algorithm to balance minimizing the original loss function and the new "penalty term." Let W_2 represent the sum of the squares of all of the weights in your model. For L2 regularization, the new loss function looks like the following:

$$L_{reg}(x, D) = L(x, D) + \lambda * W_2.$$

The rough idea is that for a model to become more complex, the values of the weights need to become larger to have more of an effect on the outcome. This new loss function balances the original loss function and the "complexity" of the model as measured by W_2. λ is known as the *regularization rate* , which controls how much the original loss function is weighed against the complexity of the model. The higher the value of λ, the more complexity is punished in the training process. Similarly for L1 regularization, the term W_2 is replaced by the sum of the absolute values of all of the weights W_1. These types of regularization can be used together in what is known as elastic net regularization. The corresponding loss function for elastic net regularization is as follows:

$$L_{en}(x, D) = L(x, D) + \lambda_1 \times W_1 + \lambda_2 \times W_2$$

Note that λ_1 and λ_2 are different constants controlling the influence of L1 and L2 regularization separately.

You now know what the definitions of L1 and L2 regularization are, but what effect do they actually have on the model? The mathematics behind this is beyond the scope of this book, though is not too complex, and the ultimate effects are easy to describe. L2 regularization tends to try to push weights to smaller values. L1 regularization tends to push weights that are not influential on the model's performance to zero. This can be very valuable when you have a large number of sparse features. An example of this scenario is when you are creating feature crosses of two features with a large number of values. This is exactly the scenario you encountered in the linear regression model trained in BigQuery ML. In general, when using feature crosses, it is usually a good idea to include L1 regularization. The regularization parameter(s) control how aggressive the push on the values of the weights are during the training process.

Dropout is a different kind of regularization in the sense that it is applied to the model itself during the training process and not to the loss function. The idea of dropout on neural networks is that a certain percentage of neurons are "turned off" for each batch of data. By *turned off* here we mean that the corresponding weighted sums for certain neurons in hidden layers are set to zero for that specific batch of data. The goal of using a technique like dropout is to hinder the model's complexity during training time. This keeps the model from becoming too complex while still letting the model learn more about the data. However, during prediction time, no dropout is used so that you have full access to the model's power.

 Over the past decade, researchers have found that using dropout at prediction time as well can be beneficial.[1] This can be used as a way to represent a model's uncertainty for both classification and regression tasks and to make a model's predictions nondeterministic.

Using hyperparameter tuning in the CREATE MODEL statement

Now that you understand a little bit about regularization, it is time to set up hyperparameter tuning in BigQuery ML. First consider the following SQL statement:

```
CREATE OR REPLACE MODEL
  `car_sales_prices.dnn_hp_car_model`
  TRANSFORM (
    * EXCEPT (int64_field_0, mmr, odometer, year, condition),
    ML.QUANTILE_BUCKETIZE(odometer, 10) OVER() AS odo_bucket,
    ML.QUANTILE_BUCKETIZE(year, 10) OVER() AS year_bucket,
    ML.QUANTILE_BUCKETIZE(condition, 10) OVER() AS cond_bucket,
    ML.FEATURE_CROSS(STRUCT(make,model)) AS make_model,
    ML.FEATURE_CROSS(STRUCT(color,interior)) AS color_interior)
```

---

1 For example, see Y. Gal and Z. Ghahramani, "Dropout as a Bayesian Approximation: Representing Model Uncertainty in Deep Learning" (Proceedings of the 33rd International Conference on Machine Learning, 2016).

```
    OPTIONS (
      model_type='dnn_regressor',
      optimizer='adagrad',
      hidden_units=hparam_candidates([STRUCT([64,32,16]),
                                      STRUCT([32,16]),
                                      STRUCT([32])]),
      l1_reg=hparam_range(0,1),
      dropout=hparam_range(0,0.8),
      input_label_cols=['sellingprice'],
      num_trials = 10,
      hparam_tuning_objectives=['mean_squared_error'])
  AS SELECT
    *
  FROM
    `car_sales_prices.car_prices_train`;
```

The statement for creating a hyperparameter tuning job is very similar to what you used before, with some key differences for the sake of hyperparameter tuning. First, notice the `hidden_units` option. Instead of just having a single list of hidden units, instead there is the `hparam_candidates` function. This function takes a list of structs with the corresponding hyperparameter tuning values and passes them along to the model during the tuning process. Here you are having the model decide the best architecture between three possibilities. The first is a neural network with 64 neurons in the first hidden layer, 32 in the second layer, and 16 in the third layer. The second option has two hidden layers with 32 and 16 neurons each, respectively. Finally, the last option has a single hidden layer with 32 neurons. Also, you are searching for the best `l1_reg` and `dropout` by using an `hparam_range`. `hparam_range` is used to find the best value in a range of floating-point values. For example, here the range for dropout is between 0 and 0.8 for the percentage of neurons in hidden layers affected by dropout at training time.

Finally, there are a couple of new options that need to be set before beginning the training. First, the `num_trials`, which was mentioned before, and the `hparam_tuning_objectives`. You want to optimize the RMSE, so set the `hparam_tuning_objectives` to be `mean_squared_error`. Go ahead, if you have not already, and start the tuning process. This tuning process will take around an hour to complete.

 In the query for the hyperparameter tuning job, you have to specify the optimizer being used with the `optimizer='adagrad'` option. The default optimizer, `adam`, does not support L1 regularization. For more details, please see the BigQuery ML documentation for creating DNN models (*https://oreil.ly/6hZQN*).

Once the training process has completed, you can explore the trial results and chosen hyperparameters by executing the following query:

```
SELECT
  *
FROM
  ML.TRIAL_INFO(MODEL `car_sales_prices.dnn_hp_car_model`)
ORDER BY
  hparam_tuning_evaluation_metrics.mean_squared_error ASC
```

An example of what your output should look like is shown in Table 8-5.

Table 8-5. The results of the trial info query for the five best trials—note the chosen hyperparameters and trial metrics (the exact values in your output will differ from what is shown here; some column names were condensed for readability)

trial_id	l1_reg	hidden_units	dropout	mean_squared_error
10	1.0	64	0.0	194784591.6
		32		
		16		
8	0.000315910340786933391	64	0.0	213445602.34905455
		32		
		16		
9	1.0	64	0.25599690406708309	218611976.60226983
		32		
		16		

If you use `ML.PREDICT` with `car_sales_prices.dnn_hp_car_model` as the model of choice, BigQuery will automatically use the best trial by default:

```
SELECT *
FROM ML.PREDICT(MODEL `car_sales_prices.dnn_hp_car_model`,
    (SELECT * FROM `car_sales_prices.car_prices_valid`))
```

Options for Hyperparameter Tuning Large Models

The frameworks and techniques discussed in this chapter are wonderful for datasets and models that are not too large. However, using scikit-learn and Keras on local machines or Colab notebooks for very large datasets and models could take a long time, or even be impossible due to memory and processing constraints. Training and tuning large models is an art of its own, and there are tools available on public cloud providers to make this much easier. This book does not do a deep dive into these products, as they tend to be much more involved from the custom code development point of view, but simply lists some options and references for those who are interested.

Vertex AI Training and Tuning

In Chapter 7 you saw how you could package up a Python module for training a scikit-learn model and submit it to Vertex AI Training. The same could be done for the scikit-learn or Keras code in this chapter for hyperparameter tuning.

Vertex AI also offers a hyperparameter tuning service as part of Vertex AI Training. This uses the `cloudml-hypertune` Python to report metrics to Vertex AI from various different trials, which can be executed in different clusters using Vertex AI Training. Like Keras Tuner, Vertex AI uses Bayesian optimization to find the best hyperparameters for your model.

For more details on how to use this service, please see the Vertex AI documentation (*https://oreil.ly/qcLDL*).

Automatic Model Tuning with Amazon SageMaker

Amazon SageMaker includes an automatic model tuning service (SageMaker AMT (*https://oreil.ly/boB_A*)) for performing hyperparameter tuning. You can use Sage-Maker AMT with built-in algorithms, custom algorithms, or SageMaker prebuilt containers for ML frameworks such as scikit-learn, TensorFlow, and PyTorch.

For more details, see the SageMaker AMT documentation (*https://oreil.ly/boB_A*).

Azure Machine Learning

Azure Machine Learning includes hyperparameter tuning as part of the Python client library and command-line interface. Like the other options mentioned, you can provide your own custom model written in the framework of your choice, make the hyperparameters for the model arguments for a function creating the model, specify the hyperparameter search space, and specify a job configuration to submit to run a hyperparameter sweep job on Azure Machine Learning. For more information, see the Azure Machine Learning documentation (*https://oreil.ly/vrKRr*).

Summary

In this chapter, you took a custom code model built by a colleague and improved it using feature engineering and hyperparameter tuning. You leveraged new transformers in scikit-learn and performed a grid search to hyperparameter tune the original linear regression model. You learned how to perform the same feature engineering in Keras using preprocessing layers and perform hyperparameter tuning using Keras Tuner for your neural network model in Keras. Finally, you learned how to perform these same tasks in BigQuery ML using SQL.

This chapter and the previous chapter on custom code models hopefully have given you a taste of what is available for building ML models. No-code and low-code solutions are at the very least a great starting point and very well may get you to your goal without having to write custom code. But you do not need to be a data scientist to explore with custom code, nor does it involve writing hundreds and hundreds of lines of code.

In the next and final chapter, you will learn about some next steps you can take if you want to go deeper into ML. You have already developed a very powerful toolkit throughout this book, but the field is ever growing, and a lot of the new tools and developments are available to more than just researchers in the field.

## CHAPTER 9

Next Steps in Your AI Journey

Throughout the course of this book, you have learned how data can drive decision making in your business with an enterprise ML workflow, how to understand your data with an eye toward building ML models, and what tools are available for building ML models. You have discovered how to use AutoML to train your regression and classification models, how to create custom low-code models using SQL in Big-Query ML, how to create custom code models using the scikit-learn and TensorFlow framework, and then finally how to improve your custom model performance with further feature engineering and hyperparameter tuning. Hopefully, you have found this journey to be equally enlightening and enjoyable. For many, that should be more than enough to enable you to infuse ML into your problem-solving processes.

For others, this is only the beginning of a longer journey into ML and AI. This chapter explores where to go next. You will learn about other important topics in data science and ML operations (or MLOps). You will also be pointed toward many wonderful resources to grow your knowledge beyond this book.

Going Deeper into Data Science

There is no universally agreed-upon definition for *data science* or a *data scientist*. A decent approximation of such a definition could be that *data science* is the discipline that uses various tools from other disciplines to extract insights from datasets. These various tools come from other areas such as mathematics, statistics, computer science, and occasionally different areas depending on the problem at hand.

All of the datasets that you worked with in this book have been *structured* datasets—datasets with a well-defined schema. Most business problems involve structured data, and you picked up a wonderful skill set for exploring structured data. However, *unstructured* datasets are becoming increasingly important as ML becomes more mature as a discipline. Recall from Chapter 2 that unstructured data includes images, videos, sound files, and text. A large amount of research over the past decade has gone into various aspects of ML for unstructured data.

A type of AI that has become increasingly important recently is *generative AI*, referring to models that generate various types of data such as images, videos, and so on. Recently, generative AI has become a very popular and fast-growing field, with image generation models such as Midjourney (*http://www.midjourney.com*) and Craiyon (*http://craiyon.com*), and chatbots (contextual text generation) such as ChatGPT (*https://openai.com/blog/chatgpt*) and Bard (*http://bard.google.com*). Additionally, generative AI capabilities are being included in many commercial products such as Bing (*https://www.bing.com*) (ChatGPT), Google Search (*http://google.com*) (Search Generative Experience (*https://oreil.ly/szZB7*)), and Amazon CodeWhisperer (*https://aws.amazon.com/codewhisperer*).

The more complex models become, the harder they are to easily understand. For example, when you learned about linear regression in Chapter 6, you saw that the weights of the model gave a clear understanding of the importance of the individual features. For even a neural network with only one hidden layer, there is no longer an easy-to-describe connection between the weights of the model and the importance of the features being used. This becomes even more difficult with the very large models that are used for problems with unstructured data and generative models.

This section dives a little deeper into various resources and offers additional resources to explore these topics if you so choose.

Working with Unstructured Data

Unstructured data is defined as data without a schema. Some classic examples were mentioned before, such as images and text. Recall that ML models are ultimately mathematical functions that take numeric inputs and have numeric outputs, which you then interpret. How do you interpret an image or a sentence as numeric input?

Working with image data

For images, the story is simpler than you may expect. Every image is represented as an array of pixel values. For example, consider the pixelated image of a handwritten digit in Figure 9-1. The image on the left is a low-resolution version of the handwritten digit 2. That image consists of a 12 × 12 grid of blocks known as pixels. The *pixel values* for this grayscale image range between 0 and 255. 0 represents black, 255 represents white, and values in between represent different values of gray. In the second image, you can see the actual pixel values for the image as an array.

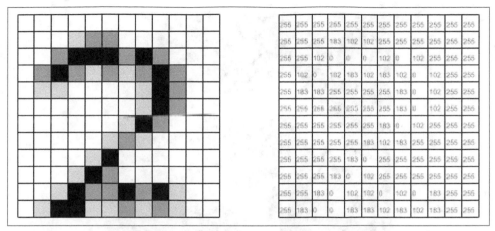

Figure 9-1. A low-resolution grayscale image of a handwritten 2 and the corresponding pixel values.

For color images, the idea is very similar. Color images consist of three *channels*: red, green, and blue. For each pixel, there is a value between 0 and 255 for each of these channels. The values for these channels together are usually called *RGB values*. For example, white is represented by [255,255,255] and yellow is represented by [255,255,0]. There are a lot of simple tools, such as the one at RapidTables (*https://oreil.ly/gby4M*), that allow you to explore different colors and see their RGB values.

Now that you understand images as either two-dimensional (black-and-white images) or three-dimensional arrays (color images) of numeric values, you may now have an inkling of how you might use these values in ML. These are your numeric inputs for your image models.

The "hello world" example for image classification is the problem of handwritten digit recognition using what is known as the MNIST (Modified National Institute of Standards and Technology) dataset. This is a dataset of 60,000 training images and 10,000 test images that are well balanced between the 10 handwritten digits (0 through 9). These images are 28 × 28 grayscale images. You can see an example of one of these images in Figure 9-2.

Figure 9-2. An example of a handwritten 7 in the MNIST dataset.

Classifying each image as the corresponding number is an example of a multiclass classification problem. We did not explore beyond two classes in the examples in this book, but the rough idea is similar. The model will predict a probability for each digit, and the most likely digit will be taken as the predicted label. You can use linear classification and neural network classifiers in a similar manner to what you used in Chapter 7, but there are also additional tools, such as convolutional layers, that are very useful when working with image data. These additional tools are beyond the scope of this book, but here are a couple of useful resources for those who want to learn more:

- Kaggle competition and tutorials for working with the MNIST dataset (*https:// oreil.ly/Vvp1d*)
- Google's ML Crash Course on Image Classification (*https://oreil.ly/_ea_0*)

Working with text data

Another common type of unstructured data that you may encounter in your ML models is text data. For example, what if you wanted to use comments in reviews to understand why your customers gave certain positive or negative ratings? You need to have a method to turn text data into numeric data.

The simplest way of performing this task is to use one-hot encoding like you have already done for categorical data in previous problems. For example, you could have the vocabulary ['red', 'blue', 'green']. If you have the word 'blue', then the corresponding value would be [0,1,0].

This can become tricky very quickly, however. If every different word has a different corresponding value, then you can end up with a very high-dimensional feature. Certain words will appear rarely, or not at all, in the training set, so the model may struggle to learn the meaning of those words.

One strategy is to use *n-grams* instead of individual words. n-grams are continuous sequences of *n* words. For example, in the sentence *The cow jumped over the moon*, the 2-grams (or *bigrams*) are ['The cow','cow jumped', 'jumped over', 'over the', 'the moon']. For spam detection, 3-grams and 4-grams tend to be more useful features than individual words. Intuitively we can see this in an explicit example. A spam email may have a sentence like "You have won the lottery and are now rich!" as part of the body. 1-grams and 2-grams will look at fragments of the sentence that are too granular to capture context, except for "now rich!", which could tip off a person or model that the email is spam. For example, "won" ,"the", and "lottery" are missing context individually needed to confirm the email is spam. On the other hand, the 3-gram "won the lottery" would throw up an immediate red flag for most people looking out for spam emails.

Another strategy is to use word embeddings. A *word embedding* is a representation of a word in some number of dimensions to try to capture its meaning and relationship to other words. For example, the word *king* could be represented as [0.5, 0.7]. Ideally, a word embedding will place words that are similar close to each other. For example, as shown in Figure 9-3, the embedding for *dog* and *puppy* will be close to each other, as will *cat* and *kitten*.

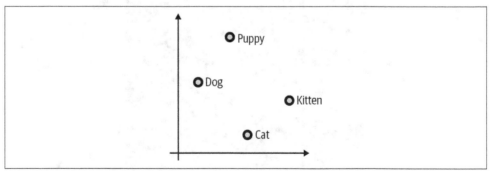

Figure 9-3. An example two-dimensional word embedding of "dog," "puppy," "cat," and "kitten."

Also note that the distance and direction between the pair "dog" and "puppy" and the pair "cat" and "kitten" are very similar. With a word embedding, you would expect a similar relationship between any animal and their babies (say, "sheep" and "lamb").

Word embeddings are models in their own right and are often trained within the context of a specific problem. More generally, different preprocessing models and tools exist for converting words and sentence fragments into numeric inputs. BERT (Bidirectional Encoder Representations from Transformers) preprocessing is a popular way of converting text input into numeric input for input into your model.

To learn more about working with text in ML models, here are a few useful resources:

- Word embeddings in Keras/TensorFlow (*https://oreil.ly/WQesS*)
- Preprocessing data in TensorFlow using BERT (*https://oreil.ly/Sqn-7*)
- Working with text data in scikit-learn (*https://oreil.ly/4EgWi*)
- Yelp review dataset (*https://oreil.ly/-NlFC*): A great dataset for working with text data to predict review scores

Generative AI

The classification models we have discussed so far in this book were discriminative models. *Discriminative* models have the goal of predicting which class an instance belongs to. For example, predicting whether a transaction is fraudulent or legitimate. Generative models are in some sense the inverse problem. The model generates the instance from the label instead. For example, given the label "a cat playing a banjo," an image of a cat playing a banjo is generated.

There are free tools, such as craiyon.com, which can be used to have fun playing around with these sorts of models. An example of this is shown in Figure 9-4.

Figure 9-4. An image generated using the prompt "a cat playing a banjo." This image was generated using craiyon.com.

Generative AI has become a major topic of discussion recently due to its use in chatbots. ChatGPT and Bard are two such examples of generative AI being used for chatbots. Underlying these products are large language models, or LLMs. The term *LLM* is a bit vague, but it is used for language models trained on large datasets with massive amounts of parameters. For example, GPT-3.5, the original model underlying ChatGPT, had more than 175 billion parameters and a corpus of over a half trillion tokens.

There are a lot of interesting conversations about the role of generative AI in society and how we as a society should be interacting with it. A deep conversation about the ethics of responsible use of generative AI is beyond the scope and purpose of this book, but these are important conversations moving forward.

If you're interested in learning more about generative AI, ChatGPT 101 on Coursera (*https://oreil.ly/KrRFm*) is a great resource to explore the use and implications of this new technology.

Explainable AI

Chapters 4 and 5 introduced feature attributions for your models, and Chapter 6 introduced the field of *explainable AI*, or XAI, in general for structured data. Many XAI techniques also exist for unstructured data such as images and text data.

XAI techniques can be broken down into intrinsic and post hoc techniques. *Intrinsic* techniques leverage the structure of the model to give explanations for predictions. Certain types of models, such as linear models and decision trees, are intrinsically explainable. For linear models, explored in detail in Chapters 6 and 7, the weights give the relative importance of the features.

Post hoc techniques, on the other hand, use the model's predictions to understand its behavior. These techniques are applied after a model has been trained, and often they are trained on part of the evaluation dataset. Post hoc techniques can be broken down into two main categories: local and global techniques. *Local* techniques focus on a single instance and attempt to explain why a specific prediction was made for that specific instance. *Global* techniques focus on the model's behavior over an entire dataset. In general, local techniques can be turned into global techniques by aggregating the results of a local technique over the dataset.

Both local and global techniques can be further broken down into model-agnostic and model-specific techniques. *Model-agnostic* techniques tend to alter the data and understand how it changes the predictions being made. A great example of this is the feature attributions that you saw in Chapters 4 and 5 when using AutoML. How are these feature attributions computed? They are computed using a technique called *permutation feature importance*, or PFI. PFI is computed in the following manner: first compute the loss of the model for the dataset you want to use. Next compute the loss again when you permute the first column of data in place. That is, you permute the first column while leaving the other columns alone (see Table 9-1). The difference between the loss on the original dataset and the dataset with the first column permuted gives a "score" for the importance of the first feature.

Table 9-1. Permuting a column in place; in this example, Column A is the column being permuted

Column A	Column B	Column C
1	4	7
2	5	8
3	6	9

Column A	Column B	Column C
3	4	7
1	5	8
2	6	9

Repeat this process for every column. The PFI for a column is the normalized score received from this process. *Normalized* here means that the scores are rescaled so that all of the normalized scores add up to one. PFI is easy to interpret and to compute in practice, but it does depend on some randomness due to the permutation. Often, when using PFI, you will compute the score for a column with multiple different permutations and average it out to try to minimize the effect of randomness.

The other type of technique is a *model-specific* technique. For example, *directional feature importances/contributions* are specific to tree-based models like decision trees, random forests, and gradient-boosted trees. On the other hand, a popular technique for neural networks is the technique of integrated gradients. *Integrated gradients* take advantage of the fact that neural networks are differentiable models. *Differentiability* is an important mathematical property that is also leveraged when minimizing loss functions using the gradient descent algorithm. The exact mathematics is beyond the scope of this book, but the idea is fairly straightforward.

Take the example of an image classification model. Suppose you have trained a model to classify images based on their main subject. Your model takes in a picture of a fireboat and correctly predicts that the image was of a fireboat. But why did it make this prediction? Roughly speaking, the integrated gradients method looks at how the predictions change as you change the features and accumulate those changes for each individual feature. For image models, those features are the individual pixel values. For integrated gradients, you define a starting point or a *baseline*. In image models, that baseline is often a completely black image, though other baseline images (such as a completely white image or random noise) can be used depending on the circumstance. You start off with the predicted probability of the label for fireboat for the purely black image and then brighten up the pixels proportionally until you get the original image in steps. For each step, you compute how much the predicted probability of fireboat has changed based on the pixel values. This can be done by computing the *gradient*, a mathematical tool for understanding the rate of change of an output based on many inputs. Finally, you accumulate (or *integrate*) these rates of change for every pixel. The pixels with the highest accumulated rates of change correspond to the most important pixels for the prediction. In Figures 9-5 and 9-6, you can see this interpolation of images and the corresponding pixel importances using integrated gradients.

Figure 9-5. The baseline image on the left with the original image of the fireboat on the right. The middle image is an interpolation between the two.

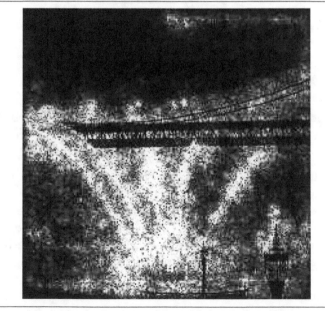

Figure 9-6. The image of the fireboat; the most important pixels, as identified by integrated gradients, are brighter. Note that integrated gradients highlight the streams of water from the boat as the explanation of why this is a picture of a fireboat.

To learn more about XAI, *Interpretable Machine Learning: A Guide for Making Black Box Models Explainable* (*https://oreil.ly/4CyIF*) by Christoph Molnar is a wonderful resource.

ML Operations

In Chapter 7 you trained an ML model for predicting customer churn and were able to serve predictions in your notebook environment. However, this is only one step in the journey to an ML model being put into production. As you saw, there was work to be done to ensure that the data was ready for training. But this does not take into account the underlying compute infrastructure needed for both training and serving models, managing and optimizing the consumption of resources being used, thinking about how to make your model usable for consumers, and how to monitor that model over time. Figure 9-7 shows the relative effort involved in ML code compared with the other aspects of productionizing ML models.

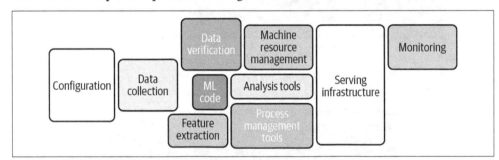

Figure 9-7. The hidden complexities of making ML models usable.

ML operations, or MLOps, is the discipline of managing all of the different tasks beyond the model itself. This includes managing the infrastructure, deciding how the model is deployed and accessed, and monitoring and updating the model as appropriate.

MLOps is usually the responsibility of ML engineers, data engineers, and data scientists to manage. However, even if you are not in one of these roles, having a high-level understanding of the various concerns in using ML models in production is very valuable. As someone building models, you can share good notes on what tools and data sources you are using, what data preprocessing needs to be done, and what features the model expects at prediction time. Doing things like including the preprocessing logic in the model itself, using something like transformers in scikit-learn or preprocessing layers in Keras, can make the deployment of training and prediction pipelines easier for engineers if the model is going into production. At most companies, there will not be a single person doing everything, so good communication is key.

For more details on topics around MLOps, see the following resources:

- Introduction to MLOps (*https://oreil.ly/E1K_3*)
- MLOps: Continuous Delivery and Automation Pipelines in Machine Learning (*https://oreil.ly/X6jv0*)
- *Designing Machine Learning Systems* by Chip Huyen (O'Reilly, 2022)

Continuous Training and Evaluation

In Chapter 5, you trained a model using AutoML to classify transactions as either fraudulent or legitimate. Your model performed well on the dataset that was provided, but after the model was being used in production for a few months, your company's support teams shared that they were getting more reports of fraudulent transactions after the fact from customers. Your model did not flag many of these fraudulent transactions though. What happened?

Over time, different types of *drift* can occur and affect the performance of your model. For example, there could be a new type of fraudulent transaction that was not present in your original training dataset. Your model would likely not pick up on this. This would be an example of *data drift*, a change in the underlying data distribution.

Another type of drift, called *concept drift*, can occur. Concept drift is where the relationship between the features and the labels change over time. A great example of this is in demand forecasting for retail. Shopping trends change over time, and the exact same product will sell differently at different times depending on the current trends. The product did not change, but the relationship between the product and the sales has changed.

Continuous training is the process of retraining the model automatically based on some criterion. Most often, this criterion will depend on either time or model performance. For example, you may want to retrain the model weekly, or you may want to retrain the model when a certain percentage of fraudulent transactions are being missed and reported by customers. For most models being used in production, this is a very common and important practice.

Continuous evaluation is often an important component in deciding when to retrain a model and is an important part of monitoring your model's performance. As the model is predicting results on new data, a sample of the new data is labeled. Often domain experts determine these labels. The model is then evaluated on this data against the new labels. If the performance of the model wanes over time, then that could be a sign that there has been some sort of drift and it may be time to retrain the model.

If you are part of the intended audience for this book, then likely you will be working with others when thinking about these concerns. However, even if it is not your responsibility, it is important to be aware of the concerns and tools that others are working with. This allows you to make more informed decisions in your own approach to make their job easier and to make you a better collaborator.

Summary

You have been on quite the ML journey working through this book! The hope is that you now feel comfortable thinking about how to turn your questions into ML projects and feel ready to start building models using the tools you used in this book. You can employ different resources and go in many directions from here, and you should feel empowered to follow those into topics of your interest. ML and AI is a rapidly growing field whose demand has exponentially grown over the past decade and likely will continue to do so in the years to come.

Index

A

A/B testing, 104
accounts
    authorizing Colab to access Google Cloud account, 240
    signing up for GitHub, 27
accuracy metric, 132-134, 223, 231, 235
activation functions, 185-187, 231, 234
adapt() method, 266-267, 269, 272
adjusted R-squared, 99
advertising media channel sales use case, 17, 71-110
    using AutoML to train linear regression model, 85-110
    dataset, 73
    exploratory data analysis, 75-83
    exporting dataset, 83-85
    loading data into Pandas DataFrame, 74-75
    overview, 19-20
    schema and data type, 24
    schema and field value information, 73
    workflow, 72
aggregate functions, 156
Amazon Aurora ML, 68
Amazon Redshift ML, 68
Amazon SageMaker, 50, 68
    automatic model tuning, 286
    interface, 65-66
anomaly detection problems, 5
APIs (application programming interfaces), 14
astype() method, 203
attrition rate, 21, 193

audio files, definition and common file extensions, 26
Auto-PyTorch, 70
Auto-sklearn, 69
AutoKeras, 69
AutoML
    benefits of, 64
    model selection, 11
    overview, 58-62
    training classification model using, 134-145
    training linear regression model using, 85-110
Azure ML (see Microsoft Azure ML)

B

bar charts, 121-122
batch() method, 233
batches and batch data
    batch processing, 26
    data collection, 6-7
    defined, 3, 27
    model deployment, 14
Bayesian search/optimization tuning method, 262, 274, 281
BETWEEN operator, 158
BigQuery ML, 21, 22, 67, 148-160
    CREATE MODEL statement in, 175-178
    explainable AI in, 179-182
    exploring data using SQL in, 154-160
    free tier, 149
    loading dataset into, 149-153
    selecting as data source, 136

templated notebooks, 166
training deep neural network in, 187-189
binary classification model, 51
bucketization
in BigQuery ML, 277-279
as category column, 215
using cut() function for, 209-212
defined, 6
hyperparameter tuning and, 261, 263
one-hot encoding, 257
preprocessing layers in Keras, 266, 269
visualizing data by, 123-125
build_model() function, 273-275
business objective, defining, 5

C

callbacks, 236
canary deployments, 105
cat command, 191
categorical features, 42, 52-53, 119, 121
encoding with scikit-learn, 215-218
exploring combinations of categorical columns, 205-208
exploring summary statistics, 204-213
interactions between numeric and categorical columns, 208-213
CCPPs (combined cycle power plants), 21, 147
(see also power plant production prediction use case)
chatbots, 290, 295
ChatGPT, 295
chi-square test, 206
classification models
using AutoML to train, 134-145
defined, 132
metrics and, 132-134
threshold, 132-134
classification problems, 5, 12
cloud platform pyramid, 62
Cloud Shell, 190-192
cloud storage
defined, 6
reasons for using, 90
clustering problems, 5
Colab
bringing query results from BigQuery to, 166-170

connecting to GitHub, 251
creating directories, 238
creating Python Jupyter notebook, 31-32
data validation, 36-42
exploratory data analysis in, 42-48
importing libraries and dataset using Pandas, 32-36
loading data into Pandas DataFrame in
advertising media channel sales, 74-75
customer churn prediction, 196-199
fraud detection, 116-117
overview, 30-31
plotting feature relationships to label, 170-174
collinearity, 170, 213-214
color channels, 291
ColumnTransformer() transformer, 229-230, 254, 263
combined cycle power plants (see CCPPs)
computation graphs, 231
computational complexity, 162
concatenate() function, 217
concept drift, 299
confusion matrices, 133, 224
continuous evaluation, 299-300
continuous processing, 26
continuous training, 299-300
correlation coefficient, 79
correlation matrices, 9-10, 78-79, 168-169
correlations
defined, 78
power plant production prediction model, 163-166
CPUs, 106
Cramer's V coefficient, 206
CREATE MODEL statement, 175
using hyperparameter tuning in, 283-285
modifying, 179-180
CREATE OR REPLACE MODEL statement, 175, 179
CREATE TABLE statement, 158
cross entropy, 220-221, 235
curvature, 222
custom model performance improvement use case, 18, 249-286
building neural network model, 270-271

creating dataset and preprocessing layers for model, 267-270

exploring scikit-learn linear regression model, 253-255

feature engineering, 256-261

hyperparameter tuning
in BigQuery ML, 276-285
in Keras, 272-276
options for large models, 285-286
in scikit-learn, 263-266
strategies for, 261-263

improving preprocessing pipeline, 256-261

loading datasets and training-validation-test data split, 251-253

loading notebook with preexisting model, 251

overview, 22-23

schema and field value information, 250

customer churn
defined, 21, 193
prediction of, 2
reducing, 2-4

customer churn prediction use case, 18, 193-248

building custom ML models on Vertex AI, 237-248

building logistic regression model using scikit-learn, 218-231

building neural network using Keras, 231-236

choosing among no-code, low-code, or custom code ML solutions, 194-196

cleaning dataset, 199-213

loading data into Pandas DataFrame, 196-199

overview, 21-22

schema and field value information, 194

transforming features using Pandas and scikit-learn, 213-218

cut() function, 209, 227

D

data
collecting, 6-7
exploratory data analysis, 9-10
file types, 25-26
preprocessing, 7-8
processing, 26-27
quantitative and qualitative, 23
role in decision making, 18
structured, unstructured, and semistructured, 24-25
transformation and feature selection, 10-11
validating in Colab, 36-42

data analysis algorithms and models, 5

data centers, 6

data definition language (DDL) statements, 158-160

data drift, 14, 299

data models, defined, 24

data repository, using GitHub to create, 27-30

data science, 289-298
explainable AI, 295-298
generative AI, 294-295
unstructured data, 290-294

data splitting, 218, 251-253

data types
checking and converting, 199-203
incorrect, 42

data understanding, 1

data warehouses
benefits of using for SQL-ML, 67
BigQuery ML, 67
defined, 67
Redshift ML, 68
serverless, 148

databases, 67

datasets
descriptive analysis of, 75-77, 118-120
exporting, 83-85, 131
heat maps for, 78-79
histogram distribution plot, 81-83
importing with Pandas, 32-36
scatterplots, 79-81

DDL (data definition language) statements, 158-160

decision making
identifying goals and use cases, 1-4
using ML workflow, 4-15
process of, 4
role of data in, 18

default values, 157

describe() method, 76-77, 118-119, 200, 204

descriptive analysis

advertising media channel sales dataset, 75-77

fraud detection use case, 118-120

dictionaries, 202

differentiability, 296

directional feature importances/contributions, 296

discretization (see bucketization)

discriminative models, 294

drop() function, 213

dropout, 282-283

dropping (deselecting) features, 59

E

EDA (exploratory data analysis), 9-10, 78, 166, 170

in Colab, 42-48

fraud detection use case, 120-131

heat maps, 78-79

histogram distribution plot, 81-83

scatterplots, 79-81

encoding categorical features, 215-218

endpoints, defined, 103

epochs, 235, 274

evaluating ML models, 12

advertising media channel sales model, 98-101

fraud detection model, 140-141

power plant production prediction model, 175-177

evaluation (validation) datasets, 12-13, 252

explainable AI (see XAI)

exploratory data analysis (see EDA)

exporting datasets

advertising media channel sales, 83-85

fraud detection, 131

F

F1-score, 133-134

feature crossing, 130-131, 259-261

feature engineering, 10, 59, 120, 164, 256-261

feature importances, 296

advertising media channel sales model, 101-102

fraud detection model, 141-142

plotting feature relationships to label, 170-174

feature selection

customer churn prediction model, 213-215

defined, 10

power plant production prediction model, 163-166

fit() method, 230, 235

fit_transform() method, 216, 223, 228, 230

forecasting model, 51

fraud detection use case, 17, 113-145

using AutoML to train classification model, 134-145

classification models and metrics, 132-134

dataset, 115

exploring, 116-131

exporting, 131

overview, 20

schema and field value information, 115

workflow, 114

FROM statement, 180

FunctionTransformer() transformer, 228-230, 253-254

G

gcloud storage commands, 191, 240

generalization, 218

generative AI, 290, 294-295

GitHub

benefits of collaboration with, 30

connecting to Colab, 251

creating data repository for projects using, 27-30

defined, 6

goals, identifying, 1-4

Google BigQuery ML (see BigQuery ML)

Google Cloud Shell, 190-192

Google Colaboratory (see Colab)

Google Vertex AI (see Vertex AI)

GPUs (graphics processing units), 106

gradient descent, 163

grid search tuning method, 261-262

groupby() function, 206

H

halving grid search tuning method, 264

harmonic mean, 133

hashing functions, 270

head() method, 75, 199, 252

heart disease campaign use case, 17
    copying file path for input, 39
    data analysis, 42-44
    loading dataset, 33-36
    overview, 18-19
    renaming dataset, 38
heat maps, 9, 10, 78-79, 169
hidden layers, 184-189
hidden units, 188
histogram distribution plots, 81-83
hyperparameter tuning
    in BigQuery ML, 276-285
    in Keras, 272-276
    options for large models, 285-286
    in scikit-learn, 263-266
    strategies for, 261-263
hyperparameters, defined, 189, 261

I

IaaS (infrastructure as a service), 62
IF function, 154
ill-conditioned systems, 163
image data, 290-292
image files, definition and common file extensions, 26
importing libraries and datasets, 32-36
imputation, 155, 209
incorrect data types, 42
info() method, 76, 118
information theory, 221
infrastructure as a service (IaaS), 62
integrated gradients, 296-297
inverse_transform() method, 217
isnull() method, 77
iterations, defined, 221

J

joblib library, 228, 230, 266
JSON (JavaScript Object Notation), 157
json.loads() function, 226-227
Jupyter Notebooks, 17, 18, 23, 27, 30, 31, 33, 47, 48, 59, 63, 68, 74, 116, 147, 182, 196

K

KBinsDiscretizer() transformer, 257, 263
Keras, 22

building neural network model, 270-271
    coding neural networks, 61
    defined, 197
    hyperparameter tuning in, 272-276
    origin of, 231
    overview, 231
    preprocessing layers in
        creating for model, 267-270
        overview, 266-267
    training neural network classifier using, 232-236

L

LabelEncoder() transformer, 232
labels, plotting feature relationships to, 170-174
libraries, importing with Pandas, 32-36
linear regression, 160-178
    using AutoML to train, 85-110
    common evaluation metrics, 99-101
    defined, 88
    exploring scikit-learn model, 253-255
    feature selection and correlation, 163-166
    prediction intervals, 109-110
    visualizing as neural networks, 183-184
LLMs (large language models), 295
logistic (sigmoid) function, 219-220
logistic regression
    classification evaluation metrics, 223-225
    overview, 219-221
    serving predictions with trained model in scikit-learn, 225-228
    training and evaluating model in scikit-learn, 221-223
loss functions, 162
low-code approach
    benefits of, 1
    compared to other approaches, 195
    defined, 50
    model selection, 11
low-code AutoML, 66-70
    open source ML libraries, 68-70
    SQL ML frameworks, 67-68

M

machine learning (see ML)
machine learning as a service (MLaaS), 62-66
MAE (mean absolute error), 101, 255

magic numbers, 157
MAPE (mean absolute percentage error), 101
marketing campaign use case, 17, 19
    baseline prediction, 49-52
    workflow, 58
masks, 201
Matplotlib
    with advertising media channel sales dataset, 73-85
    with customer churn prediction dataset, 196-218
    with fraud detection dataset, 116-131
Max function, 156-157
mean absolute error (MAE), 101, 255
mean absolute percentage error (MAPE), 101
mean squared error (MSE), 99, 271, 274
Microsoft Azure ML, 50, 286
    model deployment, 107
    Studio interface, 65
Min function, 156-157
min-max scaling, 227
MinMaxScaler() transformer, 222, 228, 229, 254
missing values, 41-42
ML (machine learning)
    identifying goals and use cases for, 1-4
    problems and model types, 12
ML frameworks
    AutoML, 58-62
    low-code AutoML, 66-70
    machine learning as a service, 62-66
    no-code AutoML, 49-58
ML workflow, 4-15
    using AutoML, 11
    data collection, 6-7
    data preprocessing, 7-8
    data transformation and feature selection, 10-11
    defining business objective or problem statement, 5
    exploratory data analysis, 9-10
    maintaining models, 14
    model deployment, 14
    model testing, 13
    model training, evaluation, and tuning, 12
    researching model selection, 11
ML.EXPLAIN_PREDICT function, 181-182

ML.GLOBAL_EXPLAIN function, 180
ML.PREDICT function, 177-178
MLaaS (machine learning as a service), 62-66
MLOps (ML operations), 298-299
MNIST (Modified National Institute of Standards and Technology) dataset, 291-292
model deployment, 14, 103
model feature attribution, 56-57
model research, 11
model testing, 13
model training, 12
    linear regression models, 279-281
    time required for, 56, 96-98, 235
    Vertex AI, 54-56, 93-98
modularity, 257
MSE (mean squared error), 99, 271, 274
multi-class classification model, 51
multicollinearity, 79, 170

N

n-grams, 293
neural networks
    activation functions and nonlinearity, 185-187
    classical machine learning vs., 62
    hidden layers, 184-189
    using Keras to build, 231-236
    nonlinear relationships, 59-62
    overview, 183-185
    training in BigQuery ML, 187-189
    typical, 60
neurons, 188
no-code approach, 49-58
    benefits of, 1
    compared to other approaches, 195
    defined, 49
    using Vertex AI, 86
node hours, 96
nonlinear relationships
    activation functions, 185-187
    neural networks, 59
normal distribution
    defined, 7
    histograms, 82
normal equation, 162
normalization, 8
Null function, 154-155

null values, 41, 154-155
numeric columns, 208-213
NumPy, 217
nunique() method, 215

O

one-hot encoding, 42
    defined, 59
    at prediction time, 227
    in scikit-learn, 215-218
    setting output as, 269
OneHotEncoder() transformer, 216, 228, 229, 254, 263
open source ML libraries, 68-70
overfitting, 12, 261, 280-282

P

PaaS (platform as a service), 62
Pandas
    DataFrames, defined, 35
    importing libraries and datasets, 32-36
    loading data into DataFrames
        advertising media channel sales, 74-75
        customer churn prediction, 196-199
        fraud detection, 116-117
partitions, defined, 153
PaySim, 115
Pearson correlation, 165
periodic processing, 26
PFI (permutation feature importance), 295-296
pickle library, 230
pip package-management tool, 272
pipelines, in scikit-learn, 228-231
pixel values, 290-291
platform as a service (PaaS), 62
power plant production prediction use case, 17, 147-192
    cleaning dataset using SQL in BigQuery, 148-160
    using Cloud Shell to view cloud storage file, 190-192
    explainable AI, 178-183
    linear regression models, 160-178
    neural networks in BigQuery ML, 183-190
    overview, 21
PR (precision-recall) curve, 134
precision, 132-134, 231, 235

in customer churn example, 223-225
in fraud_detection model, 141
using with recall metric, 132-134
precision_score function, 225
predictions
    advertising media channel sales model, 103-110
    using ML.PREDICT function for, 177-178
    of fraud detection model, 142-145
    serving with trained model in scikit-learn, 225-228
preprocessing layers
    creating for model, 267-270
    overview, 266-267
preprocessing pipeline, 256-261
problem statement, defining, 5
product pricing use case, 2-3, 17, 18
Python
    benefits of using online and cloud-based resources to learn, 30-31
    coding neural networks, 60
Python Jupyter Notebook, 59
Python Jupyter Notebooks, 18, 31-32

Q

qualitative data, 23
quantitative data, 23

R

R-squared, 99, 255
random search tuning method, 262
real-time processing, 26
recall, 132-134, 231, 235
    example of, 121
    in customer churn example, 223-225
    in fraud_detection model, 141
    using with precision metric, 132-134
recall_score function, 225
Redshift ML, 68
regression algorithms, 62
regression model, 51
regression problems, 5, 12, 50, 72, 88, 161
regularization, 282-283
reinforcement learning, 5, 12
ReLU (rectified linear unit) function, 185
replace() method, 202, 209
researching model selection, 11

RGB values, 291
RMSE (root mean squared error), 101, 162-162, 255, 271, 280
    decrease in, 258, 261, 274
    using neg_root_mean_squared_error score, 265
RMSLE (root mean squared log error), 101
ROC (receiver operator characteristic) curve, 134

S

SageMaker (see Amazon SageMaker)
sample() method, 254
scaling data, defined, 8
scatterplots, 79-81, 129-130, 165, 171-174
scikit-learn, 22
    building logistic regression model using, 218-231
    data splitting, 218
    defined, 197
    encoding categorical features using, 215-218
    exploring linear regression model, 253-255
    hyperparameter tuning in, 263-266
    loading datasets and training-validation-test data split, 251-253
    loading notebook with preexisting model, 251
score() method, 222, 255
Seaborn, 9-10
    with advertising media channel sales dataset, 73-85
    with customer churn prediction dataset, 196-218
    with fraud detection dataset, 116-131
    violin plots, 43-44
search() method, 274
semistructured data, 6-7
    comparison with other types of data, 25
    defined, 25
    examples of, 25
server infrastructure, 6
serving models (see model deployment)
Shapley values, 56, 182
sigmoid (logistic) function, 219-220
spreadsheet files, definition and common file extensions, 26
SQL ML frameworks, 67-68

cleaning dataset in BigQuery using, 148-160
    exploring data in BigQuery using, 154-160
staleness, 14
statistical bias, 155
statistics, dataset, 136-137
streaming data
    data collection, 6-7
    defined, 3, 27
    model deployment, 14
structured data, 6-7
    comparison with other types of data, 25
    defined, 24
    examples of, 24
SUM() function, 155
supervised ML, 50, 88

T

table partitioning, defined, 153
TensorFlow, 197, 231
tensors, defined, 231
testing ML models, 13
text files, definition and common file extensions, 26
Theano library, 231
toarray() method, 217
TPUs (tensor processing units), 106
traffic splitting, 104-105
training ML models, 12, 134-145, 139
TRANSFORM clause, 279-281
transform() method, 217, 228, 230
tuning ML models, 12

U

unbiased estimators, 177
undeploying models, 145
unstack() function, 206
unstructured data, 6-7, 289
    comparison with other types of data, 25
    defined, 24, 290
    examples of, 24
    image data, 290-292
    text data, 292-294
unsupervised ML, 4
use cases
    advertising media channel sales, 19-20
    custom model performance improvement, 22-23

customer churn prediction, 21-22
fraud detection, 20
heart disease campaign, 18-19
identifying, 1-4
overview, 17-18
power plant production prediction, 21
product pricing, 18
utility energy campaign, 19
utility energy campaign use case, 19

V

validation (evaluation) datasets, 12-13, 252
value_counts() method, 205, 206
Vertex AI
    analyzing datasets, 136-137
    building custom ML models on, 237-248
    choosing compute resources, 105-106
    creating managed datasets, 86, 135-136
    Dashboard, 86
    defined, 50, 85
    feature importances, 101-102, 141-142
    generated statistics, 53
    getting predictions from model, 103-110
    interface, 65
    model deployment, 103-107, 142-145
    model objective, 87-91
    model performance evaluation, 98-101,
        140-141
    model testing, 108-109
    model training, 54-56, 93-98, 137-139
    selecting training methods, 54
    temporary resource provisioning, 237
    workflow, 50
Vertex AI Training, 286
video files, definition and common file exten-
    sions, 26
violin plots, 43-44

W

webpage files, definition and common file
    extensions, 26
wget bash command, 252
word embeddings, 293-294

X

XAI (explainable AI), 178-183
    in BigQuery ML, 179-182
    intrinsic techniques, 295
    local vs. global techniques, 178, 295
    model-agnostic techniques, 295
    model-specific techniques, 296
    post hoc techniques, 179, 295

About the Authors

Gwendolyn Stripling, PhD, is an artificial intelligence and machine learning content developer at Google Cloud, helping learners navigate their generative AI and AI/ML journey. Stripling is the author of the successful YouTube video "Introduction to Generative AI" and author of the LinkedIn Learning video "Introduction to Neural Networks." Stripling is an adjunct professor and member of Golden Gate University's Masters in Business Analytics Advisory Board. Formerly, Stripling served as a data analytics engineer, cloud architect, and technical trainer for Qlik, a data analytics company. Stripling enjoys speaking on AI/ML, having presented at Dominican University of California's Barowsky School of Business Analytics, Golden Gate University's Ageno School of Business Analytics, Google Cloud NEXT, and Google's Venture Capitalist and Startup program.

Michael Abel, PhD, is the technical lead for the specialized training program at Google Cloud, working to accelerate and deepen Cloud proficiency of customers through differentiated and non-standard learning experiences. Formerly, Abel was a data and machine learning technical trainer at Google Cloud and has taught the following Google Cloud courses: "Machine Learning on Google Cloud," "Advanced Solutions Labs ML Immersion," and "Data Engineering on Google Cloud." Before joining Google, Abel served as a Visiting Assistant Professor of Mathematics at Duke University, where he performed mathematics research and taught undergraduate mathematics.

Colophon

The animal on the cover of *Low-Code AI* is a green frog (*Lithobates clamitans*). Its call is known for its explosive "bong" sound that is akin to a loose banjo string.

Green tree frogs have a range of colors: green and greenish brown to yellow-green and, on rare occasions, blue. Some frogs even look bronze, earning the name *bronze frog*. The front part of their bodies are generally a brighter green and they have white bellies. They also tend to have small black spots and black leg bands. Males have a bright yellow throat. While green tree frogs appear similar to bullfrogs, they are distinguished by a distinct fold of skin on either side of their body called a *dorsolateral fold*.

Green frogs are native to North America and are found in a variety of habitats: swamps, grasslands, forests, lakes, ponds, rivers, streams, bogs, and marshes. During the winter, they hibernate in mud at the bottom of bodies of water. They are predators that can hunt for food on land and in water. Their diet is varied, including spiders, flies, caterpillars, snails, moths, and small snakes and frogs.

The green tree frog population is abundant and widespread. While there are some abnormalities inflicting the population due to water contamination, green tree frogs have a conservation status (IUCN) of "Least Concern." Green tree frogs kept in captivity can even live up to ten years. Many of the animals on O'Reilly covers are endangered; all of them are important to the world.

The cover illustration is by Karen Montgomery, based on an antique line engraving from a loose plate from an unknown source. The cover fonts are Gilroy Semibold and Guardian Sans. The text font is Adobe Minion Pro; the heading font is Adobe Myriad Condensed; and the code font is Dalton Maag's Ubuntu Mono.